FIGURES OF DESIRE

# Figures of Desire

## A THEORY AND ANALYSIS
## OF SURREALIST FILM

## Linda Williams

UNIVERSITY OF CALIFORNIA PRESS
BERKELEY · LOS ANGELES · OXFORD

University of California Press
Berkeley and Los Angeles, California
University of California Press, Ltd.
Oxford, England

PICTURE CREDITS

The Museum of Modern Art / Film Still Archives
for photographs on pp. 91, 93, 115, 119, 123, 125, 127
Museo del Prado for *The Executions of May 3, 1808,* by Francisco José de Goya on p. 157
Films Incorporated for photographs on pp. 161, 164, 165, 189, 192, 202

LIBRARY OF CONGRESS
CATALOGING IN PUBLICATION DATA

Williams, Linda, 1946–
    Figures of desire: a theory and analysis of surrealist film /
Linda Williams.
        p.    cm.
    Originally published: Urbana: University of Illinois Press, 1981.
    Includes bibliographical references (p.        ) and index.
    ISBN 0-520-07896-9 (pbk.)
    1. Surrealism in motion pictures.    2. Buñuel, Luis, 1900–
3. Dalí, Salvador, —1904–    I. Title.
[PN1995.9.S85W5    1992]
791.43'61—dc20                                                      91-35727
                                                                   CIP

1    2    3    4    5    6    7    8    9

*I dedicate this book to my mother
who stayed up with me to watch the late show
and taught me to enjoy a good movie.*

# Contents

# Acknowledgments

I WOULD LIKE to take this opportunity to thank Christian Metz, who made this work possible through his own work and by encouraging my early attempts to understand rhetorical figures in Surrealist film. I am also indebted to Sophia Morgan and Bruce Kawin for creative, careful criticism, sound advice, and moral support. Ben Brewster and Phillip Drummond have been very helpful in their critique of an early part of chapter 2. Thanks also go to James Monaco, Julia Lesage, and Judy Gardiner for useful criticism; to Marilyn Kann and Aladeen Smith for typing; to Charles Nilon for a place to work; to Paul Fitzgerald for timely prodding; to the Research Board of the University of Illinois at Chicago Circle for a grant to work on chapter 4; and to Frank Williams and Rita Zelewsky of the University of Illinois Press, whose cheerful help made the final book possible. Final thanks go to Kaye Howe, who has been a constant source of personal and professional encouragement over the past ten years.

Chicago, January 1, 1980

# Preface to the Paperback Edition

SURREALIST cinema was my first intellectual passion. Like many before me, I was drawn to this artistic movement for its paradoxical combinations—what the Surrealists themselves liked to call fortuitous encounters. These encounters, which famously shocked the sensibilities, were invariably thought to be subversive of rational bourgeois civilization. Yet the investigation of how this subversion took place was considered anathema to the spontaneity and freedom of the entire Surrealist enterprise. Imbued with the infectious spirit of Surrealism, two generations of Surrealist-inspired critics extravagantly praised the revolutionary power of the work of Buñuel and Dali. This praise was often vehemently anti-formalist, and Freudian in only the grossest, symbol-mongering, ways. The basic lesson of the French return to Freud—of what Lacan called the insistence of the letter in the unconscious—was not applied to the very works which had taken their direct inspiration from that insistence.

It was against this dominant, anti-formalist critical tendency that I undertook this psychoanalytic-semiotic study of the key works in the Surrealist canon. First published in 1981, *Figures of Desire* was an attempt to take seriously the dreamlike form of Surrealist cinema by exploring the rhetorical figures of condensation and displacement so crucial to Freud's analysis of dreams. The book was written out of the conviction that Surrealist film offered a privileged example of the rhetoric of unconscious desire operating as formal principles in the image-discourse of these most dreamlike of films. My thesis was that rather than simply imitating the illogic of dreams, these films are about the signifying processes of desire in the human subject. Lacan's theory of the splitting of the subject and the subsequent quest for "obscure objects of desire" describes both the content and the form of the original canon of Surrealist cinema as well as much of Luis Buñuel's later work.

I wrote this book under the powerful influence of a psychoanalytic semiotics that has become one of the major paradigms of cinema study.

If I were writing this book today I would be more critical of this paradigm, more concerned to question an unrepentantly phallocentric theory of subjectivity, not to mention the problematic sexual politics of Surrealism itself. I would write, in short, a *feminist* theory and analysis of Surrealist cinema. Such a study would investigate the problematic of gaze and gender in a body of works obsessed with vision and sexual difference and it would be as concerned with probing the methods of analysis as applying them.

I would not abandon, however, the valuable insights of the Lacanian-semiotic approach. For I believe that the only mode of film that could ever truly lend itself to a post-structuralist psychoanalytic method of analysis is Surrealist cinema. The Surrealist fascination with the image derives from the same theoretical roots and the same generational esprit as Lacanian psychoanalysis. Lacan himself flirted with and participated on the fringes of the Surrealist group. These films are a rich source of the figures of unconscious desire—not to be taken (as they sometimes have) as the quests of personal subjects for attainable objects, but as what has come to be known as the unattainable quests of displaced and de-centered postmodern subjects. While certainly not the last word, or the most nuanced analysis, of these figurations, this book has served to initiate such analysis. I am delighted that it is now being made available in paperback by the University of California Press; I hope it will sustain the interest of readers who find these films as compelling as I do.

Linda Williams
Irvine, California
September 1991

# Introduction

ANDRÉ BRETON once wrote that criticism can exist only as a form of love. Though Breton is ultimately right, it is nevertheless true that many studies of Surrealism have been hindered by an overabundance of such love. Even today Surrealism retains the polemical qualities of a political-aesthetic attitude that one is either committed to or excluded from. Those on the side of Surrealism tend to defend it with the kind of enthusiam that precludes careful and close analysis. In doing so, they imply that Surrealism is by definition that which cannot be analyzed.

The analysis of Surrealist film has been equally hindered by the presence of a very similar excess of love in the tradition of film criticism. Here again it is a surfeit of love—in this case love of the medium itself—that impedes analysis. Christian Metz[1] has shown that this kind of love is really a defense constructed against the possibility of falling out of love, an overenthusiasm that arises from the lingering orthodoxy that the film medium is somehow not as legitimate or serious an art form as literature, art, and music. This defense usually takes the form of an unreasoning exaltation of the film medium as intrinsically rich or effective, an idealization of the love-object and all the mysteries of its production. When a film genre or subgenre has been deemed particularly illegitimate or when it has been banned, reviled, and even physically assaulted by audiences as was a 1930 projection of L'Age d'or, this reactionary enthusiasm for a revolutionary cinéma maudit becomes particularly aggressive and begins radically to interfere with an understanding of the texts.

Surrealist film has thus been doubly condemned to an enthusiastic love, both as Surrealism and as film. Both enthusiasms were needed at one time to assert the legitimacy of their objects. Today they only interfere with the very love they have tried to protect. One

[1] Christian Metz, "The Imaginary Signifier," trans. Ben Brewster, Screen 16 (Summer 1975): 14–74.

purpose of the present study is to revitalize the love of Surrealist film by giving it a basis in close, formal analysis. With this analysis I reverse the method of study most often employed in the past. Previous studies have taken a broad, inclusive view of the subject, citing examples of a Surrealist attitude or quality in many different kinds of films along with the actual Surrealist films themselves.[2] These studies include the films of Méliès, Dadaism, Expressionism, and figures peripheral to Surrealism—such as Cocteau—within their scope. They have succeeded in delineating recognizably Surrealist qualities in a great many films, including the so-called involuntary Surrealism of works as diverse as the Keystone Cops, the Marx Brothers, and Josef von Sternberg. But in the process they have failed both to give the few films that grew directly out of the movement the close scrutiny they deserve and to define adequately the true characteristics of this film movement.

One reason for the very broad scope of these past studies is that, strictly speaking, there are very few films that did grow directly out of the Surrealist movement. *Un Chien andalou* and *L'Age d'or* are perhaps the only unquestionably Surrealist films.[3] But even if *Un Chien andalou* and *L'Age d'or* are the only "pure" examples of filmic Surrealism, these two films alone constitute a solid achievement deserving of much more thorough attention and rigorous analysis than they have received in the past. So, while acknowledging that a much broader approach to the relations between Surrealism and film is entirely possible, my own focus in this study is intentionally narrow. It is limited to an examination of the scenarios and

[2] I refer especially to Ado Kyrou's pioneering works, *Le Surréalisme au cinéma* (Paris: Editions arcanes, 1953) and *Luis Buñuel* (Paris: Seghers, 1962); J. H. Mathews, *Surrealism and Film* (Ann Arbor: University of Michigan Press, 1971); Jean Mitry's chapter on Surrealist film in *Le Cinéma expérimental* (Paris: Seghers, 1974); Freddy Buache, *The Cinema of Luis Buñuel*, trans. Peter Graham (New York: A. S. Barnes, 1973); and, most recently, Michael Gould, *Surrealism and the Cinema* (New York: A. S. Barnes, 1976).

[3] The film version of Antonin Artaud's *The Seashell and the Clergyman* remains problematic. Although it is the first film version of an intentionally Surrealist script, its direction in 1928 by Germaine Dulac, who had no affinity with the Surrealist group, and its almost laughably poor acting—Artaud himself should have had the title role—make it a poor example of the visual qualities of Surrealist film, although many of the ideas in Artaud's scenario are unquestionably Surrealist. Man Ray's *Etoile de Mer* (1928), based loosely on a poem by Robert Desnos, has closer affinities to Dada than to Surrealism, although some critics have seen it as the turning point between the two movements.

films that grew out of the actual heyday of the Surrealist movement and out of a direct contact with its theories. Only in the final chapter do I begin to open up the study to a broader examination of Surrealist film. But here, too, I opt for a close look at a limited selection of works—Buñuel's two most recent films and their relation to his early Surrealist classics—rather than the entire thread of Surrealism running throughout this director's work.

In a similarly narrow way I focus on the origins and theoretical development of the Surrealist concept of film, in particular on how the early pre-Surrealist poetic theory of the image and the later Freudian influences on this theory in Surrealism proper combined to form a new concept of film art. Chapter 1, therefore, attempts to isolate the origins of a not always fully articulated theory of film in the writings and screenplays of the pre-Surrealists—Reverdy, Soupault, and Apollinaire—and then in the later, more properly Surrealist, writings of Artaud, Desnos, Breton, and Dalí. I don't pretend that these writings constitute a theory in the true sense of the word, but I do hope to show that the common participation of these writers in a movement with such a strong Freudian basis does give their writing on the film a special coherence.

With respect to this Freudian influence, I have also tried to get to the bottom of the fundamental analogy between the film and the dream that runs through all Surrealist writings on the film as well as most critical analysis. Here I suggest that it is not enough simply to point to obvious similarities between the film and the dream. Nor is it enough to describe the film as destined to perform Surrealist functions because of these obvious similarities. I do not share the belief of many critics that the film is in essence a Surrealist or dreamlike art form. This seems no more true than the equally popular notion that the film is "essentially" realistic. I think, rather, that the history of the cinema has been largely the history of its models[4] and that the dream has certainly been a tremendously significant model in this history. The real question, however, is just how this model operates: in what sense does Surrealism use the model of the dream in its film theory and practice? In answering this question I have found it both

[4] See David Cook, "Some Structural Approaches to Cinema: A Survey of Models," *Cinema Journal* 14 (Spring 1975):41.

helpful and appropriate to employ certain Freudian notions relating to the rhetoric of dreams, as well as certain key notions central to Jacques Lacan's reinterpretation of Freud.

The Lacanian reading of Freud stresses the ways in which the unconscious can be compared with language and the way in which the self is situated in and produced by this language. Recent work by Christian Metz on psychoanalysis and the cinema[5] has explored Lacan's idea of the formation of the self as a process of identification with an image. Metz shows how this early identification with an image operates to structure many of our responses to film, especially the way we identify with the characters of a given fiction. It is my belief that Surrealist film differs from other kinds of film precisely in the nature of this identification.

Surrealist film focuses on the process of identification without reproducing its effect in the spectator. Rather than simply using the identification process to create an illusion of a fictive time, space, and character in the way most fictional films do, Surrealist film exposes the fundamental illusion of the film image itself to focus on its role in creating the fictive unity of the human subject. It is thus both a visual art form that takes into account the problematics of the subject's relation to the image and a very sophisticated attempt to work against the identification process inherent in this relationship.

Chapter 1 deals with the theoretical and descriptive side of the topic: What is Surrealist film? How did it develop out of the literary poetics of the image? What are its visual qualities? How does it operate on the spectator? This chapter deals only with Surrealist writings about the cinema and with unproduced screenplays.

Chapters 2 and 3 are very close analyses of the two undisputed classics of Surrealist film: *Un Chien andalou* and *L'Age d'or*. Chapter 4 continues this close analysis in the contemporary Surrealism of Buñuel's *The Phantom of Liberty* and *That Obscure Object of Desire*. In all these chapters I have focused on the ways in which metaphoric or metonymic figures take precedence over diegesis or plot,

---

[5] Metz's work on psychoanalysis and film is collected in the volume *Le Signifiant imaginaire: Psychanalyse et cinéma* (Paris: Union générale d'éditions, 1977). The title essay of this volume, "The Imaginary Signifier," has been translated for *Screen*. Another essay from this volume, "The Fiction Film and Its Spectator: A Metapsychological Study," trans. Alfred Guzzetti, appears in *New Literary History* 8 (Autumn 1976):75–102.

as well as the specific ways in which they figure the latent desires that are the true subjects of each film. The term *desire* is understood here in a rather special way. It does not refer to the pursuit and possession of a love object—Pierre Batcheff's pursuit of Simone Mareuil in *Un Chien andalou* or Gaston Modot's pursuit of Lya Lys in *L'Age d'or*—but to the visual figures of the text that elaborate a structure of opposition which expresses not so much the desire *for* an object as the psychic process of desire itself. It is thus the ultimate purpose of this study to show how Surrealist film "figures" desire. This, for me, is the continual fascination of Surrealist film.

FIGURES OF DESIRE

# The Image

## THE IMAGE IN PRE-SURREALISTIC POETIC THEORY[1]

IN 1918 Pierre Reverdy made the following remarks regarding the importance of the image in poetry:

The image is a pure creation of the mind. It is not born from a comparison but from a juxtaposition of two more or less distant realities.

The more distant and true the relationship between the two realities, the stronger the image will be—the more emotional power and poetic reality it will have.

The emotion thus provoked is poetically pure because it is born outside of all imitation, all evocation, all comparison.

It is the surprise and the joy of finding oneself before a new thing.

One can create . . . a powerful image, new to the mind, by bringing together two distant realities whose relationship the mind alone has grasped.[2]

Though Surrealist poetic theory would later revise some of this—especially the part about "pure creation of the mind" and the "true relationship" between the two realities—many of the essentials of the Surrealist theory of poetic language are already stated. These include the opposition to ready-made rhetorical formulas or to any use

---

[1] A thorough historical treatment of the various French avant-garde literary theories and their contributions to film theory may be found in Richard Abel's excellent article "The Contribution of the French Literary Avant-Garde to Film Theory and Criticism (1907–1924)," *Cinema Journal* 14 (Spring 1975). My own focus here is on the particular notion of the image in pre-Surrealist and Surrealist thought on the film, some of which may be found in the recently published collection of Surrealist writings on cinema, *The Shadow and Its Shadow*, trans. and ed. Paul Hammond (London: British Film Institute, 1978). I also refer the reader to Standish D. Lawder's account of the relations between Cubism and film in *The Cubist Cinema* (New York: New York University Press, 1975).

[2] Pierre Reverdy, "L'Image," *Nord-Sud* 13, pages are unnumbered. (The translation is my own.)

of language for the imitation of past experience, and the concrete notion of the image as composed of distant realities whose combination produces a surprise.

Given these concerns, it may seem contradictory to find, a few weeks later, another article by Reverdy praising the American film *La Petite Marchande de Journaux* for its realism and naturalism of gesture.[3] Why does Reverdy praise the naturalness of the American film's imitation of life when he deplores this same naturalness in his theory of poetry?

Part of the answer lies in the fact that the relatively new invention of the "cinématographe" had had its greatest success in the American development of narratives modeled on the realism of the nineteenth-century novel. This was already a given of film construction by the time Reverdy was writing. Reverdy is not, like later Surrealists, fighting these conventions in the name of a fully developed theory of textual production. But in his praise of a now forgotten American movie, he is beginning to discover the relevance of his own poetic theory of the image to film, as well as the possibility for a dialectical use of montage. In the same article Reverdy notes that if a film shows first a woman looking out a window and next a cloudy sky, even a child would draw the conclusion that the woman is looking at the sky: "One has simply and directly obtained the essential result."[4]

Reverdy's praise of this elementary montage derives from the discovery that one of the fundamental procedures of filmic creation consists in the concrete juxtaposition of distant realities. What really excites him about the procedure of combining already significant chunks of reality is the potential surprise of their combination.

Of course, he does not yet grasp the way in which film could achieve this effect, because as his example illustrates, he does not yet question the "essential" narrative result of cinematic montage. But because he does understand the structural potential for surprise (though he doesn't fully grasp the possibility of a dialectical collision in the way Soviet film theorists would do later), Reverdy sees good reason for modern poets to look to the film for the further development of his own poetic aims.

[3] Id., "Cinématographe," ibid., 16 (1918):7.
[4] Ibid.

The Image

A few months before Reverdy began to think of the cinematic applications of his theory of the image, Philippe Soupault had explored a slightly different aspect of the medium.[5] Soupault points
out that the difference between *l'art cinématographique* and *l'art du
théâtre* lies in the striking ability of the cinema to upset the natural
laws of space and time.[6] The scenario that follows this article is an
illustration of the powers of the cinematic medium. Entitled *L'Indifférence*, this *poème cinématographique* is a Méliès-inspired flex-
ing of cinematic muscle, in which special effects—especially trans-
formations of people and objects—dominate: "I sit down on a
bench . . . suddenly there appears beside me a man who changes
into a woman, then into an old man. Just then another old man
appears who changes into a baby then into a woman. . . . I get up
and they all disappear."[7]

Reverdy's concept of the image looks to the cinema's power to
combine elements of concrete reality. This power alone he finds
surprising. But it is clear, by the example he uses, that the surprise
only emanates from a knowledge of how montage operates. Because
of narrative habits of interpretation, the viewer feels no real surprise
at the combination of shots Reverdy describes. Thus Reverdy finds
no way to create the surprise he sees as so fundamental to the filmic
process. Soupault's time-space exercises, on the other hand, succeed in creating surprise, but the surprise exists only in relation to
the laws of the real world.

In another article, also published in 1918, Louis Aragon, with
somewhat greater sophistication, praises Chaplin's ability to create a
decor that transforms the function of objects into something completely new and surprising.[8] Though both Soupault and Aragon aim
at Reverdy's surprise effect, Aragon's reference to Chaplin's use of
natural settings and contexts that are transformed by the game of the
action represents an advance over Soupault's simple recourse to special effects. It opens the way to an understanding of the more subtle
ways in which the film medium can be used, working both in har-

[5] Philippe Soupault, "Note I sur le cinéma," *Sic* 25 (January 1918):4.
[6] Ibid.
[7] Id., *L'Indifférence*, ibid. (The translation is my own.)
[8] Aragon writes that Chaplin transforms inanimate objects into living beings and living
beings into mannequins. Louis Aragon, "Du Decor," *Le Film* (September 1918); reprinted in

mony and in conflict with already existing conventions of narrative representation to create a surprise on the level of textual expectations rather than on the level of Soupault's transformation of the "real."

*Apollinaire's Screenplay* La Bréhatine. Soupault, Reverdy, and Aragon were not the first pre-Surrealist poets to cast a favorable eye on the potential of the new art of film. Much of the impetus for their enthusiasm had already been provided by Apollinaire's review *Les Soirées de Paris*. In many ways these younger poets simply followed the lead of the older master in their enthusiasm for a new, seemingly more direct, language as yet untainted by a long history of rhetorical formulas and "realistic" representation. Though *Les Soirées de Paris* did not articulate a new theory of film, its film columns praised Feuillade's *Fantômas* serials and the unprecedented popularity of a medium that, unlike the other arts, still seemed fresh and new. For Apollinaire, who along with Picasso and Max Jacob belonged to the Societé des amis de Fantômas, the very crudeness and popularity of this new form of mass entertainment represented an opportunity to establish an art expressive of the emerging *esprit nouveau*, unfettered by the compartmentalizations and specialized audiences of the current avant-garde.

Yet, in spite of Apollinaire's enthusiasm for film, his actual pronouncements on how to achieve this esprit nouveau in film are disappointing.[9] As Richard Abel points out, Apollinaire's theory does little more than reaffirm the prewar credo of the mixture of epic and lyric qualities.[10] Nevertheless, in light of his role as theoretical spokesman for a new postwar poetics of modernity whose influence on Reverdy and the later Surrealist poetics of the image is undeniable, it is of special interest to see what Apollinaire did, when—in a little known and only recently published manuscript—he tried his hand at screenwriting.

---

*Le Point* 59 (1912):32. See Richard Abel's discussion of this article in "Contribution of the French Avant-Garde" for an analysis of Aragon's early development of the concept of mise-en-scène.

[9] Apollinaire's pronouncements on the film appear in "Interview avec Guillaume Apollinaire," *Sic* 8, 9, 10 (1916).

[10] Abel, "Contribution of the French Avante-Garde," p. 26.

Apollinaire's *La Bréhatine*[11] (written in 1917) is the first scenario written by an important modern writer. Though it was never produced, it was clearly written with the intention of being produced and thus should not be considered along with the various cinematographic poems (of which Soupault's *L'Indifférence* is the first example) that would later flourish with Surrealism. Since it was written for an actual producer within an established industry, for a public that uncritically accepted the conventions of this industry, and not for distribution within a limited avant-garde circuit as would be the case later with Dada and Surrealist films, it is not surprising that the scenario takes the form of conventional melodramas in vogue at the time. *La Bréhatine* has long been regarded a hack work[12] without interest or relation to Apollinaire's other writings. In 1971 Alain Virmaux partially revised this opinion in an article accompanying publication of the screenplay.[13]

Virmaux's aim is to rehabilitate the scenario in spite of its melodrama, which he can forgive but not justify. He points out that, although the work is a pathetic tale of betrayed love and tragic suicide, it nevertheless offers an intriguing mixture of the real and the imaginary. The story is as follows: A Breton girl (la Bréhatine) awaits the return of her sailor fiancé in a lonely lighthouse, while in a parallel development this same fiancé abandons himself to a life of crime in Paris. A writer who has heard her tale uses it to write a novel, which he freely embellishes with his own contribution of the fiancé's death and la Bréhatine's subsequent suicide. When by chance la Bréhatine comes across the novel as it is being published in installments, she reads it with fascination and dread. As she reads, she envisions the events of her past life, along with those that had been imagined; and after reading the story's tragic ending, she writes the author informing him that she recognizes the woman's story as her own. She then throws herself over a cliff just as the heroine of the novel had done. The remorseful writer then brings the fiancé to the cliff, where—in an attempt to catch la Bréhatine's engagement ring,

[11] Guillaume Apollinaire and André Billy, *La Bréhatine*, Archives des lettres modernes 7 (1917):10–96.

[12] Michel Décaudin, for example, judges the screenplay totally unoriginal. "Les poètes découvrent le cinéma," *Etudes cinématographiques* 38–39 (1965):75–82.

[13] Alain Virmaux, "*La Bréhatine* et le cinéma: Apollinaire en quête d'un langage neuf," *Archives des lettres modernes* 7 (1971):97–115.

7

which has fallen—he (only half accidentally) slips and falls to a similar death.

Virmaux's essay on this scenario concludes that, by virtue of the intrusion of the "imaginary" into the realm of the "quotidian," Apollinaire's scenario deserves better consideration by both film lovers and Apollinaire critics in spite of its melodramatic limitations. I would add that the scenario's melodrama is not an unfortunate concession to a conventional genre but an extremely sophisticated use of this convention against itself. In this sense it is a precursor of the kind of textual deconstruction that Buñuel and Dalí were to develop ten years later in their films—a deconstruction central to most Surrealist film. For what impresses in this scenario is not so much the pathos of the girl's fate as the mechanism by which she meets it. This is a mechanism of repetition in which the imaginary not only intrudes into the quotidian but completely takes it over, causing the distinction between the two to break down.

The fact that this fusion of imaginary and real only takes place in the mind of a character, rationalized as a plot device in the representation of a world that still keeps these two categories separate, is what separates *La Bréhatine* from later, truly Surrealist, works. Nevertheless the work displays the essential quality that Artaud, Desnos, Buñuel, and Dalí were later to present in their own works: the identificatory function of the image in the construction of the human subject.

In the Apollinaire and Billy scenario the woman identifies with her own image as she reads the novelist's story. Half of the story is derived from past events of her own life and half is imagined by the novelist himself. The image—of events both remembered and imagined—appears as a vignette superimposed on a corner of the screen, with no visual differentiation within vignettes between what is real and what is imagined. This procedure reveals the power of an actual, remembered image to link up with and generate an imaginary one, blurring the distinction between the two. The effect is analogous to Freud's description of *perceptual identity*—a process in which a subject repeats various visual perceptions that have been linked to the satisfaction of needs in the past[14]—and also to Freud's

---

[14] Sigmund Freud, *The Interpretation of Dreams*, trans. James Strachey (New York: Avon Books, 1965), p. 605.

definition of *screen memories*.[15] Screen memories are false recollections that mix with and condense a great many childhood memories. They are reformulations of actual memories, which serve as supports for unconscious fantasies.

Both perceptual identity and screen memories display the deceptive power of the image to obscure the distinction between fact and fiction. In the case of *La Bréhatine*, this obfuscation is not the result of the subject's own projected fantasies but of someone else's projection. But this projection is presented by the film in images that have an irresistible power to induce belief. Seduced by the apparent reality of her own image as presented in the story and viewed on the screen as no different from the remembered images of her actual life, the real woman becomes the victim of an imaginary identification. As she identifies with a false image of herself, she finally becomes that image.

Thus an apparently banal melodrama based on a Breton theme familiar to French film audiences of 1917 goes right to the heart of an issue that had already, in a much more scientific way, formed the basis of Freud's exploration of the unconscious and would in the future form the basis of the Surrealist's mining of Freudian theory: the startling power of the cinematic image considered not in its capacity for imitation but in its capacity to create an alternative reality. What Apollinaire's scenario demonstrates is the power of the visual image to elicit a poetic response that is, in Reverdy's terms, "outside of all imitation, all evocation, all comparison."[16] Because of, rather than despite, its apparent conventionality, *La Bréhatine* goes farther than Soupault's *L'Indifférence*, in its search for what Reverdy calls "the surprise and the joy of finding oneself before a new thing."[17] Only by inscribing the scenario within a conventional realism that it undercuts do Apollinaire and Billy begin to achieve the surprise that Reverdy, Soupault, and Aragon sought. This is a point the Surrealists were to discover again during the 1924–28 period. But what interests us here is that as early as 1917–18, in an initial burst of cinematic enthusiasm that had no issue in actual filmic production, the

[15] Id., "Screen Memories," *The Standard Edition of the Complete Psychological Works of Sigmund Freud*, 24 vols., ed. James Strachey (London: Hogarth Press, 1953–66), 3:305–6.
[16] Reverdy, "L'Image," pages are unnumbered.
[17] Ibid.

pre-Surrealist theory of the image was already drawing upon the existing conventions of this new art form to create the desired surprise.

Reverdy, Soupault, Aragon, and Apollinaire all point to one basic observation in their tentative exploration of the film medium: that the unprecedented realism of the image—its apparent naturalness—need not be used to achieve the illusion of reality. For, although film is composed of images that are the most meticulous imitation of already significant fragments of reality ever made possible, the very fact that these fragments are so convincing makes their combination in a structure not intended to create the illusion of reality all the more surprising. This interest in a mirror that does not reflect what *is*, but whose ability to reflect becomes the very symbol of the enigma of signification, will become central in the later development of Surrealist film. As Paul Eluard writes, "I am captivated, truly captivated by the reality of a mirror that does not reflect my appearance." [18]

### THE SURREALIST IMAGE

In the first manifesto of surrealism (1924), André Breton relates that it was a visual hallucination of a man cut in two by a window that inspired his subsequent exploration of the relation between unconscious thought and poetic production. [19] This exploration resulted in Breton and Soupault's experiments in automatic writing and the ultimate development of the notion of the surreal. This notion was a reformulation of Reverdy's earlier idea of the poetic image. But instead of discovering the hidden motive in the combination of two or more chunks of reality, Breton favored the more dialectical notion of the spark that arises from their collision. Breton discovered that this spark could be found in the discourse of the unconscious. Automatic writing, derived from the psychoanalytic technique of free association, was simply a means of reproducing in the medium of verbal language both the content and process of the unconscious. It

[18] Paul Eluard, untitled note on his dreams, *Le Surréalisme au service de la révolution* 1 (July 1930):2. (The translation is mine.)

[19] André Breton, *Manifestoes of Surrealism*, trans. Richard Seaver and Helen R. Lane (Ann Arbor: University of Michigan Press, 1974), pp. 21–22.

was a makeshift attempt by verbal language to capture what Freud had already described in the *Interpretation of Dreams* as the tendency of the unconscious to discourse visually.

Other methods would soon develop. Not surprisingly these methods turned increasingly toward the visual arts. In the first manifesto, Surrealism is described as "psychic automatism in its pure state, by which one proposes to express—verbally, by means of the written word, or in any other manner—the actual functioning of the mind."[20] Between the publication of the first and second manifestoes, this "any other manner" of visual expression became increasingly important.

In 1925, the year he took over direction of the first Surrealist review, *La Révolution surréaliste,* André Breton began publishing installments of his original *Surréalisme et la peinture,* published as a whole in 1928 and augmented in 1941 with the essay *Genèse et perspective artistiques du surréalisme.* In both Breton looks back at the works of de Chirico, Duchamp, Man Ray, and especially Max Ernst to discover an *avant-la-lettre* flowering of Surrealist principles in the plastic arts.[21] In Ernst's collages, actual objects were separated from their customary surroundings and recombined in new relationships with other objects. The result of these recombinations was the famous *dépaysement* or disorientation so typical of Surrealist art.

One of the major themes running through these works and already implicit in Breton's earlier theory of the poetic image is the notion that auditory or verbal images lack the clarity, precision, and, therefore, force of visual images. As Breton admitted in a 1935 treatment of the differences between visual and auditory images, it is in painting that Surrealist poetry found its most vast field of influence.[22] Thus, as Anna Balakian has pointed out, Surrealism established a closer bond between poetry and the visual arts than had ever before existed.[23]

[20] Ibid., p. 26.
[21] Breton writes that Ernst's collages corresponded most closely to the poetry of Lautréamont and Rimbaud. *Genèse et perspective artistiques du surréalisme* (New York: Brentano's, 1945), p. 90.
[22] Breton, *Position politique du surréalisme* (Paris: Sagittaire, 1935), p. 174.
[23] Anna Balakian, *Surrealism: The Road to the Absolute* (New York: Dutton, 1970), p. 144.

From Ernst's collages it was a natural step to the development of a similar combinative procedure in photography. Man Ray's use of montage processes in his "rayograms" gave a similar effect of dépaysement. From there it was but another step to the separation of actual objects from their natural context. Following the lead of Marcel Duchamp's "readymades," the Surrealists would circulate random objects among themselves, posing irrelevant questions about their function. A piece of rose-colored velvet, for example, elicited the question With whom should it meet on a dissection table for it to be beautiful?[24] These games, which the Surrealists called "research on the irrational knowledge of the object,"[25] were created as ways of separating the object from its functional connection to a context in order to create new associations emanating from the concrete density of the thing itself.

*The Image of the Object in Space.* The Surrealists' expansion of thepoetic image into the realm of the visual arts resulted in the readoption of conventions of figural art abandoned by Cubism. Recognizable objects were once again given a certain existence in space. But these objects were often composite creations or strangely deformed. Whether in Magritte's eerie confluence of indoor-outdoor settings or in the contradictory perspectives of de Chirico, the relation of part to whole and whole to the space it occupied was intentionally rearranged.

Thus the Surrealist artistic image only pretends to create the illusion of real space, no matter how meticulously drawn (Magritte) or even photographed (Man Ray) the objects in it might be. Like the dissection table in Lautréamont's often quoted "as handsome . . . as the fortuitous encounter upon a dissecting table of a sewing machine and an umbrella,"[26] the image is simply the space of an encounter and never the illusion of a previously existing place.

*The Image of the Object in Time.* In André Breton's example of the

---

[24] Paul Eluard, "Recherches expérimentales," *Le Surréalisme au service de la révolution* 6:12.

[25] Ibid.

[26] Lautréamont, *Maldoror,* trans. Guy Wernham (New York: New Directions, 1965), p. 263.

image of a man cut in two by a window,[27] it is important to note that Breton's initial impulse was to continue this production of images in *time*: the original phrase gave way to a whole succession of phrases almost without pause.[28] Though the phrase came to Breton in verbal form, he adds that it was sustained by "the faint visual image of a man walking cut half way up by a window perpendicular to the axis of his body."[29] He adds in a note that had he been a painter this visual representation would have undoubtedly dominated the verbal one: "It was most certainly my previous predispositions which decided the matter."[30]

But, whether visual or verbal, what most interests Breton is not the medium in which the static image can be captured but the possibility of developing it in time as a succession of illogically evolving images. Automatic writing, whose primary technique is the acceleration of the speed of writing, elicits this flow of mysteriously linked images "in the absence of control exercised by reason."[31] This is a process dependent upon the temporal dimension inherent in all verbal arts but radically opposed to the more typical practice of creating the illusion of events taking place in time.

*Poisson soluble* (*Soluble Fish*), published as an accompanying illustration of Breton's theoretical defense of Surrealism in the first manifesto, combines both these Surrealist qualities of the spatial image (and its effect of dépaysement) and the temporal qualities of a *récit* in which narrative time is deconstructed in favor of the time of the textual unfolding.[32] *Poisson soluble* does in verbal language what the best Surrealist films would do in images a couple of years later: it unites the spatial elements of image and the temporal elements of narrative in a discourse that deconstructs the usual function of each. . This deconstruction of space and time is similar to the use of space and time in the dream.

[27] Breton, *Manifestoes of Surrealism*, p. 21.
[28] Ibid.
[29] Ibid., pp. 21–22.
[30] Ibid., p. 21.
[31] Ibid., p. 26.
[32] *Soluble Fish* begins: "The park, at this time of day, stretched its blond hands over the magic fountain. A meaningless castle rolled along the surface of the earth, close to God the register of this chateau was open at a drawing of shadows." André Breton, *Soluble Fish*, in *Manifestoes of Surrealism*, p. 51.

*Surrealist Film Aesthetics: The Language of Film and the Language of Dream.* The privileged position of the dream throughout all Surrealist art is, of course, well known. The dream unites the two divergent directions of the verbal (temporal) and visual (spatial) arts in the most perfectly "automatic" of textual productions. The proliferation of dream accounts that filled the pages of the Surrealist journals of the period is sufficient testimony to the Surrealists' interest in this form of access to the unconscious. To a very large extent the development of the aesthetics of Surrealist film grows out of the model of the dream. It is important to determine, therefore, just how this model operates. In what way did the Surrealists who enthusastically turned to the new medium of film in the 1920s and 30s propose to "imitate" the dream? And, since their motive for turning to the film was at least partially to escape the rigid codifications of verbal language and encounter the relative freedom of a seemingly more direct expression of desire, this first question encounters another that is even more complex. To what extent do the film and the dream actually escape the codified structures inherent in language, or to what extent are they themselves structured? In exploring the Surrealists' answer to the second question, I hope to show that the Surrealist discourse on film is the first theoretical treatment of questions that have recently been re-posed by semiotic and psychoanalytic theories of film currently developing in France.

Christian Metz's use of Lacanian psychoanalysis extends his original study of film language to include the unconscious structures that affect our experience of film. Although the Surrealists did not employ this specifically Lacanian interpretation of film and dream language, I hope to show that the Surrealist discourse on film can most fruitfully be interpreted in light of Lacan's theory of the languagelike structure of the unconscious. This theory helps us understand the very profound ways in which the Surrealists proposed to cultivate not the *content* of unconscious desire—as many critics have maintained—but its *form.*

The following pages in no way attempt to present a complete history of Surrealist film aesthetics or even of this aesthetics as practiced in the two or three classics of Surrealist film. I am concerned in this chapter only with the theoretical side of the problem: how the Surrealists conceived of film art. For this reason I have omitted discussion of the occasional interviews with the makers of Surrealist films, in order to focus on those Surrealists who, although they made no films themselves, sustained a fairly high level of theoretical discourse on the cinema. I have also purposely omitted discussion of the early pre-Surrealist cinematographic poems, as well as some of the more famous pronouncements of Breton and Aragon on the film, because they are presented in other works on the subject, most notably in Ado Kyrou's *Le Surréalisme au cinéma* and J. H. Mathews's *Surrealism and Film*, and because, in spite of their obvious and infectious enthusiasm, they tend to be among the least illuminating of the Surrealist writings on the film.

Instead my focus is on some of the lesser known contributions to Surrealist film aesthetics—Goudal, Artaud, and Desnos—and on their rather tricky use of the model of the dream. In so doing I hope to counter what has been until now a dominant tendency in analyses of Surrealist film. This is the tendency, evident in both Kyrou and Mathews, to confuse an important Surrealist goal—Breton's famous psychic automatism freed from all *reasoning control*—with the more general freedom from all *form*. Surrealist film has often been viewed as the absolute freedom of expression of certain privileged poetic subjects, and as the "free" expression of desire. My own view is not only that form is important in both Surrealist film and Surrealist discourse on film, but also that the notion of "subject," as these critics have understood it, does not really exist. For, whether in the subject of unconscious erotic desire or in the human subject considered as a psychological entity, Surrealist film is a radical questioning of the supposed integrity of these subjects and of the enigmatic relations between content and form. In the following examination of what certain Surrealists had to say about the film, I hope to show that desire functions much less as a subject-content than it does as a form—a structured process in which the work of the image is of central importance.

It is obvious that dreams and films are experienced in similar ways—in darkened rooms in which the dreamer or spectator passively perceives, identifies with, and believes in a flow of images that appear real but have no corporeal existence. But it is not so obvious just how the Surrealist filmmaker might *use* these similarities in the making of an actual film. For example, should the filmmaker try to imitate the dreamer's passivity before and belief in the image? Or should the model of the dream be interpreted more loosely? It is also obvious that the contents of films and dreams often act out the most secret desires. The Surrealists were fond of extolling the erotic virtues of silent film stars, such as Pearl White and Louise Brooks, as if the passions experienced on the screen by these stars were an appropriate enactment of their own unconscious desires. But they were also well aware that the dream, unlike the film, is a private production of meaning.

Although the dreamer seems to understand and accept the illogicalities of dream discourse, it is really only the manifest content that is understood. The true desire is often latent. Thus the dream is a closed system that can only be decoded by external knowledge— of both the dreamer's life and psychoanalytic methods of interpretation. If, for example, the recollection of an actual dream were filmed, the result would be a totally opaque reproduction of the manifest content of a dream, with no clue to its latent meaning. To the outside spectator such a film would appear even more senseless and chaotic than the actual dream appeared to the dreamer,[33] and the wish-fulfillment at its center would remain unrevealed. On the other hand, to produce a dreamlike discourse in which the latent content or wish-fulfillment can be easily decoded is to run the risk of planting psychoanalytic clues or conventionalized symbols that aid in interpretation but violate the unconscious and irrational ambience so important to the dream.

The problem of the dream model in the development of a Surrealist film aesthetic is thus more complex than it first seems. But precisely because the Surrealists did break away from some of the more literal applications of the dream model, they were able to go beyond the simple violations of time and space that had characterized both the early screenplays of Philippe Soupault and Benjamin Peret and the overly symbolic dream sequences of the commer-

---

[33] Most of the original work on psychoanalysis and the cinema by Metz, Bellour, Kuntzel, and others has been presented in *Communications* 23 and recent issues of *Ça Cinéma*, especially vol. 7/8 (May 1975) in homage to Christian Metz. More recently, Metz's work on psychoanalysis and cinema has been collected in the volume *Le Signifiant imaginaire*. Two essays from this volume have been translated: the title essay, by Ben Brewster, for *Screen* 16 (1975); and "The Fiction Film and Its Spectator," by Alfred Guzzetti, for *New Literary History* 8 (1976). All subsequent references will be to these translations.

cial cinema. As we shall see, the real contribution of the dream model in the development of a Surrealist theory of film is not based on the more obvious imitation of dreams but on a more profound attempt to understand their similarities as systems of communication that differ in important ways from verbal language.

## GOUDAL, ARTAUD, AND DESNOS
## IN SEARCH OF THE "LANGUAGE" OF DREAMS

In a remarkable and little known article published in 1925 soon after the first manifesto and *Poisson soluble*, Jean Goudal provides a surprisingly insightful and thorough analysis of film's resemblance to dream and its Surrealist possibilities.[34] Goudal was not himself a Surrealist. Yet his understanding of Surrealist goals and his ability to foresee some of the effects of the movement on filmmaking make this essay an illuminating document.

In this article[35] Goudal poses the important question How can we envision the future of the cinema on the basis of its most fundamental technical conditions? He then stresses that in many modern arts the basic material of the art form is brought into play, that literary Surrealism brings the "matter" of *language* into play at the expense of reality, and that film is especially privileged in its capacity to do the same.

While Goudal questions the ability of verbal language to achieve the defeat of the real (since language for him is primarily rational), he sees the experience of film as a merging of conscious and unconscious states. In the very way we experience it, film takes us out of ourselves and into a hallucinatory realm: "Let's go into a cinema . . . On entering, our gaze is guided by the luminous ray to the screen . . . Life on the street outside no longer exists. Our problems

---

[34] Hugo Münsterberg's 1916 work, *The Film: A Psychological Study* (New York: Dover, 1970), had already explored many of the issues raised by Goudal. Although Münsterberg's brilliant analysis demonstrated the many ways in which film was capable of reorganizing the representation of space, time, and causality in the interest of portraying an inner world of memory, imagination, and emotion, he was not interested in using these capabilities for anything other than heightened dramatic effect.

[35] Jean Goudal, "Surréalisme et cinéma," *La Revue hébdomadaire* 8 (February 21, 1925). Reprinted as "Surrealism and Cinema" in Paul Hammond, ed. and trans., *The Shadow and Its Shadow*. All subsequent references are to this translation.

evaporate, our neighbors disappear. Our body itself submits to a sort
of temporary depersonalization. . . . We are nothing but two eyes
riveted to ten square metres of white sheet."[36] Thus the image takes
us out of our own reality, luring us into an identification with the
other on the screen that is much stronger than any identification
produced in language. Identification with an image defeats the system of differences inherent in language and its appeal to reason: "In
language the foremost factor is always the logical thread. The image
is born according to this thread, and contributes to its embellishment, its illumination. In cinema the foremost factor is the image
which, on occasion . . . drags the tatters of reason behind it."[37] For
Goudal such images function as images in a dream, because we absolutely believe in their existence no matter how illogical they
seem.

Goudal therefore surmises that Surrealism is privileged by the
very techniques of the film medium. Consequently, the surest way
to make existing Surrealist literary works acceptable for a larger public would be to treat them as film scenarios. Though he is wrong
here—the particular surreality of a work like *Poisson soluble* is inextricably bound to its verbal discourse—his description of the illogicality of the image and the way in which film is experienced is
central to all Surrealist thinking about the cinema. Goudal never
assumes that a Surrealist use of film would amount to a *trompe l'oeil*
representation of the dream. In fact, he is quick to note the differences between the film state and the dream state, as when he
likens the film to a form of conscious hallucination rather than the
unconscious hallucinatory state of sleep. What interests Goudal is,
therefore, more the resemblance between the film and the dream *in
language* than *in content*: the fact that each proceeds through a succession of images that is a simulacrum of the real world but is also
at the same time radically artificial. It is this quality of being
both more and less real than reality that film and dream have in
common.

Comparing the film with the theater, Goudal anticipates a point
central to Christian Metz's essay "The Imaginary Signifier"[38]: that

[36] Ibid., p. 51.
[37] Ibid., p. 53.
[38] *Screen* 16:14–76.

in the dream and the film one sees the image of something that is not really there in an illusion similar to that of a mirror. Thus, in a paradoxical way the film and the dream are more purely visual than is, for example, the theater.[39] Goudal suggests that the exploitation of similarities between film and dream is the surest way to achieve surreality in film. This means that illogical successions of images could come to replace the usual fictional goal of inspiring belief in the fiction that is *behind* the image in order to concentrate on the unconscious properties of the image itself.

The period of Antonin Artaud's involvement in film as actor, scenario writer, and essayist stretches from 1924, when he first abandoned the stage to become a screen actor, to 1933, when he wrote the article "La Vieillesse précoce du cinéma."[40] But it was primarily during his often stormy involvement with the Surrealist group, while serving as director of the Bureau de Recherches Surréalistes,[41] that his creative talents as a writer were concentrated on the film. Desnos' affiliation with the Surrealist group lasted longer than that of Artaud. He had been the star dreamer during the heroic pre-Surrealist *periode des sommeils*[42] that preceded publication of *La Révolution surréaliste*. But, like Artaud, by the time of publication of the second manifesto, he was no longer a member of the group. (Artaud's acting and Desnos' journalism, both of which served other gods than Surrealism, constitute the main reason for these expulsions.) Both Artaud and Desnos maintained a steady production of screenplays and writing on the cinema, though neither had much success producing their work. Only one scenario by Artaud was ever

[39] Goudal writes: "The individuals performing on a theater stage have a physical presence that strengthens the *trompe l'oeil* of their setting—while the camera aspires to give the illusion of reality by means of a simulacrum of a uniquely visual kind. An actual hallucination is needed here which the other conditions of cinema tend to reinforce, just as, in the dream, moving images lacking three dimensionality follow each other on a single plane artificially delimited by a rectangle which is like a geometrical opening giving on to the psychic kingdom." "Surrealism and Cinema," p. 349.

[40] Antonin Artaud, *Collected Works*, trans. Alastair Hamilton, 5 vols. (London: Calder & Boyars, 1972), vol. 3.

[41] Id., "L'Activité du Bureau de Recherches Surréalistes," *La Révolution surréaliste* 3 (April 15, 1925). Artaud was a full-fledged member of the Surrealist group from 1924 to 1927. After that he was only sporadically involved, as, for example, when the Surrealists joined him in booing Germaine Dulac's direction of his screenplay *The Seashell and the Clergyman*.

[42] Sarane Alexandrian, *Le Surréalisme et le rêve* (Paris: Gallimard, 1974), p. 103.

19

filmed and none by Desnos, though Desnos' poem "Etoile de Mer" was interpreted in a film of the same title by Man Ray in 1928.

Artaud's writings on the cinema tend to be more probing than are those by Desnos. His essays and scenario[43] go to the heart of the issue of film's existence as a language. Artaud's own attitude toward film is encapsulated in the fate of the hero of his first published scenario. In it an actor "has been stricken by a strange malady. He has become incapable of keeping up with his thoughts. . . . He is at a loss for words; they no longer answer his call, and all he sees is a procession of images, masses of contradictory, disconnected images."[44] The objectification of these images forms the basis of this scenario in a time-expansion structure similar to Cocteau's *Le Sang d'un poète* but predating that film by five years.

This failure of words and the reasoning thought processes carried out by language is central to all of Artaud's work, not only his work in film. But, during this period of his work, it is responsible for the appeal of film as a means of avoiding language's separation of the word from the thing. What Artaud wanted was a language that would not only *express*, but also—impossibly—*be* the very flesh and blood of his thought. It is not my purpose here to delve into the specifics of Artaud's "malady."[45] It is clear, however, that his rejection of normal verbal language as a tool in the quest for thought both parallels and differs from the Surrealists' own rejection of cliché-ridden logical language and the world-views it perpetrates. For Artaud the rejection of language and the recourse to a nonverbal image-discourse derives from a fundamental sense of the absence of any essential being he could call his own and, similarly, of any discourse that, once spoken, belonged to him.

As Derrida sees it in *L'Ecriture et la différence*, signification for Artaud was by its very nature a kind of robbery in which the speaking subject is never located at the center of his discourse but is always absent, stolen away by the already existing structures of a lan-

---

[43] Artaud, *Collected Works*, vol. 3. This volume contains all of Artaud's essays, scenario, and correspondence concerning the cinema.

[44] Ibid., p. 11.

[45] See Maurice Blanchot, *La Part du feu*, 5th. ed. (Paris: Gallimard, 1949); Jacques Derrida, *L'Ecriture et la différence*(Paris: Seuil, 1967); Naomi Green, *Antonin Artaud: Poet without Words* (New York: Simon & Schuster, 1970).

guage that makes the discourse understandable but never his own.[46]
Derrida explains that Artaud's sense of an original alienation,
caused by an Other that has stolen his word and separated him from
his body, seeks an outlet in his dream of a "life without difference"[47]
and, similarly, an art that would never separate itself from his
body—the dream of an art without an *oeuvre*.[48]

Artaud's obsession with film, like his later development of the
theater of cruelty, was an impossible attempt to prevent his work
from being stolen away by the Other, by placing it in a medium that
did not have the "differences" of language, e.g., the arbitrary and
conventional association of a particular sound with a particular
sense. The apparent absence of difference between the image and
what it expresses meant that the cinema seemed to appeal directly
to the imagination without the separation between sound and sense
so endemic to language: "So nothing interposes itself any longer
between the work and the spectator. Above all the cinema is like
an innocuous and direct poison, a subcutaneous injection of
morphine."[49]

The notion of the immediacy of film, of its ability to bypass the
usual coded channels of language through a visual short circuit that
acts "almost intuitively on the brain,"[50] is Artaud's attempt to rediscover what he terms the primitive arrangement of all things. It is
also a partial way of escaping the need to produce an actual work.
For the film image, unlike an accumulation of words on the page or
an enactment of these words in a theater, cannot be pointed to as a
thing that is actually *there*. In other words, the film (as Christian
Metz has shown, but as the Surrealists had already intuited) is an
*imaginary signifier*. This idea of an imaginary signifier is central
to Metz's psychoanalytic film theory. Briefly, the term refers to the
paradoxical fact that, although film is the most perceptual of all the
arts and even though its signifier (the play of light and shadow on

[46] Derrida writes: "La lettre est toujours volée . . . parce que toujours ouverte. Elle n'est jamais propre à son auteur ou à son destinataire." *L'Ecriture et la différence*, p. 262.
[47] Ibid., p. 268.
[48] Artaud writes, "pas d'oeuvres, pas de langue, pas de parole, pas d'esprit, rien." Quoted from Derrida, *Le Pèse nerfs*, in *L'Ecriture et la différence*, p. 268.
[49] Artaud, *Collected Works*, 3:60.
[50] Id., "Cinema and Reality," ibid., p. 20.

21

the screen representing the objects of the real world) gives a powerful impression of reality, this impression is only an illusion.

The projected illusion of past photochemical registrations, the cinema is "profoundly stamped with unreality, from its very beginning."[51] By *imaginary signifier* Metz does not mean a signifier that is *really* not there. As will become clear below, he means to stress that filmic signifiers—as opposed to those of theater and literature—are more inscribed in a specific relation to what Lacan calls "the Imaginary."

For Artaud, precisely this absence of the cinematic signifier seemed to offer a possible protection against the robbery of his speech by the Other. In a major article published along with the scenario of *The Seashell and the Clergyman*, Artaud describes just how he envisions the future development of film. Explaining that his concept of film follows neither the lead of the dominant "psychological cinema" nor the then current avant-garde of "pure cinema," Artaud adds:

> We must find a film with purely visual sensations the dramatic force of which springs from a shock on the eyes, drawn, one might say, from the very substance of the eye, and not from psychological circumlocutions of a discursive nature which are nothing but visual interpretations of a text. We are not trying to find an equivalent of the written language in the visual language, which is simply a bad interpretation of it. We are trying to bring the very essence of the language and transport the action into a level where every interpretation would become useless and where this action would act almost intuitively on the brain.[52]

This nondiscursive, nontranslatable, visual "essence" of language is a language that refuses to *represent* anything, even the dreamlike content of the unconscious. Instead, it approximates the *form* of the unconscious, the direct and seemingly uncoded way in which unconscious "language" operates. Thus Artaud states that his scenario of *The Seashell and the Clergyman* is not a reproduction of a dream and should not be regarded as such:

> I shall not try to excuse the apparent inconsistency by the facile sub-

[51] Metz, "Imaginary Signifier," p. 48.
[52] Artaud, "Cinema and Reality," *Collected Works*, 3:20.

terfuge of dreams. Dreams have more than their logic. They have their life where nothing but a sombre truth appears. This script searches for the sombre truth of the mind in images which emerge exclusively from themselves, and do not draw their meaning from the situation in which they develop but from a sort of powerful inner necessity which projects them into the light of a merciless evidence.[53]

Artaud understands what Robert Desnos, in a much more naïve view of the powers of film, does not: that it is the "mechanics of a dream,"[54] its *way* of signifying, that the film must imitate if the desired effect of surreality is to be achieved. It is interesting to compare Desnos' writing on the cinema with Artaud's in relation to this fundamental issue. Desnos' writing, collected in the volume *Cinéma*,[55] is more limited in scope than Artaud's: analysis and theory interest him much less. With a radical and intentional subjectivity, a loose and not very consistent terminology founded on the opposition between aestheticism (bad) and poetry (good), Desnos is an excellent example of the kind of *critique synthétique*[56] that had been practiced by the pre-Surrealists ever since the days of the review *Sic*. Desnos writes: "I have always tried not to do criticism. In everything that relates to the cinema I have only expressed desires. . . . However bad the scenario, however detestable the direction, it is still about a flesh and blood hero no less real than those of our dreams."[57]

For Desnos, too, it is the film's resemblance to dream that fascinates. To him the film is an artificial dream that can provide new and exciting images for dreamless nights. As with Artaud, the illusory and elusive quality of the projected image fascinates him: "You die and yet your doubles captured in the fragility of the celluloid survive you and continue to carry out your ephemeral actions. The projection does not stop at the screen. It goes beyond it, and ever-increasing, continues to infinity like two mirrors reflecting each other."[58]

A true Surrealist, Desnos refuses to consider the film as simply

[53] Ibid.
[54] Ibid., p. 63.
[55] Robert Desnos, *Cinéma*, ed. André Tchernia (Paris: Gallimard, 1966).
[56] Marguerite Bonnet, "L'Aube du surréalisme et le cinéma," *Etudes cinématographiques* 1 (Spring 1965):85.
[57] Denos, *Cinéma*, p. 110. (All translations from Denos' writing on the film are my own.)
[58] Ibid., p. 156.

another art form, an object of contemplation endowed with aesthetic virtues. As the above passage indicates, he prefers to model the film upon the dream's function of wish-fulfillment, as a mirror reflecting our desires rather than what is. For Desnos the heroes of film would ideally act out the spectators' own repressed desires, daring to commit the crimes they are too timid to commit themselves.[59]

In theory at least, Desnos differs from Artaud as to how the wish-fulfillment of dreams is achieved. In a very literal way, he speaks of film as the reproduction of the dream[60] and of the projection of the dream onto the screen.[61] For Desnos the appropriate Surrealist use of film would be as a medium to defeat the constraints of the real world through the disruptive antisocial tumult of *amour fou* (mad love): "Look out censor! Look out for that woman's hand in close-up . . . your son will dream of it tonight and . . . escape the life of a slave."[62] Desnos' description of the essential characteristics of the dream as sensuality, absolute liberty, and an atmosphere of infinity and eternity[63] could equally be a description of André Breton's concept of amour fou.[64] But where Breton focuses on the shapes and forms of the amour-fou experience, Desnos seems to view it as a kind of absolute content, a poetry of the subject freed from all form.

Desnos' antiaestheticism becomes a predominant theme in much subsequent criticism of Surrealist film. Ado Kyrou, Jean Mitry, and J. H. Mathews[65] have all maintained similar notions concerning the absence of a Surrealist aesthetic form in film. I would like to take a moment here to explore this issue as it developed in subsequent analyses of Surrealist film, because I think it is an attitude that frequently impedes the understanding of Surrealism. What often happens is critics like Desnos, Kyrou, Mitry, Mathews, and Sadoul confuse an important Surrealist goal—Breton's famous psychic automatism freed from all *reasoning* controls—with a general

---

[59] Ibid., p. 110.

[60] Ibid., p. 132.

[61] Ibid., p. 150.

[62] Ibid., p. 159.

[63] Ibid., p. 151.

[64] In *L'Amour fou* (Paris: Gallimard, 1937), André Breton exalts the tumultuous and disorienting experience of "mad love."

[65] Ado Kyrou, *Le Surréalisme au cinéma*; Jean Mitry, *Le Cinéma expérimental*; J. H. Mathews, *Surrealism and Film*.

freedom from *any* form. Surrealist film has thus been viewed as the absolutely free expression of certain privileged poetic subjects that have been liberated from the constraints of logic. Mathews, for example, quoting Kyrou, Brunius, and Bonnet for support, maintains that for the Surrealist the ideal film is simply a "storehouse for visual images" that will satisfy the viewer's hunger for the marvelous. "Exactly how these images are to be assembled, and with what display of technical finesse, is therefore less important to him than that their presence be felt, providing his imagination with something it can digest and transform surrealistically."[66] He elaborates:

> To the surrealist mind, undue respect for the container—from which, surrealists believe, aestheticism is born—represents far more than formal preoccupations only. . . . To a man, surrealists are far more likely to be moved, therefore, when a film appears to be a vehicle for a content that overspills the mold in which it has been cast. To the extent that aestheticism directs attention away from the poetic potential of film material, it merits denunciation, they contend. They consistently reveal themselves too concerned with seeing things anew to tolerate practices designed to rearrange reality, perhaps, but never to disrupt its familiar orderliness. While contrivance is the hallmark of artistry, they allege, liberation is the consequence of poetry. Just as they distinguish between literature (the exercise of literary technique) and verbal poetry (the revelation of an aspect of the world, previously concealed, which the poet captures with words), so they separate the art of the cinema from the poetry of film. They align themselves with Desnos in regarding "poetic action," not technical skill, as the ingredient most likely to lend a movie distinction and give it lasting value.[67]

It is true that in his writings on the film, Desnos does seem to favor the "contained" over the "container," content over form. But I think Mathews is wrong to assume that this preference is dominant in the Surrealist concept of film or even, for that matter, in Desnos' own screenplays. This false dichotomy has been in use ever since the Surrealists themselves reacted against the avant-garde movement of *cinéma pur* that preceded Surrealist film. These proponents of pure cinema—Viking Eggeling, Walter Ruttman, and Fernand

[66] Mathews, *Surrealism and Film*, pp. 14–15.
[67] Ibid.

Léger—avoided recognizable subjects, narratives, or even shapes in their pursuit of near-abstract forms that would approximate the effects of music. Only in relation to these radical nonrepresentational efforts does Surrealism appear content-oriented. Thus, although it is true that Dalí, Buñuel, Artaud, and Desnos have all at different times denounced the formal aestheticism of "pure cinema," their own interest in reinstating recognizable contents should not be interpreted as a lack of concern for the "container." Even if one wanted to accept Mathews's separation of container and contained, it is clear that the terms he uses—*testing*, and *overspilling the mold* in which a content has been *cast*—betray an inevitable preoccupation with form and with tensions arising within a given form.

Although Desnos, Artaud, and Goudal all agree that the model of the dream is essential to the development of a specifically Surrealist film practice, they disagree as to the most important features of this model. Artaud and Goudal stress the structural and formal resemblance between film and dream, basing their theory of Surrealist cinema on the exploitation of the film's ability to imitate the special language of the dream. Desnos, on the other hand, bases his theory of Surrealist cinema on the development of a wish-fulfilling content of amour fou. Taken separately, neither of these theories comprises an adequate theory of Surrealist film that corresponds to the practice that follows. But combined with each other and with the theoretical implications contained in some of the screenplays of Artaud and Desnos, we can sketch a much fuller development.

Superficially at least, Desnos' film theory would seem to reduce to the following formula: the film, like the dream, should reverse our expectations of the real world by presenting the accomplishment of our most secret desires for passion, adventure, and even murder. In practice one would therefore expect that Desnos' screenplays need only exaggerate melodramatic and passionate qualities already inherent in the films of his day. But in three of Desnos' published screenplays surreality arises not from the presentation of passionate or murderous wish-fulfilling contents, but from the playful way in which he first sets up and then transgresses the narrative forms that embody these contents.

In *Minuit à quatorze heures*,[68] for example, the initial dramatic situation of a love affair that develops between a man and woman in the presence of the woman's original lover is a straightforward and rather banal narrative. But this love affair and its narrative complications—the old lover accidentally drowns while fishing—is soon quite literally swallowed up by what at first seem to be inconsequential formal repetitions. These formal repetitions appear first as rings in the water where the old lover drowns, then in circular reflections from the sun, then in the round pupils of the lover's eyes and the round shape of the moon, until gradually, after many intricate variations, both the lovers and their house are swallowed up by a concrete and all-devouring round ball. Thus a purely formal shape existing initially as the form of other objects—in the water, the eyes, and the moon—takes on greater and greater materiality, until it becomes a subject in its own right, swallowing up everything else in the scenario, including (literally) the incipient psychology of the characters. This round form-become-subject is an ominous and inexplicable presence one would be tempted to interpret as the couple's guilt if it were not so whimsically unsymbolic and so gratuitously formal a development.

Desnos' screenplay is typical of much later Surrealist film: the usual identification of spectator with character is intentionally disturbed by intruding formal similarities. The spectator's belief in the previous reality of place, time, and character is quite literally obliterated by the mysterious and all-engulfing round shapes that first arise out of and finally take over the narrative world posited at the beginning. (It is no accident that three years later Buñuel and Dalí's *Un Chien andalou* commenced another rupture of narrative space and time with a quite similar analogy between round shapes seen in the moon and the eye of a woman seated on a balcony. Here, too, as we shall see in the next chapter, the spectator's identification with the character on the screen is ruptured by the similarity between round moon "sliced" by clouds and round eye literally sliced by a razor.)

These round forms-become-objects are Desnos' way of approx-

[68] Denos, *Cinema*, pp. 21–28.

27

imating the quality of latency so important to our experience of the dream. They hint at latent meaning without either the slavish imitation of the dream or the heavy-handed implanting of symbolic clues to interpretation mentioned above. The ball interrupts the progress of the narrative in much the same way unconscious desires shape the ordinary thoughts and memories of the preconscious and conscious in dreams: one incomprehensible but insistent level of "meaning" intrudes upon and takes over another. Desnos' screenplay offers an analogue of the tensions between the manifest and latent contents in a dream. Although Desnos makes us feel its presence as a force in his text the actual meaning of unconscious desire remains a mystery.

Three of the four Desnos scenarios published—*Les Mystères du Métropolitaine, Y a des punaises dans le rôti de porc,* and *Minuit à quatorze heures*—begin as either melodrama or farce, which before the end is transformed into surreal visions. As the scenarios now stand, they are only sketchy outlines of one possible realization of the Surrealist goal with respect to film. But they demonstrate that Desnos' occasionally naïve pronouncements concerning the "reproduction" of the dream amount to neither a slavish representation of actual recollected dreams nor a literal accomplishment of wish fulfillment, but to a film aesthetic that draws on the established conventions of narrative film. Desnos understood, as Buñuel and Dalí were also to understand, that unconscious desire, if it is to be present in film in the way in which it is present in dreams, cannot also be "represented" there as a subject: it must be perceived, as the unconscious desires of dreams are perceived, through the transgression of a more familiar discourse.

We have already seen that Artaud's writings on the film reveal an even more sophisticated understanding of the uses of the dream model. In these writings Artaud saw the importance of using the film medium to create an analog of dream language. Artaud's practice—insofar as we can infer it from unproduced scenarios that are even sketchier in visual detail than are those of Desnos—is equally clear on this matter. In his first published scenario, *Eighteen Seconds,* Artaud's theory that Surrealist film should imitate the "mechanics" of dream is excitingly demonstrated. The hero of this scenario is an actor incapable of keeping up with or attaining his own thoughts. We have already seen how this dilemma is an expression of Artaud's sense of alienation between being and saying. Standing under a street lamp, watch in hand, the actor counts as eighteen seconds tick by. During this period, events taking up to an hour to occur on the screen take place. The actor identifies himself with the first person at hand, a hunchbacked newspaper vendor. But, just as fast as he takes on the identity of this other person, the imagined self-possession of the other disappears. In this way one futile identification follows another, as the actor's centerless self goes from double to double until he finds himself on the stage of a theater, where he imagines himself an actor who is merely playing the part of a hunchback. In other words, the actor has finally hit upon an identification with the actor in himself—with an aspect of himself that is perpetually a reflection of the Other. Artaud has here created a structure *within* the film that parallels the structure described by Desnos as the experience of viewing the film—a structure which, Desnos writes, "continues into infinity like two mirrors reflecting each other."[69]

In Artaud's screenplay, this infinite reflexivity of the series of mirrors that constitute the actor's identity is the focus of the work. Each identification represents another stage in the pursuit of the actor's perpetually elusive self. The pursuit leads him on a wild-goose chase through a maze of images, none of which contains or ever can contain the unified self he desires to possess. The last moments of this scenario show how this process of identification reverses itself. After coming face to face with the mirror identification of actor with actor, we are led back to the original image of the actor standing under a street lamp:

> And there he is, on the stage, with his hump, at the feet of his mistress who is acting with him. And his hump is also false: it is feigned. And his mistress is his real mistress. . . . But he is also acting the part of the king. He is king, he hears and sees himself on the stage at the same time. And the king has no hump. He has realized that the hunchback on the stage is none other than his own effigy, a traitor who took his wife and stole his mind. . . . And at the same time the two characters dissolve into each other on the screen. The whole auditorium trembles . . . and against this trembling background all

[69] Ibid., p. 165.

the images file past, also trembling, the king, the newsvendor, the hunchback actor, the lunatic, the asylum, the crowds, and the man finds himself on the pavement under the lamp-post, his watch in hand.[70]

Eighteen seconds have gone by. He pulls out a revolver and shoots himself in the head.

Although the logical incoherence of *Eighteen Seconds* gives it a much greater dreamlike appearance than Desnos' *Minuit à quatorze heures*, Artaud's method is much less a matter of representing an actual dream than of finding a filmic analogue to certain dream procedures. Artaud has done this by making the identification process that is central to the dream mechanism the subject of his film. This, of course, is very different from what most fictional films and dreams do. The fiction film, as Christian Metz has shown, resembles the dream insofar as the spectator is encouraged to passively accept, believe in, and identify with images projected on the screen. The fiction film thus uses the identification process that is so basic to the dream to involve the spectator in the false reality of the image. Artaud's screenplay disrupts this illusion through a textual enactment of an identification process gone berserk. Rather than using identification to involve us in a representation, Artaud exposes the mechanics of this process to our scrutiny. The image of the Other is revealed as a seductive illusion of wholeness which the dreaming (and desiring) subject can never attain.

Artaud's theory and practice suggests that the Surrealist celebration of the unprecedented reality of the film image derives paradoxically from the desire to expose its ultimate falseness. Artaud's special contribution to Surrealist film lies in his ability to connect this particular paradox with the larger paradox of the role of the image in the formation of the self. Thus, although Artaud's writings about the film seem on the surface to betray a desire for a system of nonverbal communication in which the cleavage between word and thing characterizing verbal language can be overcome, his actual use of nonverbal communication to portray a character's thoughts does not avoid but, rather, reencounters the problem of linguistic

[70] Artaud, "Cinema and Reality," p. 14.

alienation. Both *Eighteen Seconds* and, later, *The Seashell and the Clergyman*[71] act out the drama of an alienation more profound than that inherent in language, an alienation already located in and portrayed by the image.

The linguistic alienation that Artaud first locates in his theoretical writings on the film and that the film seems capable of overcoming turns out in his screenplays to be even more profoundly embedded in the elemental and seemingly more direct "language" of the image. So, although Artaud's recourse to film arises out of the basic sense that our situation *in* language prevents us from ever in any essential way being ourselves *through* language, his exploration of the film medium leads right back to a further encounter with language in the discovery that images—in the primitive, dreamlike, *directly* significative way in which he understands them—are only illusions of a unity between signifier and signified that has never really existed.

In this Artaud anticipates what Jacques Lacan—himself no stranger to Surrealist sensibility—more fully articulated almost forty years later.[72] Lacan writes that, although the unconscious seems to be composed of a direct, primitive, and narcissistic relation to prelinguistic identification with hallucinated, dreamed, or real images, this category (which Freud calls the primary processes and which Lacan renames the Imaginary) is, in fact, penetrated from the very beginning by symbolic structures akin to those at work in verbal language. Lacan shows that the human subject immersed in the Imaginary cannot recognize the true state of affairs. The subject must believe in the reality of the image, just as the dreamer believes in the reality of the dream. This fundamental misrecognition (*méconnaissance*) is as central to Lacan's thinking about the Imaginary as it is to

---

[71] *The Seashell and the Clergyman* is the only one of Artaud's scenarios ever to be produced. This production, directed by Germaine Dulac, remains highly problematic. The sketchiness of the original screenplay makes it hard to determine whether Dulac did justice to Artaud's original conception. It is clear, however, that the resulting film—perhaps in part because it lacked Artaud in the title role—is far from being a classic of the genre. Artaud himself joined Desnos in ridiculing it at the premiere. He bitterly opposed Dulac's original strategy of introducing the film in the opening titles as Artaud's personal dream.

[72] Jacques Lacan, *Ecrits* (Paris: Editions du seuil, 1966); trans. Alan Sheridan, *Ecrits: A Selection* (New York: Norton, 1977).

the Surrealist's understanding of the function of the image in film.

Lacan shows that the imaginary relation of narcissistic identification so important in what he calls the mirror-stage is a misrecognition of the human subject's situation in language. It is the peculiar genius of Surrealist film and of the Surrealist discourse *on* film, that it did not itself succumb to the seductive appeal of the Imaginary, even though the model of the dream seems to point to a literal imitation of the dream's effect upon the dreamer. Instead, the Surrealists' discourse on film suggests that this Imaginary is itself an appropriate subject for their films. Thus, whereas in the fiction film everything happens so as to cover up the misrecognition at the heart of our relation to the image and to make us believe in the reality of the fiction, in Surrealist film everything happens so as to show that the film does not *represent* a world so much as it *constructs* one. What's more, Surrealist film shows that this construction of a world and a self takes place within an already existing language system. We have seen, for example, how Artaud and Desnos' screenplays indicate a very clear understanding of the predominantly narrative nature of film language. Both Artaud and Desnos saw that only through rupture of the established codes of narration could Surrealists hope to achieve film texts that could imitate the structure of unconscious processes as revealed in our dreams.

In other words, this early Surrealist understanding of the dream model as it applied to film was to imitate the *structure* of the dream rather than its content. Since the dream consists of the disruption of one level of discourse by another (i.e., the condensation of psychic material into one single image or the displacement of the psychic material from its natural place onto insignificant or indifferent elements), the Surrealist practice with respect to film was to imitate these condensation and displacement processes. But, instead of condensing and displacing the individual's *private* store of visual psychic material, the film condenses and displaces a more *public* store of visual material contained in the film's already evolved code of narrativity.

Although the full development of the Surrealist aesthetic becomes evident in the actual films of Surrealism, particularly in Buñuel and Dalí's *Un Chien andalou* and *L'Age d'or,* Goudal, Desnos, and Artaud were already pointing, each in their own way, toward a film aesthetic based on the rhetorical model of the dream. Desnos and Artaud's screenplays approximate the structure of the dream through the effect of rhetorical rupture. In these scenarios Artaud and Desnos create dreamlike procedures approximating the ways in which the unconscious articulates desire. If Surrealist film can be said to be about anything, it is about the *forms* taken by this desire. To understand the nature of this desire as it operates in Surrealist film, the next section looks more closely at the psychoanalytic investigation of dreams and the unconscious.

### FREUD, LACAN, AND THE UNCONSCIOUS

In *Le Surréalisme et le rêve,* Sarane Alexandrian details the history of the influence of the psychoanalytic study of dreams on surrealism. Alexandrian shows that in all basic features—e.g., condensation, displacement, and wish fulfillment—the Surrealists accepted the Freudian conception of the unconscious as revealed in dreams. As Breton explains in *Les vases communicants,* the Surrealists were interested in using the dream as a means of access to their own unconscious, considered both as a source for their texts and as a formal model of expression. As we have seen, the dream model appealed to them as a special form of communication without what seemed the rigidities of ordinary language, offering a form of expression in which a given signifier referred not simply to a given signified, but to a multiple chain of often contradictory associations. On the model of this different kind of language, the Surrealists developed their initial experiments in automatic writing and began to produce the various automatic texts, dream accounts, and group experiments, including the trancelike dream-hallucinations of the famous *séances de sommeil.*[73]

*The Model of the Unconscious.* In *The Order of Things* Michel Foucault compares the Renaissance relation of word to thing with this same relation in the Neo-Classical period. He finds that during the Renaissance language was considered to exist as a *thing* in its

[73] Alexandrian, *Le Surréalism et le rêve,* pp. 103–32.

own right. Thus words were considered as signs pointing toward things or ideas, but also as opaque, dense objects in themselves. The proof of this density lay in their power to evoke a secondary language of exegesis aimed at interpretation of these word-objects.

As language became increasingly invested with the rational values of the Neo-Classical age, words lost the ability to exist as things participating in the mystery of creation. Foucault goes on to say that, as a result of this loss of density, language ceased to exist in this period and began merely to function as a transparent vehicle of representation no longer requiring exegesis. Not until the modern period and a new realization of the inadequacies of rational thought was an attempt made to rediscover how language could again *exist* in its own right.[74]

It is precisely to this existence of language as a thing that Freud points in his exegesis of dream language in *The Interpretation of Dreams*. One of its most persistent themes is that dreams (and the unconscious) carry out thought processes through the hallucinatory perception of images: "What are truly characteristic of dreams are only those elements which behave like images, which are more like perceptions, that is, than they are like mnemic presentations."[75] Freud adds that the reason for this recourse to visual, pictorial "language" in dreams comes from the fact that "in every language concrete terms, in consequence of their history and development, are richer in associations than conceptual ones."[76]

Freud's conception of the language of dreams is similar to Foucault's conception of language as it existed during the Renaissance rather than as it functioned during the Neo-Classical era. His attention is directed primarily to the letter of the unconscious—its form of expression. Interpretation is not achieved through a one-to-one translation, but through attention to configurations of elements within the manifest content. Dream images differ from the procedures of normal language precisely because to the dreamer these images are more like things. They lack the quality of rigid codification characteristic of language. This lack of strict codification—the fact that an image is both indissolubly itself and open to association

---

[74] Michel Foucault, *The Order of Things* (New York: Pantheon Books, 1971), pp. 42–44.
[75] Freud, *Interpretation of Dreams*, p. 82.
[76] Ibid., p. 375.

with whatever it (metonymically) comes in contact with or (meta-phorically) associates with—privileges image-discourse as the ideal form of expression for desire.

The Surrealists' attraction to the image is inseparably linked with the Freudian notion that the image-presentation of dreams is a psychic shortcut to the satisfaction of desire. But it is important to clarify the exact sense in which this desire can be understood if we are to avoid the assumption that wish fulfillment in Surrealist film means the simple possession of a love-object. To do this we must delve a bit deeper into Freud's distinction between *primary* and *secondary processes* and between what Jacques Lacan later reformulated as a distinction between the Imaginary and the Symbolic.

Freud divides the psychic apparatus into two basic functions: (1) that of the unconscious, characterized by the primary processes of dreams and fantasies; and (2) that of the preconscious and conscious, characterized by the secondary processes of waking thought and memories. In each of these processes, psychic energy flows differently. In the primary process it flows more freely, according to the condensing and displacing mechanisms of the dream-work described in chapter 6 of *The Interpretation of Dreams.*[77] In *displacement*, important elements of the latent content of the dream are displaced onto insignificant or indifferent but often more figurable elements. Displacement is a decentering of psychic values effected by the agency of censorship. *Condensation*, which is often prepared for by the work of displacement, is a combination of several associated ideas in one single dream representation. This commonly occurs in the combination of qualities from two or more persons into one composite fixture in the dream. Irma in Freud's own "Dream of Irma's Injection" is an example of such a condensed figure. She is composed of Irma herself (Freud's patient), Irma's friend (a woman Freud would have preferred to have as a patient), and many other associated figures, including Freud's wife and child.[78]

The primary processes aim at the most direct satisfaction of desire. The baby, for example, will hallucinate an image of the mother's breast (or whatever object has provided satisfaction in the past). This hallucination merely repeats, as nearly as possible, the

[77] Ibid., p. 311.
[78] Ibid., pp. 138–53.

35

perception linked to the satisfaction of a need, establishing what Freud calls a relation of "perceptual identity"[79] between the image remembered and imagined. Perceptual identity is a shortcut to satisfaction that in the long run, of course, fails to satisfy the baby's real hunger. Secondary processes, on the other hand, are governed by the reality principle, which teaches the baby not to be fooled by the intensity of these perceptual identities. Here the child modifies, defers, and inhibits the initial urge for immediate satisfaction.

*Lacan's Reinterpretation of Freud.*[80] Where Freud pointed to the differences between verbal language and the image-presentation of the primary process, French psychoanalyst Jacques Lacan, using the tradition of structural linguistics, reestablishes the analogy with language. His key point that the discourse of the unconscious is structured like a language[81] relies on Saussure's notion of the doubleness of all language. Saussure shows that every utterance implies the preexistence of a system which renders that utterance possible. Thus for language to operate, the system that gives sense to a word cannot be present with the word as it is spoken.

Lacan shows that the unconscious, too, has a similar structure. On this point Lacan and Freud differ most. Freud believed that the Primary Process—similar to what Lacan later calls the Imaginary—was competely separate from the Secondary Process—similar to what Lacan calls the Symbolic. For Lacan, however, this Primary Process or Imaginary is already structured by a systematization akin to that of language, since the moment the infant enters a rela-

[79] Ibid., pp. 605–6.

[80] It has often been said that it is a travesty of Lacan's work to attempt to rephrase it in simple terms. But these warnings are often followed by just such rephrasing, and I will venture to add my own. For the following discussion I have drawn from Lacan, *Ecrits*, trans. Sheridan, *Ecrits: A Selection* (all subsequent references are to this translation); id., *Le Seminaire de Jacques Lacan* 20 vols. to date, ed. Jacques-Alain Miller (Paris: Seuil, 1972– ), vol. 11, *Les Quatre concepts fondamentaux de la psychanalyse* (1973), trans. Alan Sheridan, *The Four Fundamental Concepts of Psycho-analysis* (New York: Norton, 1978). I have also referred to the following works of commentary: Anika Lemaire, *Jacques Lacan*, trans. David Macey (London: Routledge & Kegan Paul, 1977); Jacques Lacan, *The Language of the Self: The Function of Language in the Unconscious*, trans. Anthony Wilden (Baltimore: Johns Hopkins, 1968); *Screen* 16 (Summer 1975), special issue on psychoanalysis and cinema; *Edinburgh '76 Magazine: Psycho-Analysis/Cinema/Avant-Garde* 1 (1976).

[81] Lacan, "The Freudian Unconscious and Ours," *Four Fundamental Concepts of Psychoanalysis*, p. 20.

tionship with another human being, it enters a domain structured by language. For example, the infant child's need for milk passes through a linguistic system based on the opposition between crying and not crying. What begins as a simple cry soon becomes linked for the infant with the satisfaction of its need for milk. When this happens, the cry becomes a sign, which, every time it is uttered, implicates the opposing sign of not crying. In other words, the initial need of milk launches the baby into a preexisting system of signification that is not under its control. An initial need is transformed into a demand addressed to the Other. This demand is part of a chain of unconscious signification implied in the very act of crying.

The moment an initial need becomes a demand, the child enters a whole new realm of structured opposition. Collin McCabe writes: ". . . insofar as the sign is defined by what it is not, it exists within a chain of signification in which its opposite and different, not-crying, is inevitably implicated. Thus if the cry is to function as a conscious *demand* addressed to another, it must bring with it a chain of signification which is not under the subjects' control and opens up the world of the unconscious—of *desire*." [82]

The most famous illustration of the above situation is Freud's analysis, in *Beyond the Pleasure Principle*, of a game played by his own grandson. The child associated his own playful manipulation of the appearance and disappearance of a toy attached to a string with the vowel sounds *o* and *a*. Freud interpreted these vowels as elements of the German words meaning *gone (Fort!)* and *here (Da!)*, suggesting that the game is a symbolic manipulation of the alternating disappearance and return of the mother. Lacan points to this game as the moment in which the child is born into language:

We can now grasp in this the fact that in this moment the subject is not simply mastering his privation by assuming it, but that here he is raising his desire to a second power. For his action destroys the object which it causes to appear and disappear in the anticipating *provocation* of its absence and its presence. His action thus negatives the field of forces of desire in order to become its own object to itself. And this object, being immediately embodied in the symbolic dyad of two elementary exclamations, announces in the subject the diachronic inte-

[82] "Presentation of 'The Imaginary Signifier,'" *Screen* 16:9.

gration of the dichotomy of the phonemes, whose synchronic structure existing language offers to his assimilation; moreover, the child begins to become engaged in the system of the concrete discourse of the environment, by reproducing more or less approximately in his *Fort!* and in his *Da!* the vocables which he receives from it.

*Fort! Da!* It is precisely in his solitude that the desire of the little child has already become the desire of another, of an *alter ego* who dominates him and whose object of desire is henceforth his own affliction.[83]

Thus the symbol is that which destroys the original object (the presence of the mother) to become a substitute object structured by the opposition between presence and absence. The "death" of the thing itself makes possible the child's desire for it.

From this hypothetical moment on, the child is caught in a language system in which satisfaction can never take place, because the sign of presence is immediately linked with the sign of absence. Fresh desire is lurking behind an always incomplete satisfaction, implicit in the laws of language or in what Lacan calls the Symbolic. As Claire Johnston explains, desire is essentially "the difference between satisfaction sought and satisfaction obtained. The object of desire is thus the memory trace of a previous gratification which can never be obtained but will always be the lost object forever reincarnating itself in a series of objects. Desire is set in motion with the first cry and the posing of the first signifier."[84] For Lacan this entrance of the signifier into the baby's life marks the first instance of linguistic alienation, the first separation of the word from the thing. It is this separation that marks the difference between Freud's Primary and Secondary Processes. For Lacan, however, these processes are not so separate. Renaming them the category of the Imaginary (a process dominated by the perceptual identity of images) and the category of the Symbolic (a process dominated by the separation of words and things as governed by language), he shows that the Imaginary is nevertheless penetrated from the very beginning by the Symbolic. In fact, one of the characteristics of the Imaginary is its misrecognition of unity, especially that of the hu-

---

[83] Lacan, "The function and field of speech and language," *Ecrits*, pp. 103–4.

[84] Claire Johnston, "Towards a Feminist Film Practice: Some Theses," *Edinburgh '76* 1 (1976): 53.

man subject. For example, the baby who hallucinates the breast that has provided satisfaction in the past, "believes" in the reality and unity of this image. It experiences a fundamental misrecognition— *méconnaissance*[85]—of the divorce between signifier and signified. This misrecognition is central to Lacan's notion of the "mirror stage" and its role in the formation of the subject.[86]

Lacan maintains that a child between six and eighteen months of age (the mirror stage) seems to recognize its own image in the mirror with a special joy. Before this moment of recognition the child has had no knowledge of its own body as a unity. But at this moment of primary narcissism the child overcomes fragmentation by identifying the image of the Other with itself, whether this Other is its own image or the image of the adult who holds it before the mirror. This supposed, fictional unity of the subject is then projected onto all the rest of the world.[87]

Thus the very constitution of the child's subjectivity is carried out by the mediation of the image of its own body and by its false recognition (*méconaissance*) of the Other who holds it as identical with its self. But this essential misrecognition of the subject as an Other is eventually disturbed by the child's Oedipal phase and the understanding of the phallus considered as a signifier of difference and not as an anatomical organ. The phallus gives access to genital sexuality and the child's desire for forbidden objects. It is the signifier par excellence of the difference that destroys the Imaginary relation of self with Other.[88] The phallus introduces a third element into the dual relationship between mother and child, the father. The interdictions of the "Law of the Father" introduce a knowledge of the Symbolic that permits the child to distinguish the difference between its own subjectivity and other pronominal categories. By entering into this Symbolic realm, the child attains the possibility of becoming like the father or the mother.

---

[85] For Lacan the term *méconnaissance* designates not a simple ignorance but a certain organization of affirmation and negation: "*Il faut bien qu'il y ait derrière sa méconnaisance une certaine connaissance de ce qu'il y a à méconnaître.*" Lacan, *Le Seminaire*, vol. 1, *Les Ecrits techniques de Freud*, p. 189.

[86] "The mirror stage as formative of the function of the I as revealed in psychoanalytic experience." Id., *Ecrits*, p. 2.

[87] Ibid.

[88] See id., "The signification of the phallus," ibid., pp. 285–86.

The Symbolic comes as an intrusion and rupture of the Imaginary unity of the subject typified by the mirror stage. From this point on, language mediates the relation to reality, forever distancing the subject from the direct grasp of his or her own psychic truth. Thus Lacan stresses the disjunction between lived experience and the sign (composed of the division between signifier and signified) that replaces it. As Anika Lemaire writes in her book on Lacan, each word in a sentence

> acquires a meaning through the inter-relational play between the elements of the sentence, but, at the same time, this meaning is never fixed in a stable manner. The single word implies a series of references to the other words in the code. . . . The anchoring point is mythical. The final signified for which one searches is radically excluded from thought as it concerns an incommensurable dimension, namely the Real.[89]

This *final signified* is the repressed, lost object upon whose trace the unconscious is formed.

As in the *Fort!/Da!* game, the reality of the thing itself—in this case the child's mother—is lost in the process of symbolization. Mediated by language, the human subject is divided from itself, alienated by the effect of the signifier. This intrusion of language, which Lacan equates with the interdictions of the Law of the Father in the Oedipus phase, marks the end of the Imaginary unity with the mother, causing the child to renounce and repress what can now be called desire. Thus the child learns to assume castration— the symbolic understanding of difference and the notion of lack that underlies it. All desire is thus, fundamentally, a desire for what has been irretrievably lost within the subject itself.

The above is, of course, only a very cursory summary of some of Lacan's key terms. The primary point is the way the signifier of the phallus leads to a further formation of the subject that radically breaks with the fictive unity of the Imaginary. Thus, whether in the dual fascination with the Other or the triple relation of the Symbolic, Lacan's primary contribution to Freudian theory has been to demonstrate that the subject is separated by language from both it-

---

[89] Lemaire, *Jacques Lacan*, p. 41.

self and the world. This fundamental linguistic alienation is an experience of loss, which desire perpetually tries to fill.

## SURREALIST FILM AND THE IMAGINARY

The notion of the image in the Surrealists' discourse on film derives from two contradictory impulses that have already been viewed in Artaud, Desnos, and the pre-Surrealists. These impulses are, on the one hand, a nostalgia for the unity of a prelinguistic Imaginary—for a moment when the separation of subject and world was not yet felt—and, on the other hand, the confrontation of the misrecognition of this Imaginary with the knowledge of difference obtained from the Symbolic. In other words, what we have seen so far as the Surrealists' fascination with the image as a means of escape from language's separation of word and thing has also been a very particular and even self-conscious use of misrecognition as an intentional specular trap sprung on the spectator. Unlike the classical narrative film, this trap is sprung not to catch and hold the viewer in replication of a mirror-stage belief in and identification with the reality of its images, but to expose the very misrecognition at the heart of the film's resemblance to the Imaginary. So, although the Surrealist poets first turned to film because it seemed to offer an escape from what they felt to be the rigidities of codified language, their exploitation of the filmic image soon became a very sophisticated attempt to expose the viewer's own misrecognition of the image. Thus, their cultivation of what Lacan calls the Imaginary aims ultimately at the revelation of the ways in which the image, too, is structured by processes similar to those at work in language.

Lacan's reinterpretation of Freud makes possible a more subtle and precise appreciation of what Surrealist film, even at this early stage, was striving to become. Previous attempts to understand Surrealist film have quite naturally derived from the obvious historical influence of Freud. In this view the main goal of all Surrealist art is the liberation of the expressive powers of the unconscious from the inhibitory and rational powers of the conscious mind. But, as André Breton suggests in *Les Vases Communicants*, surreality actually consists in the interpenetration of these two different states. Lacan's substitution of the already interpenetrating terms *Imaginary* and *Symbolic* for Freud's *Primary* and *Secondary, unconscious* and *conscious*, is thus a more appropriate designation. With these terms it becomes possible to go beyond the usual celebration of a mysterious and ineffable unconscious whose automatic procedures produce equally mysterious and ineffable outpourings. If the unconscious *is* structured like a language, it then becomes possible to trace the dynamics of this language and the role of the signifier in it. Lacan's lesson that all human growth and development take place in opposition to the fictive unity of the mirror stage suggests a more precise understanding of what Surrealist film's resemblance to the Imaginary is all about.

While most fictional film exploits the Imaginary, using our original narcissistic identification with an image to draw us into a belief in the diegetic world depicted by the film, Surrealist film makes this Imaginary identification the very subject of the work. But if the Imaginary becomes the privileged subject of these films, this is only to demonstrate the false perception on which it is based.

The Surrealist's delight in the paradox of a medium that could provide so convincing an illusion of reality—the projected illusion of a presence that is radically absent—is thus based upon the potential rupture of these illusions. Surrealist film dramatizes the human subject's relation to the image by working against the lure of the Imaginary, revealing the misrecognition of identification rather than, as in the fiction film, reproducing its effect in the spectator.

Lacan's theory of the construction of the subject in the place of the Other can help us understand, for example, the peculiar emphasis in the screenplays of Apollinaire, Desnos, and Artaud on complex structures of identification. We have seen that Apollinaire in *La Bréhatine* and Artaud in *Eighteen Seconds* devise fictions in which their heroes identify with (imagined) images of themselves. In each of these works the self is revealed as a product of an identification with the Other. The Breton girl identifies with the image of herself created by the novelist and shown to us (in Apollinaire's screenplay) on the screen. Through this identification she encounters a desire for her own death. Similarly, in an effort to possess his own alienated self, the actor standing by the street lamp in *Eighteen*

*Seconds* identifies with and becomes a dizzying series of Others. But upon assuming each new identity, he finds that what was perceived as a wholeness from the outside is from the inside only a centerless insubstantiality. Identification is revealed as the futile pursuit of his own self. Face to face with the image of an actor on the stage, he finds himself identifying with someone who is himself a reflection of others. After looking into this mirror of his own emptiness, he too kills himself.

Both of these scenarios present fictional characters involved in situations that permit an exploration of the illusory unity of the self. But although they create situations that give cinematic form to an identification process based on the desire for the Other, they are still working within the confines of the fictional film and its hypothesis of a previously existing time, space, and character. In *Eighteen Seconds*, however, the actual representation of this time, space, and character is reduced to a skeletal framing device—the actor standing under the street lamp at the beginning and end. In between is the portrayal of a whole realm of unconscious associations that obey none of the rules of traditional narrative.

We shall soon see, in *Un Chien andalou* and *L'Age d'or*, how Surrealist film found a way to rupture the film's fictional and conventional unity of the self without resorting to the usual devices of dream sequences or subjective fantasies—devices that ultimately preserve the supreme fiction of the unity of the self even while giving access to its partial fracturings.

*Lacan and Surrealism.* While still a young psychoanalyst, Jacques Lacan was a reader of, and sometime contributor to, the Surrealist journals *Le Surréalisme au service de la révolution* and *Minotaure.* In the former, his doctoral thesis on paranoia was favorably reviewed by René Crevel. Crevel criticized psychoanalysis for being insufficiently dialectical, showing the importance of dialectics to such a discipline. At the end of the article Crevel, who had praised Lacan's thesis for its subjective approach, encouraged the younger generation of psychoanalysts to accept the Surrealist challenge.[90] Lacan apparently took this appeal to heart, for Hegelian dialectics is a powerful influence on his early work.

[90] Réné Crevel, *Le Surréalisme au service de la révolution* 5 (1933):48–52.

But already in the first issue of *Le Surréalisme au service de la révolution* Salvador Dalí had been exploring the relation of paranoia with poetic and pictorial creation.[91] On the basis of their common interest, Lacan visited Dalí. Sarane Alexandrian reports that when the young doctor was received by Dalí at his hotel, the artist had a piece of cigarette paper glued to his nose. Although Alexandrian doesn't give an account of what was said at the meeting, he does say that Dalí did most of the talking.[92] Subsequently, in the first issue of *Minotaure*, an early version of Dalí's article "Interpretation paranoiaque de l'Angélus de Millet"[93] was followed by Lacan's related article "Les problèmes du style et les formes paranoiaques de l'expérience."[94]

What fascinates Dalí in paranoia is the way it invests the entire perceptual field with double significance: that of the objects themselves and their ordinary meanings and that of their repressed meanings. Citing an image from his film *Un Chien andalou*, Dalí points out (somewhat ingenuously) that even the tangible rotting flesh of a dead ass can become the sign of something beautiful. The images, or *simulacra* (Dalí's term), of reality are interesting to him only because of their lack of coherence with reality. Through a conscious cultivation of paranoia, Dalí sought to develop his own ability to produce such doubly significant images.

In 1936, three years after Dalí and Lacan published their accompanying articles on paranoia in *Minotaure*, Lacan delivered his first important contribution to psychoanalysis—his original version of the famous conference on the mirror stage. Thus it may not be an exaggeration to state, as Alexandrian does, that many of Lacan's most important contributions to psychoanalytic tradition—his theory that the unconscious is structured like a language, his concept of desire, and the rhetoric of the Imaginary—are all drawn from the poetic well-spring of Surrealism.[95] Though I do not wish to make a grand point of such influences (they are, after all, only a manifestation of Lacan and the Surrealists' common interest in psycho-

[91] Salvadore Dalí, "L'Ane pourri," ibid., 1 (July 1930):9–12.
[92] Alexandrian, *Le Surréalisem et le rêve*, pp. 67–68.
[93] Dalí, *Minautaure* 1 (February 15, 1933):11–67.
[94] Lacan, ibid., p. 68.
[95] Alexandrian, *Le Surréalisme et le rêve*, p. 68.

analysis), the fact remains that Lacan's fascination with the role of the signifier, his devaluation of any preexisting category of the "real," and his emphasis upon the role of desire are all natural concerns of the Surrealist sensibility.

Thus it is certainly not accidental that Surrealist poet Louis Aragon's poem "Contre-Chant" becomes a key point of reference throughout Lacan's *Four Fundamental Concepts of Psycho-analysis* (pp. 17, 79). This poem, the themes of which are the scopic drive and the poet's role as mirror-reflector to an always absent object, is an open acknowledgment of Lacan's affinity with the Surrealist awareness of the misrecognition inherent in the Imaginary relation to the Other. Neither is it accidental that a major point of Lacan's essay "The agency of the letter in the unconscious" (*Ecrits*, pp. 156–57) contains an attack against the Surrealist concept of the figure in the name of a substitution theory of metaphor. In this essay, Lacan's quarrel with Surrealism is really a refinement of the Surrealists' own attempts to base production of their texts upon the rhetorical model of the unconscious. In this essay Lacan draws the significant parallel between the processes of condensation and displacement in the unconscious, and metaphor and metonymy in poetic language.

The nature and significance of these analogies will be explored later. My point here is simply that Lacan was not merely interested in and sympathetic toward Surrealism; he was also very much a product of that generation's *esprit*. Not the least aspect of this esprit is Lacan's often maddeningly obscure, capriciously associative, imperious style—a style that keeps one ear cocked to the play of signifiers in the unconscious.

*Disruption in the Theater.* Yet another way in which the Surrealists exposed the workings of the Imaginary was their peculiar method of going to the movies. André Breton relates this film-going practice in his famous 1951 essay, which sums up the Surrealist involvement in film: "When I was 'at the cinema age' . . . I never began by consulting the amusement pages. . . . I agreed wholeheartedly with Jacques Vaché in appreciating nothing so much as dropping into the cinema when whatever was playing was playing, at any point in the show, and leaving at the first hint of boredom—of surfeit—to rush off to another cinema where we behaved in the same way. . . . I have never known anything so *magnetising*."[96] The attention to an "imaginary" signifier experienced in a darkened room in a state of passive acquiescence is akin, Christian Metz has shown, to a baby's underdeveloped motor reactions before its own image in the mirror.[97] But Vaché and Breton's sudden, noisy, and disruptive entrances and exits aimed to defeat the passivity inherent in the filmgoing experience. In the same essay Breton describes how he and Vaché would ceremoniously eat full meals in movie houses to the stupefaction of the other spectators. Joseph Delteil, in like spirit, would use the cinema to induce more vivid dreams or, if not sleepy, would read by the light of the flickering images.[98]

The effect of these inattentive and impolite movie-going habits was to disrupt the spectators' identification and belief in the fiction. Robert Desnos also outlines an interesting variation on the above method designed to achieve the same effect. He hopes for an impossible and absolute belief in the fiction of the film: "The masterpiece of the screen will be the one in which audiences puncture the screen with revolver shots aimed at a disagreeable character, the one, unfortunately utopian, in which the projectionist removes the traces of kisses from the screen."[99] Though this hope seems at first rather juvenile, Desnos is really suggesting a very subtle argument: that the process of identification with the fiction encoded in the film can be used against itself to disrupt this passive receptivity and belief in the fiction. For the act of shooting or kissing the screen could only, as Godard later shows in *Les Carabiniers* or as Buster Keaton was already showing in *Sherlock Jr.*, have the effect of breaking with the very same fictional identification that inspires such a naïve response. This is so because any act on the part of a spectator, even if it originates as a confusion between fiction and reality, must ultimately eliminate this confusion by calling attention to the imaginary nature of the cinematic signifier, to the absurdity of a flesh-and-blood spectator kissing or shooting the screen. So what begins

---

[96] André Breton, "Comme dans un bois," *L'Age du cinéma* 4–5 (August–September 1951):27; trans. Paul Hammond, "As in a Wood," in *The Shadow and Its Shadow*, pp. 42–43.

[97] Metz, "Imaginary Signifier," pp. 15–17.

[98] Joseph Delteil, "Le Cinéma," *La Revue européene*, March 1, 1925, p. 68.

[99] Desnos, "La Morale du cinéma," *Cinéma*, p. 111.

as a confusion of fiction with reality ends as a reinforcement of the separation between them.[100]

In 1930 a manifestation of this very mechanism came to the aid of Buñuel and Dalí's film *L'Age d'or*. Ado Kyrou recounts how members of two fascist groups had come to protest the anti-Christian and antipatriotic elements of the film. While these groups successfully destroyed the canvases of Dalí, Ernst, Man Ray, and Tanguy displayed in the lobby, their attack on the film was less successful. At the moment in the film when a reliquary is placed in a gutter beside a car, the groups threw ink on the screen.[101] But the ink had no damaging effect on what was only a *projected* image, and the film itself (the actual celluloid) remained unharmed. The fascists had fallen victim to a trap similar to that described by Desnos but were powerless against the imaginary signifier that so offended them.

*Signifier and Signified.* The Surrealists' movie-going habits were extrinsic methods of disrupting the cinematic mode of reception. These habits offered yet another way to achieve a rupture with the film's fiction, the identification with which, Christian Metz has shown,[102] has been made possible by the child's initial identification with its own image in the mirror phase. We have already seen some instances of how this rupture is achieved within Surrealist film-scripts. In the next chapter we will look more closely at this phenomenon in Buñuel and Dalí's *Un Chien andalou*. But for the moment it may be useful to explore other ways in which ruptures are achieved.

The fictional film and the dream resemble each other insofar as they both inspire belief in what we see on the movie or the mind's screen.[103] But the degree and emphasis of this belief differ. Christian

---

[100] Christian Metz describes this phenomenon in "The Fiction Film and Its Spectator," pp. 75–76.

[101] Kyrou, *Luis Buñuel*, p. 30.

[102] Metz, "Imaginary Signifier," p. 15.

[103] Bruce Kawin, *Mindscreen* (Princeton: Princeton University Press, 1978). Kawin's excellent book outlines a theory of filmic subjectivity ranging from simple first-person subjectivity to what Kawin calls systemic reflexity—the film as a field of thought in itself rather than the expression of any one character's thought. As we shall see, the rhetoric of Surrealist film belongs to this second, more complex, form of "mindscreen."

Metz shows that in the fictional film we experience the *signified* as real, whereas we always remain vaguely aware—Desnos' utopian schemes to the contrary—that the *signifier* is imaginary.[104] But in the dream, as well as in the entire realm of the imaginary, as Freud shows again and again,[105] it is the signifier that is first believed. The signified remains latent.

If Breton and Desnos devised schemes to disturb the fictional signified of non-Surrealist films by calling attention to the imaginary nature of the medium, in the Surrealist films and screenplays this was not necessary. In these works the signified of the fiction is not emphasized. What happens instead is a very peculiar and paradoxical phenomenon: the Surrealist goal with respect to the cinematic signifier is to approximate as closely as possible the dreamer's belief in the reality of the signifier, a signifier that the dreamer *thinks* is perceived but is really only imagined. If the film is to inspire belief in the signifier, it must provide images that are easily perceived, that are clear and straightforward *as* images even (or especially) if their content is bizarre in the extreme. Buñuel, for example, relates in a 1955 interview that he has always avoided fancy camera effects that call attention to the filmmaker's artistry.[106] This is one source of Surrealist film's paradoxical "realism"; the realism Surrealist filmmakers take away on the level of the fiction or signified they restore on the level of the image or signifier. As a result, Surrealist film has been relatively unmarked by the kind of obvious photographic distortion that has characterized the Expressionistic and Fantastic modes.

Expressionistic, Fantastic, and Dadaistic films, as well as the dream sequences in some traditional narrative films, use photographic distortions (e.g., split screens in *Entr'acte*, superimpositions in *Le Phantom de la Moulin Rouge*, jump-cuts in the carriage ride in *Nosferatu*) to convey particular kinds of strangeness. But Surrealist film, as it developed out of Dada, moved away from this kind of photographic distortion early in its development. Although *The Seashell and the Clergyman* (1928) and *Etoile de mer* (1928) are

---

[104] Metz, "Fiction Film and Its Spectator," p. 85.

[105] Freud, *Interpretation of Dreams*, p. 83.

[106] Buñuel, quoted in François Truffaut, interview, *Arts*, July 21, 1955; reprinted in Kyrou, *Luis Buñuel*, p. 117.

The Image

both early Surrealist-influenced works marked by photographic distortion, the more mature and properly surreal *Un Chien andalou* (1929) and *L'Age d'or* (1930) are, for the period, relatively free of such distortion.

Of course, these more mature developments of the Surrealist mode are not without their own kinds of special effects, as any viewer who has squirmed at the famous eye-slicing or ants-in-a-hole-in-the-hand sequences of *Un Chien andalou* will attest. But the special effects one finds in these later works tend to be of the kind Christian Metz calls profilmic.[107] Profilmic effects are special effects achieved before the actual shooting of the film. They differ from specifically cinematographic effects achieved in the camera or laboratory. (The shark in *Jaws* or the severed hand in *Un Chien andalou* are profilmic effects, while the gelatin lens distortions of *Etoile de mer* or the superimposition of matches on Marcel Duchamp's head in *Entr'acte* are both cinematographic effects.) Elaborating on a section in Bela Balázs's *Theory of Film*,[108] Metz explains that profilmic effects differ from cinematographic effects in that the viewer experiences no sense of distortion or difference in the most fundamental process of the film medium: in the perception of the image. Thus, even though all special effects inevitably call attention to their strangeness, they do so in different ways. In *Un Chien andalou* much is strange, but this strangeness—the eyeball cut by the razor and the ants emerging from a hole in a hand—is paradoxically more believable as signifier than as signified.

Beginning with *Un Chien andalou*, Surrealist film discovers a visual style that best approximates the way in which the Imaginary is experienced rather than the way it appears to the logical mind. This distinction is important. In the dream it amounts to the difference between the way in which we represent and recollect the strangeness of a dream to ourselves or others in a waking state and the way in which we accept and *believe in* this very same strangeness during the course of the dream. The entire history of dream sequences in film, until the innovations of Surrealist film began to have an influence, has been just this *representation* of the dream to a waking

---

[107] Christian Metz, *Essais sur la signification au cinéma*, 2 vols. (Paris, Klincksieck, 1972), 2:178.
[108] Bela Balázs, *Theory of Film*, trans. Edith Bone (New York: Dover, 1970), p. 143.

consciousness. In non-Surrealist dream representation, distortion of vision is used as the sign of a conscious awareness of the strangeness of the dream.

Pabst's *Secrets of a Soul* (1926), for example, was released as an "official" psychoanalytic dramatization of the workings of the unconscious. Pabst was advised by Karl Abraham, a Berlin psychoanalyst and member of Freud's close circle of colleagues. (Freud and Abraham had a falling out over the question of their participation in the film. Freud was adamantly against it; he had already refused Samuel Goldwyn's $100,000 offer to advise the filming of a psychoanalytic potboiler. Abraham, who was in favor of it, did advise the director, if only to prevent an even worse vulgarization by the uninitiated.) In a good example of the photographic distortion typical in dream sequences of the period, the film visualizes the dreams and compulsive thoughts of an impotent scientist who is married to a younger woman.

Murnau's *The Last Laugh* (1924) is another example. In this film, when Emil Janning's demoted doorman passes out after a night's drinking, a double exposure emanating from his head gradually reveals an elongated dreamlike distortion of the revolving hotel door that had figured prominently in previous scenes. Similarly, the double exposure that begins Keaton's extended dream sequence in *Sherlock Jr.* and the movement from black and white to color in *The Wizard of Oz* are well-known Hollywood examples of the prevalent practice of employing photographic difference to cue audiences to a *conscious* awareness of a dreamlike representation.

This is not to say that some specifically cinematographic effects do not remarkably resemble the visual qualities of dreams. Superimposition, for example, is at least a partial filmic equivalent of the dream process of condensation.[109] But such effects, because of their very specific alteration of our perception of the photographic image, call attention to the cinematic signifier in such a way that they betray the *experience* of the Imaginary—its inducement of belief in the signifier, experienced as though it were a real perception. Thus, in relation to previous filmic attempts to present poetic, unconscious, or irrational structures, the relatively straightforward visual

[109] Metz, "Fiction Film and Its Spectator," p. 92.

presentation begun by *Un Chien andalou* and continued with *L'Age d'or* and the later Surrealist work of Luis Buñuel marks an important turning point in the cinematic approximation of the discourse of the unconscious.

Surrealist poets and filmmakers were thus the first to take seriously the striking resemblance between the film's imaginary signifier and that of the unconscious. The exploitation of this essential resemblance led to the development of a film mode that reverses the usual fictional goal of inspiring belief in the fictional signified to focus instead on a primary belief in the image itself—its signifier. As in the mirror stage, this image seduces the viewer into a narcissistic identification with the Other on the screen. This new focus on the image as a source of narcissistic identification led to a totally new way of representing subjective or unconscious experience in film. The imitation of the procedures of dream as experienced (and believed) by the dreamer during the act of dreaming, rather than as represented later to waking consciousness, resulted in the creation of a new and more realistic visual style, a radical departure from previous visual cues to the presence of subjectivity, unconscious thought, or fantasy.

At the same time, the exploitation of the film's resemblance to the dream image led to a new kind of film content: the film itself considered as an image-generating process of unconscious thought. This too was a radical departure from the more typical Expressionist procedure of showing either glimpses (in *The Last Laugh*) or extended sequences (in *Caligari*) of a given character's subjective or unconscious thoughts. Instead of showing what a character thinks, the Surrealist tendency in film was to show how images themselves can "think" and how the apparent unity of the human subject is really a succession of identification with such "thinking" images. Already Apollinaire's *La Bréhatine* reveals an early effort in this direction, while Artaud's screenplays *The Seashell and the Clergyman* and *Eighteen Seconds* are more radical and mature examples of the filmic exploitation of the image's ability to constitute human subjectivity and to think visually the hidden thoughts of the unconscious. Finally, in *Un Chien andalou* this exploitation reaches its fullest and most successful development. *Un Chien andalou* is a film composed entirely of visual formulations of (sexual) desires and fears.

But these desires and fears are not anchored in a character; they are figures generated by film text itself—a text whose dynamics are modeled upon the rhetorical figures of unconscious thought. The following chapter will examine the work of these figures.

# CHAPTER TWO

# Un Chien andalou

New images will come to follow the free bent of desire
at the same time as they are vigorously repressed.

SALVADOR DALI [1]

Un Chien andalou (The Andalusian Dog) 1929

Production: Luis Buñuel.

Director: Luis Buñuel.

Script: Luis Buñuel, Salvador Dalí.

Photography: Albert Duverger.

Design: Pierre Schilzneck.

Editor: Luis Buñuel.

Music: At its first performance the film was accompanied by gramophone records, including Wagner's *Tristan and Isolde* and some Argentine tangos. In 1960 Buñuel advised on the compilation of a score for a synchronized version based on the 1929 musical selections.

Leading Players: Pierre Batcheff (The Man); Simone Mareuil (The Woman); Jaimé Miratvilles; Salvador Dalí (Marist Priest). 17 minutes. Black and White.

IN 1929 Luis Buñuel and Salvador Dalí's short film *Un Chien andalou* [2] burst upon the Paris scene, an instant success in Surrealist and

[1] Dalí, "The Stinking Ass," trans. J. Bronowsky, *This Quarter* 5 (September 1932):49–54; reprinted in Lucy Lippard, ed., *Surrealists on Art* (Englewood Cliffs, N.J.: Prentice-Hall, 1970). Originally published as "L'Ane pourri," in *Le Surréalisme au service de la révolution* 1:12.

[2] Buñuel directed from a scenario written by himself and Dalí. Much has been written about the respective contributions of each man. Although Dalí was present only on the last day of shooting, Buñuel gives him equal credit for creation of the scenario: "'The film was 50% of each of us. . . . I did the cutting of the eye and the ants in the hand; Dalí did the garden scene and the cocktail shaker bell.'" Francisco Aranda, *Luis Buñuel: A Critical Biography*, trans. and ed. David Robinson (New York: Da Capo Press, 1976), p. 60. Many com-

other avant-garde circles and the apparent fulfillment of the many Surrealist hopes for the cinema. Ever since, this short seventeen-minute film has enjoyed a privileged position in film history, considered variously as: the primary source for the spread of a Surrealist style in the commercial cinema, the first film to assault its spectator systematically, the classic example of cinematic poetry, and an important precursor of the current American avant-garde.[3]

In an extended article Philip Drummond shows how the above accolades have, for half a century, replaced and obscured any serious understanding of the text by so many "presumed moments of historico-aesthetic impact and effect."[4] Drummond's detailed analysis of the film is an important corrective to the kind of impressionistic rewriting to which the film has so often been subjected, and I highly recommend it on that account.

The aim of my own analysis is somewhat different. If, as Artaud suggests, Surrealist film can offer the cinematic equivalent of the "mechanics of the dream" and if, as is widely recognized, *Un Chien andalou* is the most successfully oneiric of Surrealist films, it is important to discover what these mechanics are all about. The aim of the following section is to establish the methodological groundwork for analysis of the dreamlike rhetoric that dominates the film. With this groundwork I hope to offer: (1) a close analysis of the peculiar form of the Surrealist figure in film, (2) a subsequent analysis of the latent meaning of these figures in relation to the text as a whole, and (3) a rhetorico-psychoanalytic reading of the entire film.

*The Rhetoric of the Unconscious.* Unconscious desire cannot be named. As Freud defines it, it is forbidden a normal mode of dis-

---

mentators, Aranda included, tend to attribute positive credit to Buñuel, negative credit—for snobism and avant-garde preciosity—to Dalí (ibid., p. 60). This is a tempting view, since Dalí had much less to do with their following "collaboration" on *L'Age d'or* and since he appears to have a long history of behaving irresponsibly toward Buñuel. Nevertheless, as far as the scenario goes, it seems more reasonable to accept Buñuel's word on their equal collaboration than to allow current anti-Dalí sentiment to lead us astray.

[3] Philip Drummond cites the sources for these prevalent views in "Textual Space in *Un Chien Andalou*," *Screen* 18 (Autumn 1977): 55.

[4] Ibid., p. 56.

course; it can only be registered by its transgressions. For the psycho-analyst these transgressions are the slips and repetitions that do violence to originally intended speech. In dreams they are memory traces divested of their original meaning by the hidden discourse of the unconscious.[5]

The way in which the unconscious accomplishes these transgressions is not in itself codified in the same way a linguistic system is codified. Emile Benveniste points out that it is only in the broad sense of a general linguistic capacity, as *langage* rather than *langue* (a specific system or code), that one can speak of "language" in dreams or other unconscious expressions.[6] Benveniste continues that it is really in the secondary procedures of what is commonly referred to as *style* that one encounters the qualities that constitute unconscious *langage*. He explains that the unconscious makes use of a rhetoric which, like style, has its figures. The old catalog of tropes can thus provide an inventory suitable to it.[7]

Jacques Lacan, in his essay "The agency of the letter in the unconscious or reason since Freud" carries Benveniste's original observation a step further by drawing an analogy between the primary figures of new rhetoric—metaphor and metonymy—and the procedures of condensation and displacement in dreams.[8] Lacan suggests that condensation and displacement in dreams are primary processes that temporarily bind the psychic energy of desire in ways similar to the temporary poetic binding of meaning in metaphor and metonymy. This is not to say that metaphor and metonymy are the same as condensation and displacement. Dreams are unconscious productions, and poems are for the most part conscious productions. For this reason I prefer to retain the poetic/rhetorical terms *metaphor* and *metonymy*, but with the ultimate purpose of discovering how a specifically Surrealist use of these rhetorical procedures resembles the unconscious procedure of "dream work."

---

[5] Lacan, *Le Seminaire*, vol. 1, *Les Ecrits techniques de Freud*, p. 270.

[6] Emile Benveniste, "Remarques sur la fonction du langage dans la découverte freudienne," *Problèmes de linguistique générale* (Paris: Gallimard, 1966), p. 86.

[7] Ibid.

[8] Lacan, *Ecrits*, pp. 146–75.

## JAKOBSON'S METAPHOR AND METONYMY:
## RHETORICAL FIGURES IN FILM

When Lacan first noted the resemblance between Freud's condensation and displacement and Roman Jakobson's rhetorical concept of metaphor and metonymy, he acknowledged the importance of Jakobson's reformulation of the old catalog of tropes into a more modern, restricted rhetoric consisting of two main figures: metaphor and metonymy.[9] This restricted rhetoric[10] was composed of two basic kinds of figures modeled on the binary oppositions of structural linguistics: paradigm and syntagm. Since the rhetorical notions of metaphor and metonymy derive from the parallel with the linguistic function of paradigm and syntagm, it is important to describe what these linguistic functions are.

The structural linguistics of Ferdinand Saussure show that language has two fundamental axes. The first, a *paradigmatic axis*, functions to select the elements of any given utterance according to certain rules or paradigms. A paradigm is the theoretical reconstruction of the linguistic choices made by every speaker of a language. These choices are made among similar things. "'Did you say *pig* or *fig*,' said the cat. 'I said *pig*,' replied Alice." Thus Jakobson explains that phonologically the cat was attempting to recapture a linguistic choice made by Alice. "In the common code of the cat and Alice . . . the difference between a stop and a continuant, other things being equal, may change the meaning of the message."[11] Alice has made a paradigmatic selection from similar—phonological—elements. The second, a *syntagmatic axis*, refers to the way in which the elements actually present in the verbal chain are arranged. Here the key function is the combination of *contiguous* elements along

---

[9] Roman Jakobson has written several articles on aphasia, all of which are reprinted in volume 2 of his *Selected Writings*, 2 vols. (The Hague: Mouton, 1971). The most famous of these, the one to which I refer, is the 1956 article "Two Aspects of Language and Two Types of Aphasic Disturbances," pp. 239–59. For a brief history and description of the "old catalogue of tropes" that Jakobson is reformulating, see Roland Barthes, "L'Ancienne rhétorique: Aide-mémoire," *Communications* 16 (1970): 172–230.

[10] The term *restricted rhetoric* is Gérard Genette's. See his "La rhétorique restreinte," *Communications* 16 (1970): 158–71.

[11] Jakobson, *Selected Writings*, 2:241.

the chain of discourse: how Alice put together the contiguous phonological, morphological, and syntactical elements she has already
chosen. Every speech act, Saussure shows, encompasses both these
functions.

Jakobson's article on language and aphasic disturbances shows
how this binary division of structural linguistics applies to two very
similar divisions in aphasic speech disorders. Jakobson suggests that
two rhetorical figures selected from the catalogs of classical rhe-
toricians can be used to simplify and revitalize rhetorical analyses
in literature and the visual arts. Thus, he proposes that metaphor
and metonymy are the two quintessential rhetorical figures, because
they have polar axes similar to those of paradigm and syntagm.[12]

Jakobson explains that the one thing (linguistic) paradigms, (rhetorical) metaphors, and the so-called aphasic "contiguity disorder"
have in common is *similarity*: all derive from the selection of features from among similar things. On the other hand, syntagms, metonymies, and the aphasic "similarity disorder" are all marked by the
function of *contiguity*, the combination of contiguous and present
elements. Aphasic similarity disorder affects a speaker's ability to *select* words or phrases from the paradigmatic language code that
is organized according to similar categories. Contiguity disorder affects a speaker's ability to *arrange* these elements contiguously. The
speaker with a contiguity disorder will therefore rely heavily on the
other pole of language, choosing similar or "metaphoric" formulations from the paradigm. In response to the word *microscope*, such
an aphasic might substitute the similar word *spyglass*, but he or she
would have difficulty providing the linguistic context for the word in
a full sentence. On the contrary, a speaker with a similarity disorder
would find it difficult to select similar terms from a paradigm. Such
speakers would find it hard to name, provide synonyms for, or meta-
linguistically define a given term. For example, when shown a pen-
cil, an aphasic with similarity disorder would not be able to name it
but would, instead, veer off to a contiguous quality or function and
say something like "to write."[13]

Jakobson applies the underlying linguistic categories of similarity

[12] Ibid., pp. 244–56.
[13] Ibid., p. 247.

57

and contiguity (or selection and combination) to larger stylistic (or aphasic) idiosyncrasies of metaphor and metonymy.[14] In so doing he draws the important lesson that similarities that underlie metaphor have been given much attention in stylistic analyses, while contiguities that underlie metonymy have been rather ignored. We hardly notice, for example, that Anna Karenina's handbag becomes a metonymic figure for the heroine herself in her famous suicide scene in Tolstoy's novel. Jakobson's point is that we tend not to notice that metonymies are figures, because the fact that they are based on real or virtual spatial contiguities makes them seem so much more realistic than metaphoric associations based upon similarity alone.

At the end of his article Jakobson suggests that metaphoric and metonymic poles of stylistic expression occur in film. But he does not say how this is so other than that the work of Griffith is predominantly metonymic, while the work of Chaplin and Eisenstein is predominantly metaphoric.[15] Although this statement is extremely suggestive, Jakobson does not tackle the very difficult problem of tracing the differences between verbal and visual figurations. Yet, often when we talk about metaphors in film, we really think of the model of verbal metaphors. Verbal metaphors are built out of the transgression of coded linguistic meanings. On the purely denotative, linguistic level, the phrase *my love is a flame* makes no sense, because love is not a flame. On the connotative, rhetorical level, however, the word *flame* has undergone a change of meaning. A figural meaning arises out of the discrepancy between the coded, literal meanings of the two parts of the statement. This discrepancy between what I. A. Richards[16] calls *tenor* (the underlying idea of love) and *vehicle* (the flame with which love is compared) forges the discovery of a new meaning that is based upon the *ground* of their

[14] Jakobson himself does not always keep these linguistic and rhetorical levels separate. Christian Metz, in "Métaphore/Métonymie, ou le référent imaginaire" (*Le Signifiant imaginaire*, pp. 224–29), clarifies Jakobson by stressing the difference between the coded linguistic level of the discourse and the uncoded rhetorical level of the referent. I mention this now to avoid confusion later.

[15] Jakobson, *Selected Writings*, 2:256.

[16] I. A. Richards, *Philosophy of Rhetoric* (New York: Oxford University Press, 1936, 1971), p. 96.

shared characteristic of heat. The metaphor is composed of both halves of the statement.

But in film, the image of a flame is not an arbitrarily coded link between a sound and a concept. If a filmmaker uses the image of a flame as a metaphor for love, this visual flame rather stubbornly remains a flame, at least more stubbornly than the word. (If one thinks of all the love scenes in films that take place adjacent to fireplaces, it is clear that such "figures" are only loose approximations of the love-flame equation in the verbal metaphor. In fact, they are very often partial metonymies owing to the fact that the fireplace and its flame are contiguously related to the lovers.)

One result of Jakobson's reformulation of old rhetoric into two binary figures has been to encourage a great many studies in film (and literary) metonymy.[17] Rather than the loose application of the poetic term *metaphor*, film analysis now tends to focus on *metonymy* to the extent that film has often been defined as an essentially metonymic art. Film metaphors have been pushed aside, as if to make up for all the years metaphor reigned supreme.

An extreme but typical instance of this antimetaphoric tendency is film historian and aesthetician Jean Mitry's insistence that film metaphors do not actually exist. Mitry argues that most of what are called film metaphors are not true metaphors at all but rather at least partial metonymies. He cites as an example a famous close-up of the pince-nez of the ship's doctor caught in the ropes of the ship in Eisenstein's *Potemkin*, after the doctor himself had been thrown overboard. Mitry argues that the pince-nez is not so much a metaphor founded on *similarity* between the upperclass doctor and his glasses as a metonymy based upon the fact that the glasses and the doctor have been *contiguously* associated with each other previously in the film.[18]

Here Mitry simply gives a more elaborate theoretical basis to the general notion mentioned above—that in film metaphor the flame and pince-nez, unlike the words for these things, seem to be really

<hr>

[17] One of the best analyses of metonymy in literature is Gérard Genette's "Métonymie chez Proust." *Figures III* (Paris: Seuil, 1972), pp. 41–66.

[18] Jean Mitry, *Esthétique et psychologie du cinéma*, 2 vols. (Paris: Editions universitaires, 1963), 1:120–22.

there. If they don't have a reason to be there, Mitry argues, they disrupt what is often felt to be the film's primary function of narration. Mitry generalizes this notion to proclaim that film, unlike verbal language, cannot accommodate metaphors that do not arise from the given space or imaginary world of the narrative—from what he and other French critics refer to as its diegesis.[19] In other words, since film must use images to create its diegetic illusion of a world, any figural connotation that comes from outside this world goes against the grain of filmic creation; it is a conceptual intrusion appropriate to verbal language but not to film.

Mitry's pronouncements are important because they articulate narrative norms that are often implied in analyses of films. But although Mitry is correct to show that many so-called film metaphors are in fact partial metonymies, he is wrong to deny the existence of "pure" filmic metaphor. Such a denial leads him to dismiss such metaphors as the two shots that open Chaplin's *Modern Times*. This famous metaphor—a shot of a crowd of sheep herded to the slaughter followed by a similar crowd of workers pressing into a subway entrance—points out the function of workers in a machine-dominated, depersonalized society. Metaphoric similarity between the herd of sheep and the "herd" of workers suggests that workers are as faceless and submissive as sheep herded to the slaughter. Mitry would claim that, since the sheep don't belong to the modern urban world of the diegesis (they are extradiegetic), the metaphor defeats the realistic thrust of all filmic discourse and thus weakens Chaplin's film. He adds that even this metaphor is not entirely pure, since the sheep are present in the image chain along with the workers; they have not taken their place. Thus Mitry also defines *metaphor* substitutionally: as only that instance where, in a verbal metaphor, the word *flame* replaces the word *love* (my flame burns) and, in a film

[19] *Diegesis* is an important term in the analyses of *Un Chien andalou* and *L'Age d'or* that follow. The term was first coined by Etienne Souriau to indicate the denotative material of a film. Christian Metz explains that the term is derived from the Greek διυλσις meaning *narration* but also relating to the represented instance—the ficitonal space and time dimension implied in and by the narrative. It is thus contrasted with the aesthetic instance of the film. its connotative or figural level, which, according to Metz, comes later, building upon the diegesis. Christian Metz, *Film Language*, trans. Michael Taylor, (New York: Oxford University Press, 1974), p. 97.

metaphor, where the shot of the sheep replaces the shot of the workers.

But if Jakobson's binary rhetorical division is to be useful as a way of talking about filmic or any other kind of figures, these divisions must be able to accommodate all existing practices. It is no solution to disallow metaphor in film, when the films of Chaplin, Eisenstein, and Buñuel all contain such metaphors. The real question is how these figures operate.

In this connection I would like to mention a very helpful elaboration of Jakobson's rhetoric proposed by Christian Metz.[20] Metz shows that, in spite of Jakobson's expansion of verbal rhetoric to include visual figures, there is a persistent tendency, even in Jakobson's work, to define film rhetoric in terms of verbal tropes. When Mitry says the *Modern Times* metaphor is not a metaphor because it lacks substitution, he is thinking in terms of the verbal definition of a *trope*—one word or expression used for another. Metz suggests, however, that both in language and in film there are really two ways in which a figure can be deployed, and only one of them is an actual substitution. The first and more common way is for a metaphor (or metonymy) to be arranged syntagmatically in the verbal or image chain. The second, less common way, is for the figure to be arranged paradigmatically—condensed in such a way that the given element of the figure implies the part that is not given.[21]

With this distinction, Metz suggests that we must be careful not to confuse the referential axis of rhetoric with the discursive axis of linguistics. What has often happened in past rhetorical analyses is that, since the phenomenon of contiguity is common to both metonymy and syntagm, contiguity of the discourse (syntagm) is confused with contiguity of the referent (metonymy). In like manner, since similarity or contrast is common to both metaphor and paradigm, it is easy to confuse similarity or contrast of the discourse (paradigm) with that of the referent (metaphor). In critical practice this commonly means that the observations made about metonymy are actually pertinent to a discussion of syntagm, while the observations about metaphor are pertinent to paradigm. Proof of this con-

[20] Metz, "Métaphore/Métonymie," pp. 177–371.
[21] Ibid., pp. 224–29.

fusion is often provided in the tacit assumption that metonymies, like syntagms, are always spread out along the horizontal axis of the discourse, while metaphors, like paradigms, can only appear vertically, as implied but absent terms.

Metz preserves the primary rhetorical categories of metaphor and metonymy while providing a secondary stipulation as to how the figure is deployed on the linguistic level of the discourse. Out of Jakobson's original binary division, Metz develops a four-part classification consisting of: (1) *Metaphors placed in syntagm* (similarity—or comparability—on the level of the referent plus contiguity on the level of the discourse). Such metaphors can either be pure, as in the extradiegetic example of sheep plus workers from *Modern Times*, or diegetic, as in the shot of Clive Brook and Marlene Dietrich's kiss on a train followed by the train whistle blowing in the film *Shanghai Express*. (2) *Metaphors placed in paradigm* (similarity—or comparability—on the level of the referent plus comparability on the level of the discourse). Here, a single comparable element of an originally two-part metaphor placed in a syntagm comes to stand for the thing being compared. Thus (in a diegetic example) in a love scene that takes place before a fire, the fire can come to stand for (and replace) the passion of the embracing couple. (3) *Metonymies placed in paradigm* (contiguity on the level of the referent plus comparability on the level of the discourse). Here, as above, one element replaces another, but in this case the original association of elements is based on metonymic contiguity rather than similarity or contrast. A classic example cited by Metz is the moment in Fritz Lang's *M* when a balloon, which had earlier been contiguously associated with a little girl, is shown all alone, caught in a web of telephone wires. The balloon replaces the murdered body of the girl herself in much the same way Anna Karenina's handbag comes to stand for Anna's crushed body. (4) *Metonymies placed in syntagm* (contiguity of the referents plus contiguity of the discourse). This is similar to (3), except that both elements of the metonymy are present in the image chain as, for example, the earlier moments in *M* when both balloon and girl appear together.[22]

What happens most often in narrative films is that a metaphor or metonymy first placed in syntagm will at some later point be placed

[22] Ibid.

in paradigm. Metz's elaboration allows us to keep the rhetorical and linguistic levels separate so that we can more completely describe the operations of the figure and the way it is deployed in the actual discourse. The usefulness of this distinction will, I hope, become evident in the analysis of the prologue to *Un Chien andalou* that follows.

THE PROLOGUE TO *UN CHIEN ANDALOU*:
A SURREALIST FILM METAPHOR

The famous metaphor of moon and eye that concludes the prologue to *Un Chien andalou* is perhaps the most often cited example of filmic Surrealism—to the extent that audiences usually remember it and forget the rest of the film. The image of a woman's eye cut open by a razor has been isolated as a still in countless posters, film histories, and anthologies, to become the very emblem of surreality in film in much the same way as Dalí's melting watches have functioned in painting. But this image has not been sufficiently studied as a metaphor. It is, after all, the bizarre similarity between the eye cut by a razor and the moon cut by a horizontal sliver of a cloud that is so striking in this episode. In this section I propose to concentrate exclusively on the peculiar form of this most famous Surrealist metaphor.

*Description of the Prologue.* The prologue is composed of what appears to be an entire scene played out in the space on and near a balcony bathed in moonlight. It begins with the title, "Once upon a time." Apart from this title the sequence has only twelve shots. The following is a numbered description of each shot, including a camera-distance scale.

Title: "Once upon a time . . ."

| SHOT | DESCRIPTION | SCALE |
|---|---|---|
| 1 | Fade-in on two hands sharpening a long razor on a strop attached to the door-handle of a French-window. Hands are viewed from above and behind. A watch is on the left wrist. Four strokes of the razor. | Close-up |

63

2    Head and shoulders of man, cigarette in mouth, eyes    Close-up
lowered, in three-quarter right profile. The man is
wearing a striped, collarless shirt. A curtained window is visible to right of frame.

3    As in 1. Razor blade is tested for sharpness on the    Close-up
thumbnail of the left hand.

4    As in 2.    Close-up

5    Man in left profile standing before window-door with    Medium
curtains. He looks at strop, razor, then opens French-
window to go outside.

6    Reverse frontal of balcony and man walking out onto    Medium
it. He looks out across balcony (in general direction
of spectator) and walks to edge where he leans on
railing, razor still in hand.

7    Head and shoulders of man in three-quarter right    Close-up
profile. He raises head to look up.

8    Dark sky with moon on screen left. A horizontal    Long shot
sliver of cloud approaches from the right.

9    As in 7.    Close-up

10    Direct frontal view of woman's face staring at specta-    Close-up
tor. To left and slightly behind is torso of man wear-
ing striped shirt, a diagonally striped tie, and no
watch. As his left hand holds open her left eye his
right hand moves in front of the lower part of her
face, as if preparing to draw razor across the round
exposed eye.

11    As in 8. The cloud now passes before the moon.    Long shot

12    The eye with thumb and forefinger holding it open.    Extreme
The razor slices it open. A jellylike substance spills    close-up
out.

*Shots 1−4.* The prologue opens on a high-angle close-up of a man's
hands sharpening a long razor on a strop. The four strokes of this
sharpening correspond to the four-shot alternating syntagm (1−4) of
the entire sharpening action. In shot 2 (close-up of the man's head
and shoulders, cigarette in mouth), it is only by the downward direction of the man's glance that we infer the diegetic contiguity of
shots 1 and 2, e.g., that these hands and arms are connected to the

head and shoulders which follow. Shots 3 and 4 repeat this same procedure with the slight difference in shot 4 that the razor is now tested for sharpness on the thumbnail of the left hand—the first instance of a horizontal line bisecting a circular shape. Though shots 1 and 3 (looking down on the razor and hands) are not viewed from precisely the same angle at which the man would see them, the downward angle of the shot, from above and behind the hands and a little to the left, does approximate the subjective viewpoint of his glance.

So far the diegetic action of a man sharpening a razor has been placed in an alternating syntagm characterized by the organization of isolated fragments of space leading to the inference of their connection in a larger whole. But already there are problems in this inference. If we look closely at the relation of the arms and hands to the French door and curtain in shots 1 and 3, we see that the man's position in relation to the curtained window close behind this head in shots 2 and 4 is spatially different in relation to what is presumably the same (now curtainless) window-door in shots 1 and 3.

*Shots 5 and 6.* The repetition of close-ups in shots 1–4 gives way in the middle of the prologue to two medium shots. These shots reinforce the spectator's previous inference as to the contiguity of hands and arms (1 and 3) to head and shoulders (2 and 4) by showing the whole person and the general scene through which he moves. In shot 6 the French doors behind the man form a horizontal line that runs into his head at precisely eye level. This is the second instance of a horizontal line that bisects a round shape.

*Shots 7–12.* Shots 7, 8, and 9 seem about to repeat the alternating syntagm of shots 1–4 in which the man's glance is alternated with the object he sees in a four-shot series. But there are two important differences. In the first series the order is object-seen + glance, while here it is the more usual glance (man looks upward at night sky) + object (insert of moon). In the second series, just at the point where the pattern glance + moon, glance + . . . creates anticipation of a return to the moon to continue the already begun movement of the cloud across the moon, an entirely new element is introduced, a close-up of a woman's face (shot 10). The seated woman

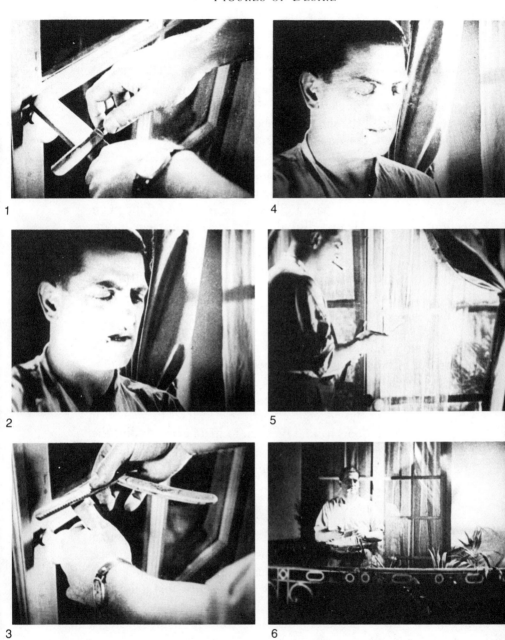

1

4

2

5

3

6

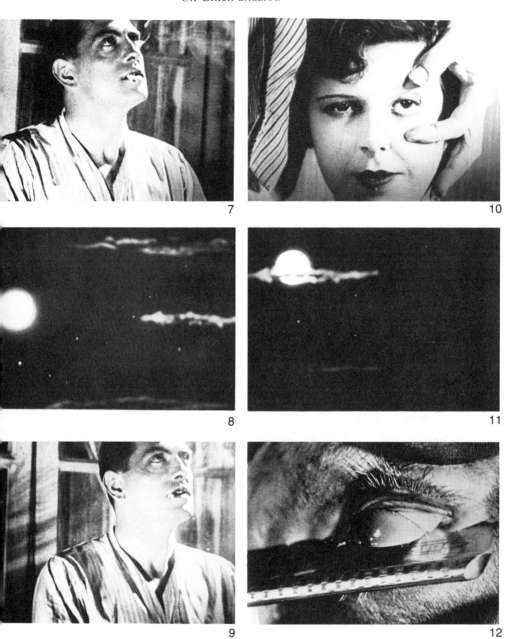

7

8

9

10

11

12

is staring directly at the camera; the torso of a (or is it the?) man stands beside her preparing to cut open her eye. Thus, instead of the anticipated completion of one diegetic action—the movement of the cloud across the moon—another, formally similar, action is introduced. This new action, like the movement of the clouds before the moon finally completed in shot 11, is also divided into two alternating shots, culminating in the final shot of the extreme close-up of the eye cutting. (The movements of cloud across moon and razor across eyeball are the third and fourth instances of round shapes bisected by horizontal lines.)

Because it is an action divided into the same kind of alternating two-shot syntagm as the movement of the clouds across the moon, this new element of the eye cutting at first seems consistent with the diegesis in the rest of the prologue. In other words, we tend to read this action as taking place in the continuous diegetic space of the balcony and night sky. But at the same time there is no real indication that this woman whose eye is about to be cut is placed in this space. We only infer it on the basis of the general contiguity of the previous syntagms. We tend to assume, for example, that the torso of the man standing beside her in shot 10 holding a razor and wearing a striped shirt is the same man we have viewed throughout the prologue. But, if it is the same man, he has suddenly lost his watch and acquired a striped tie. And, after solitarily gazing at the sky in shot 9, he is suddenly in an entirely new position as well as in modified dress in the very next shot. Our tendency to want to absorb a nondiegetic element that ultimately cannot be absorbed into the diegesis is an important feature of both this prologue and the film in general. The result is a subtle tension that seems to emanate from within the diegesis without allowing us to point to clear-cut instances of a total rupture with its apparent realism.

This initially subtle spatial discrepancy of the man's position in shots 1–4 becomes more apparent in shots 8–12, but only as a tension within a dominant pattern of alternating syntagms that describe two connected sets of actions: the sharpening and test cutting in shots 1–5, and the final bisecting (of both moon and eye) in shots 8–12. Both of these actions proceed via the division of what at first appear to be contiguous fragments of space and time in a conventional diegetic manner. But on closer examination (almost imperceptibly in the first, and more noticeably in the second) both subvert the very same assumptions about diegetic space and time they seem to want us to accept.

*The Figure: Metaphor or Metonymy.* The rupture in the diegesis that occurs in the second half of the prologue is a rhetorical figure. The only apparent motivation for the interruption of the movement of the cloud across the moon is the formal *similarity* between the round shape of the moon and eye, and the thin shape of the cloud and razor, which "cut" them. Since the motive is *similarity* of the (shapes of the) referents rather than an association of *contiguity*, this figure is metaphoric rather than metonymic.

Using Christian Metz's four-part division of filmic figuration, we can see that this is a metapor placed in syntagm. It is a metaphor in which similarities between the referents—moon and eye, cloud and razor, and the similar horizontal movements of the latter—are arranged contiguously (syntagmatically) in the image chain.

To reach an understanding of what is special about this particular metaphor, it may be helpful to compare it with the much more typical function of a similar figure in another more typically diegetic film. In the example from Josef von Sternberg's *Shanghai Express* cited above, Clive Brook and Marlene Dietrich's first kiss is followed by an exterior shot of the train's whistle blowing. These two elements, kiss (the tenor) and whistle (the vehicle) constitute a diegetic metaphor placed in syntagm, in which the vehicle "comments" upon the tenor. The usual procedure in reading such a metaphor is to construct a connotative system of the referents that can encompass both elements. Differences between kiss and whistle are minimized, while their similarities (heat, excitement, pressure) emerge in a comment upon the sexual excitement of the Dietrich-Brook's relationship.

This particular metaphor observes a structure typical of many diegetic metaphors in film: a contiguous background element, the whistle that is on the same train, is brought momentarily to the foreground as a comment upon the dominant narrative action of the kiss. The figure preserves a hierarchy of the tenor belonging to the diegesis over the vehicle brought into the diegesis momentarily. Thus the vehicle (the more properly figural element of the metaphor, brought in for purposes of comparison) rarely takes on more than momentary importance before restoring us to the main action of the tenor. In the classical metaphor this hierarchy is usually maintained by the order of appearance of the two parts of the metaphor placed in syntagm: most often, diegetic action of the tenor is followed by the comparison of the vehicle commenting upon it. The whistle emerges as connotatively significant only after the kiss; the reverse would be less effective. But if this order is reversed, as for example in the extradiegetic pure metaphor of the herd of sheep from the opening of *Modern Times,* in which the shot of the sheep preceeds the shot of the workers, there is a second way in which the dominance of the diegesis is assured.[23] The vehicle, whether present in the diegesis or not, usually belongs to natural, architectural, or otherwise nonhuman material (in this case the sheep) that seems a secondary or background element, again maintaining a hierarchy of diegesis over figure.

In the prologue metaphor, precisely this hierarchy is disturbed. The distinctive feature of this metaphor is that what would commonly constitute the tenor or comparing element of the figure—in this case the moon—is given first. But, not only is it given first, its entire function builds upon the viewer's expectation of the more common metaphoric process—of a metaphor that serves the diegesis—while actually giving a diegesis that serves the metaphor. Everything happens in this metaphor as if the formal resemblance between the moon that is "sliced" by cloud and the woman's round eye elicits the human action of slicing the eye. In other words, there is a reversal of the usual metaphoric process in which the tenor half of the metaphor belongs to the action of the diegesis and the vehicle half belongs to a part of the decor or, in the case of the pure metaphor, to an entirely extraneous element brought in from outside the narrative. Instead, the moon and cloud are precisely the kind of extraneous or background material that would usually come second and belong to the vehicle, while the eye and the razor, which here belong to the compared element of the figure, are the kind of

---

[23] The *Modern Times* metaphor is somewhat of an exception in that the vehicle part of this metaphor—the sheep—precedes the tenor part—the workers. But this unusual order is because the metaphor opens the film; it does not disturb the usual hierarchy of diegesis over figure.

human activity that would usually appear first and belong to the tenor.

So it is impossible to say that the vehicle element of this metaphor (moon and cloud) comments on another hierarchically more significant tenor element belonging to the diegesis (eye and razor). For here it is precisely the vehicle—the element that usually appears to be the artificial or consciously constructed part of the figure (the moon and clouds)—that constitutes the "action" of this sequence. In other words, the action has shifted to the vehicle part of the figure, which usually comes second and in which we notice the hand of the artist at work forging connotative meanings. Within the original denotative signifiers—the round shape of the eye and moon, the thinness of the cloud and razor, and the similar speeds with which both move across their respective objects, there is a remarkable formal similarity of the signifiers alone motivating the comparison; yet there is no immediate connotative "explanation" on the level of the signifieds.

But not only does the first part of this figure seem to create the diegesis, it also becomes a self-reflecting comment on the very process of making metaphors. In describing the first part, we tend to say that the clouds slice or cut the moon, which they do not really do— it is already a figure of speech to say so. But we say so precisely because the film has been building up to this final cutting through a proliferation of motifs emphasizing the bisection of circular shapes by horizontal lines. The first cutting of the thumbnail with the razor prepares us for the later—figural—cutting of the moon by the cloud. This figural cutting is in turn a prefiguration of the literal cutting of the eye which follows. What is so radically disturbing in this figure then is, not only the audacity of comparing one violent and sadistic image with another that is innocuous and natural, but also the fact that such a rigorous formal control exercised by the operation of the figure dictates the development of the sadistic and violent content.

To summarize the differences between the *Chien andalou* prologue metaphor and the structurally similar, and more typical, metaphor in *Shanghai Express*, we find that: (1) in the prologue metaphor a disturbed hierarchy of background and foreground creates a situation in which the figural or vehicle half of the metaphor comes first and appears to generate the diegesis; and (2) in the *Chien* figure is a deviation from the more typical semantic basis for association of the elements of the metaphor—form rather than content dictates the ground of the association. Such a figure, though formally modeled on the typical metaphor, actually functions as a deconstruction of the anticipated metaphoric process in which the denotative content of the eye-cutting refuses to be absorbed immediately into a connotative expression.

Unlike the classical figure, this seemingly autonomous figure refuses to be read as mere embellishment upon a discourse. It demands to be seen as the very cause of this discourse. The figure, which in its more usual manifestation can be dismissed as superfluous, here becomes essential. In *Un Chien andalou* this means that none of the events related by the prologue can be read as the illusion of past events, but only as configurations arising out of the act of writing, out of the desire expressed by the figure itself. Yet, what is so striking about this particular metaphor is the way the meticulous building of an apparently realistic diegesis culminates in an outrageous and metaphoric act of violence, which unlike most film violence subverts the very realism of its discourse.

*The Hand and the Eye.*[24] If, as we have seen, this figure does not permit the kind of connotative interpretation that comments on the diegesis, there is another sense in which it can be seen as a general symbol of the entire act of filmic creation. It is certainly no accident that the first shot of this prologue is a close-up of a hand sharpening a razor, while the last shot combines the elements of hand, razor, and eye. Even to a viewer unaware of the identity of the man who wields this razor—he is played by Luis Buñuel himself—and whose gaze we constantly follow, it is clear that his function in this prologue resembles that of the filmmaker. This function is double: it consists of vision and cutting, two processes that are repeated several times in the short twelve shots of this sequence.

Each new element introduced after the first shot is first viewed by the man on the balcony. We watch him looking—twice this look is

[24] In this section I am only making more explicit what Pascal Bonitzer ("Le Gros orteil: 'Realité' de la denotation," *Cahiers du cinéma* 232 [October 1971]: 15) and Joel Farges ("L'Image d'un corps," *Communications* 23 [May 1975]: 88) have already implied.

followed by the razor, once by the moon. The final look of outward regard that precedes the sudden appearance of the woman develops out of the pattern created by this vision. It is a progression to *envision*, which the diegetically contradictory elements of the tie and the absence of the watch seem to affirm. The cutting that follows this envision is nothing less than its implementation, an ironic symbol of the hand of the artist at work cutting up the continuous fabric of "reality" into newly significant combinations.

This prologue has yet another kind of vision, that of the woman. Hers is an eye that sees nothing, an eye that stares straight ahead, passive and unblinking at the approach of the razor. It is an eye that is put there to *be* seen, whose vacant stare, as Joel Farges has noted,[25] connects with our own passive voyeuristic stare, which through this connection feels the violence of the razor as a blinding assault on its own vision. But blindness, as every poet knows, can also be a *figure* for a different kind of sight. For, as the Surrealist poet Paul Eluard writes, *"Le doux fer rouge de l'aurore/Rend la vue aux aveugles"* (The gentle red iron of dawn/Restores sight to the blind).[26] And, just as Eluard employs the iron that blinds as a metaphoric figure for sight, so Buñuel and Dalí draw their razor across our eye in such a way that, by blinding us to the possibility of seeing *through* the figure, they force us to look *at* the work of the figure itself.

### LATENT MEANING

The above analysis of the formal attributes of the prologue metaphor is in no sense exhaustive. But at this point it will be more fruitful to proceed with the analysis of the rest of the film before venturing an interpretation of its latent significance.

Since metaphor and condensation, unlike metonymy and displacement, make associations between elements that may never be brought together outside the particular textual space of the metaphor, it is reasonable to ask, especially in the case of Surrealist meta-

[25] Farges, "L'Image d'un corps," p. 93.

[26] Paul Eluard, "Le Baillon sur la table," *La Vie immédiate* (Paris: Editions des cahiers libres, 1932). The translation is mine.

phors like that of the prologue, just what is the motive for these combinations: why are the moon and eye, like the umbrella and sewing machine in Lautréament's famous image, brought together? (In fact, the parallel between Lautréamont's famous comparison from *Maldoror*, "as handsome . . . as the fortuitous encounter upon a dissection table of a sewing machine and an umbrella"[27] and the filmic figure under question is itself fortuitous. In both examples male and female symbols combine with cutting motifs. Just as André Breton has noted the sexual import of Lautréamont's poetic image,[28] we will eventually see a similarly latent sexual import in the prologue metaphor.)

On the microlevel of a single metaphor, it is not possible to point to a consensus of meaning with the same facility with which we would translate the classical metaphoric formula My love is a flame. In the preceding analysis of the prologue metaphor, we have only seen that a self-referential figure seems to generate the diegesis. Although there *is* a latent meaning to this metaphor, it cannot be discovered through the kind of translation that the classical equation *love = flame* has accomplished in the past. Once again this is partly due to the absence in film, as well as in the unconscious productions of the Imaginary, of a fixed code analogous to that of language. As we have seen, the figural meaning of verbal rhetoric arises out of the discrepancy between the accepted literal meanings of the two parts of a statement. This discrepancy between the conventional coded meanings of *tenor* (love) and *vehicle* (flame) forces the discovery of a new meaning based on the *ground* of a shared characteristic (heat). But film does not possess such a fixed denotative code except insofar as rhetorical figures themselves have hardened into codelike forms.

Christian Metz's work in film semiology has shown that the narrative procedures of film have tended to develop out of connotative effects that have later become absorbed into short-lived and only partial kinds of systems: what Metz prefers to call a *grande syntagmatique*, rather than a full-fledged paradigmatique. This grande syntagmatique is a level of codification that exists only in the larger

---

[27] Lautréamont, *Maldoror*, p. 263.

[28] Breton, *Les Vases communicants* (Paris: Gallimard, 1955), p. 67. Breton suggests that the umbrella represents man, the sewing machine woman, the dissection table the bed.

organizational units of sequences and not in the minimum unit of the shot. Unlike language, the film does not begin with a code that connotation then transgresses. Instead the filmmaker begins with the raw material of the photographic registration, which connotative effect eventually shapes into a denotative code. (For example, Metz explains how an alternating montage originates as a way of making the denotation more lively and later becomes codified as one of the signifiers of simultaneity.[29]) In other words, the separation between grammar and rhetoric is not as sharp as it is in the verbal arts, although certainly even the verbal arts present problems enough on this score.

Similarly, in the dream the basic units of discourse are images that, unlike words, in themselves have no codified meanings. As seen in chapter 1, it is a common mistake in dream analysis to assume that the unconscious is a preexisting storehouse of meaning which the dream symbols simply represent. Laplanche and Leclaire, in their psychoanalytic study of the unconscious, explain that it is a misuse of the Freudian understanding of the unconscious to see dream images as the fixed symbolization of certain unconscious thoughts rather than as the production and creation of meaning.[30] This is not to say that there is not a latent meaning in every dream, but simply that this latent meaning is not an already existing entity that can be reached through mechanistic decoding.

Insofar as *Un Chien andalou* imitates the procedures of the unconscious, its figures too have a latent meaning, not just the usual connotation of most filmic figuration, like the kiss and whistle in *Shanghai Express* that can be interpreted in an instant, but a truly latent meaning that can be discovered only through a close analysis of the entire text. In the prologue metaphor we saw the peculiar way in which a figure becomes a part of the denotative diegesis through a reversal of the more typical hierarchy of diegesis and figure. The disturbance of this hierarchy is an indication that a desire simultaneously seeks to find expression and through censorship to cover this expression. On the basis of the prologue alone, we cannot yet determine what this latent meaning is. We have only been cued to

[29] Metz, "Problems of Denotation in the Fiction Film," in *Film Language*, pp. 118–19.
[30] Jean Laplanche and Serge Leclaire, "L'Inconscient: Une Etude psychanalytic," *Les Temps Modernes* 183 (July 1961):83.

the presence of an enigma by the unconventionality and self-referentiality of the metaphoric process.

As a result, we are forced to hold the process of interpretation in suspense, to look *at* the figure and the discourse it generates more closely, until on the macrolevel of the whole text we begin to see a pattern of overdetermination. Throughout the film these include a fascination with body parts that are never quite as they should be and the often related activity of cutting or mutilation—mutilation that always occurs in the context of male and female relations. The following close description and analysis of the rest of the film attempts to understand the metaphorical "statement" of the prologue in light of the figural complex of the entire film.

The prologue is followed by a second time-reference, the specificity of which, "eight years later," contradicts the earlier fairy-tale time-reference ("once upon a time") that began the film. A cyclist appears on a deserted Paris street. (I will refer to this man as *the cyclist* through the rest of the analysis to distinguish him from other nameless male figures.) In addition to a dark suit, he is wearing incongruous lacy-white frills on his head, shoulders, and waist. Around his neck, attached by a strap, is a wooden box covered with diagonal stripes. When the cyclist rides directly toward the camera the box becomes the center of the shot. The following shot is a lap-dissolve to a close-up of the same box. The diagonal stripes on the box are a visual echo (or rhyme) of the vertical stripes on the tie the razor-wielding man suddenly acquired during the eye-cutting.

The scene changes to a full view of a bed and sitting room, in which the woman of the prologue sits at a table reading a book. She is wearing the same dress but her eye is uncut. Suddenly she looks up as if startled. A shot of the cyclist outside leads us to infer that his presence must somehow be what startled her. The woman throws her book shut onto the table. In a close-up it unnaturally reopens to a reproduction of Vermeer's *The Lacemaker*, showing a seated woman intently working a piece of lace. The woman goes to the window and looks down on the cyclist. From this high perspective we watch the cyclist slowly come to a stop and, without putting out a hand or leg to break his fall, keel over onto his side in the street. There he remains motionless, one wheel of the bicycle still spinning, his box still around his neck. In reaction shots, the woman has been alternately repelled and intensely interested. She now runs downstairs, where in a great show of protective emotion she kneels beside him, holds his head, and kisses his face repeatedly. Dissolve to a close-up of a box showing a hand opening it with a key. An object wrapped in diagonally striped paper is removed. A medium shot reveals that the woman, who is now back in the room, is the person opening the box with the key, removing from it a diagonally striped necktie wrapped in vertically striped paper.

From the bed beside her, the woman picks up a white collar with a black tie attached. She removes the black tie and replaces it with the diagonally striped one from the box. A shot of the bed shows that the cyclist's frills have been carefully laid out in the position they would occupy if the cyclist were himself on the bed. The woman puts the collar with the new tie in its proper place but without tying the tie. She carefully arranges the whole effigy as the camera pulls back to reveal that the box too is in its proper place around the "neck" of the "cyclist." The woman then sits beside the bed as if watching over a sick person. Two separate shots show the bed and frills over which she watches. In each of them the untied striped tie magically ties itself—first quickly, then slowly.

This ritualized arrangement of the cyclist's bizarre garments on the bed in the woman's apartment has an unmistakable fetishistic function, which we shall examine later. For the moment it is sufficient to note that these garments evoke the absent cyclist in the form of a metonymy-placed-in-paradigm, a figural association based upon the previous contiguity of the cyclist and these garments (as the pince-nez of the ship's doctor in *Potemkin* evoked its recently drowned former owner). But, in this case, the extremely unlikely combination of these particular garments with a male cyclist on a Parisian street lends to this metonymy (unlike the more typical metonymic association of doctor and pince-nez) a good deal of the sense of artificial construction common to metaphor. This sense of artifice tends to encourage us to discover an underlying metaphoric similarity between the cyclist himself and the confused signs of gender—tie, collar, box, and frills—which evoke him.

Suddenly, the woman starts, as if sensing something. She turns her head away from the bed to see the cyclist on the other side of the room now without the frills and box. He stares with fascination at his right hand. The woman approaches, looks at the hand with him, and then recoils fearfully. The man continues to stare at his hand, glancing at her only briefly to check if she sees it too.

A *Metaphoric Series*. At this point an intricate series of similar shapes forms a transition between the space of the apartment and the street below. The metaphoric series begins by revealing the mystery of the cyclist's hand:

> Shot 1. Close-up of the man's hand with a *circular* hole in the palm, out of which ants swarm. Dissolve.
> Shot 2. Close-up of the torso of a female sunbather lying on her back with arms crossed behind her head. The shot is centered on a *round* patch of dark underarm hair. Dissolve.
> Shot 3. Close-up of a *round* sea urchin, whose stiff black spines are slowly moving. Dissolve.
> Shot 4. A *round*, iris-framed, long shot from a high angle centered on the *round* close-cropped head of an androgynous-looking woman holding a long stick. With the stick she pokes at a *round* severed hand lying in the street. The iris opens out to reveal a crowd that has formed a circle around the androgyne.

This is the end of the figure proper, although the action begun in the final shot of the androgyne continues with a close-up of the severed hand as it is prodded by the stick, a low-angle shot of the crowd as it sways slightly, and a policeman who pushes the crowd away from the androgyne. As an interior shot reveals the cyclist and woman standing before a window looking down on the scene in the street, we realize that the high-angle shot that first presented the androgyne (shot 2) was in fact the perspective from the woman's apartment and that she and the cyclist have overseen the drama of the severed hand taking place in the street below. While the cyclist and woman continue to watch from above, the androgyne places the severed hand in a ubiquitous, diagonally-striped box identical to the cyclist's box and clasps it sadly to her breast. Soon afterward she is struck by a car. The cyclist's reaction to all these events is one of mounting sexual excitement.

Like the metaphor of the prologue, the metaphoric series proper is motivated by the formal similarity of round shapes emphasized by the dissolves between shots. The round shape of the hole in the cyclist's hand and the swarming movement of the ants resemble the similar round shape of the sunbather's armpit and its tuft of hair. Thus far similarity of the referents (hollow in hand and armpit) combine with contiguity of the discourse to form a metaphor placed in syntagm.

In shot 3 the round shape of the sea urchin and its protruding spines echoes the round hole and swarm of ants in shot 1 and the round underarm and tuft of hair in shot 2. But, whereas in shots 1 and 2 the round shapes were *concave* holes or vacuums from which ants and hair emerged, the round shape of the sea urchin in shot 3 is a *convex* volume from which black spines protrude.

With shot 4 (beginning with the iris on the androgyne), the round shapes of the preceding three shots are repeated in a different way. Here the iris frame of the shot itself is round. This roundness is echoed by the round shape of the androgyne's head within the shot. Then, as the iris opens out, its shape is replaced by the round shape of the crowd encircling the androgyne and is echoed by the severed round hand with which she plays.

Comparing these images, we discover a marked development from the round concave hole of the hand (shot 1) and the equally concave round cup of the sunbather's armpit (shot 2) with the convex roundness of the sea urchin (shot 3) and the equally convex roundness of the androgyne's head and severed hand (shot 4). In this progression, the metaphor begins within the diegesis; it continues its development extradiegetically in the shots of the armpit and sea urchin. Then, in the final shot of the series, the androgyne and severed hand lead back into the diegesis through the subsequent revelation that the androgyne has been observed by the cyclist, whose own mutilated hand began the series. Thus a progression of similar shapes deviously links the contiguous space of apartment and street, leading first away from and then back to the diegesis.

THE MEANING OF THE FIGURES

Each of these enigmatic figures—the prologue metaphor of moon and eye, the metonymy of the garments placed on the bed, and the

The cyclist and woman stare at his hand. The metaphoric series begins with

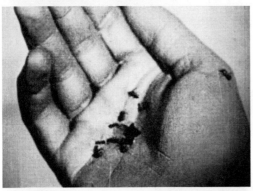

Shot 1. The cyclist's hand with ants swarming out of a hole.

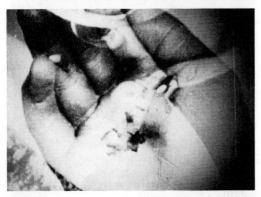

Dissolve between the hole in the hand and

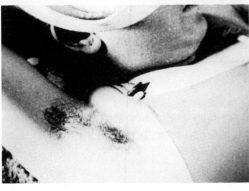

Shot 2. The underarm of a female sunbather.

Dissolve between the underarm of the
sunbather and

Shot 3. A spiny sea urchin.

Dissolve between the sea urchin and

Shot 4. The androgyne who pokes at a
severed hand with a long stick.

metaphoric series beginning with the hole in the hand—repeat motifs of cut or mutilated flesh and/or signs of male and female gender.

The cutting motif begins with the trial cut of the thumbnail before the eye-cutting of the prologue and continues with the mutilated hand and completely severed hand of the metaphoric series. The opposing signs of male and female gender appear first in the diegesis in the combination of male cyclist dressed in feminine frills, then in the metonymic manipulation of male collar and tie combined with these same frills; they continue in the more abstract concave hollows and convex protrusions of the metaphoric series, and finally culminate in the person of the androgyne "herself."

Mutilation by cutting frequently leads to the combination of the signs of male and female gender. For example, the initial mutilation of the eye-cutting in the prologue is followed by the male-female cyclist and then by the fetishized signs of his contradictory gender alone in the metonymies of the garments placed on the bed. In the metaphoric series this pattern is repeated within a single figure: the initial mutilation of the hole in the hand is followed by a shift from concave to convex roundness that culminates in the appearance of the androgyne, who combines in one person the same contradictory gender traits as the cyclist.

Most commentators have viewed the prologue metaphor variously as a symbol of sexual penetration of the female body,[31] as an assault on the viewer's own vision and a movement toward inner vision,[32] and finally, as in my own preceding analysis, as some form of metaphor for the act of cinematic construction itself. My further view does not deny any of these meanings but, rather, adds the notion that the latent meaning of the metaphor can only be castration. The significant point about this meaning is that it emerges only in the light of the other figures, as they respond to the initial metaphor of the prologue. But what these subsequent figures do, paradoxically, is attempt to deny the meaning of castration, even

[31] See Raymond Durgnat, *Luis Buñuel* (Berkeley: University of California Press, 1968), p. 24.

[32] See Ken Kelman, "The Other Side of Realism," *The Essential Cinema: Essays on the Films in the Collection of Anthology Film Archives*, 2 vols., ed. P. Adams Sitney (New York: Anthology Film Archives and New York University Press, 1975), 1:113.

though this very denial becomes itself the confirmation of the fear it is intended to allay.

The woman whose eye is cut by the razor in the prologue becomes a sexual object of the cyclist's desire in the subsequent diegesis. It is thus reasonable to interpret the woman's split eye as a metaphor for the vagina and the razor as a substitute penis. But if this is so, the metaphor of male desire is peculiarly condensed. The fact that penetration occurs through cutting opens up the possibility that it is the result of cutting—the result, that is, of castration. This only becomes apparent in the movement of the following figures to deny the consequences of this castration: to deny sexual difference.

In a 1927 article[33] Freud shows how the function of the fetish arises from the fear of castration. In the male fantasy, a woman's difference (and desirability) is the result of castration. If the fear of castration becomes a fixation, the tendency on the part of the male unconscious is to replace female love objects with fetish objects that will forever *disavow* the feared castration. Thus Freud shows that the function of the fetish is to be a substitute for the mother's "penis that the little boy once believed in."[34] He calls this substitute a *Verleugnung* or "disavowal" of the terrifying fact that women have no penis:

> In the conflict between the weight of the unwelcome perception and the force of his counter-wish, a compromise has been reached, as is only possible under the dominance of the unconscious laws of thought. . . . the woman *has* got a penis; but this penis is no longer the same as it was before. Something else has taken its place, has been appointed its substitute. . . . the horror of castration has set up a memorial to itself in the creation of this substitute. . . . It remains a token of triumph over the threat of castration and a protection against it.[35]

Frequently these substitutes—feet, shoes, underpants—are contiguous substitutes metonymically associated with the hidden and feared lack. They either cover or stop short of the part of the body that may have undergone castration. Thus the fetish allows the

---

[33] "Fetishism," in Freud, *Complete Psychological Works*, 21:153.

[34] Ibid., p. 154.

[35] Ibid.

fetishist to preserve the illusion of the female phallus. Yet, as Freud points out and as others after him have stressed even more,[36] the fetish is an object that, in its denial of what is most feared, cannot help but assert that very fear.

The feminine frills the woman lays out on the bed, to which the diagonally striped tie is significantly added, are fetishistic figures of the cyclist himself that wishfully present him as a sexually undifferentiated being, as both male *and* female. But this fetishistic assertion of the absence of sexual difference simultaneously asserts the fear that the fetish is created to deny.[37] This process of denial is repeated in the following figure of the metaphoric series. But here the metaphor also reasserts the initial fear of castration in the beginning shot of the wounded hand. Just as the wound of the eye-cutting is followed in a subsequent scene by the disavowal of the fetish garments, so here the metaphoric assertion of castration is directly followed by a progression of increasingly convex shapes that attempts to disavow the initial concave wound.

But, again, the more the text tries to disavow and cover an initial lack, the more it asserts that lack. For in the final image of the series—the shot of the androgyne on the street—the forms are convex; but the content of the convex form is, most disturbingly, a severed hand—a cut-off organ. Not only does this process of disavowal call attention to the fear of castration, it also ironically points out the double nature of the sexual symbols involved: concave and convex are two sides of the same bowl. One side is absence (the concave wound, the vagina), the other side is presence (the convex protrusion, the penis). When the convex protrusion turns out to be a severed organ, it becomes a presence that insidiously evokes an absence. Thus even a phallic protrusion becomes an ironic metaphor for the fear it is intended to allay.

The paradoxical structure of all these figures reflects the ambiguous logic of dreams, in which the assertion of any thought can be

[36] Octave Manonni, "Je sais bien mais quand même," *Clefs pour l'imaginaire* (Paris: Seuil, 1969), p. 2.

[37] A variant and even complementary interpretation of the placing of these garments on the bed could see it as an expression of the woman's desire that the sexually undifferentiated child not develop into a sexual being. thus her own disavowal would seem to be less oriented toward a specific fear of castration and more toward keeping the child a neuter (and unthreatening) object of her motherly affections.

both positive and negative in a perpetual movement between the opposing poles of signification. Contraries act in this film as they do in dreams, where, as Freud has observed, the concept *no* seems not to exist.[38] Causality in general seems to operate throughout the film in a particularly dreamlike way. Freud has observed that dreams can represent causal connection by the introduction of the dream equivalent of a "dependent clause." In certain kinds of dreams a clearly separate beginning section—the dependent clause—posits an initial condition or state of affairs, which the rest of the dream—the "principal clause"—then develops. Freud's point is that the seemingly disjointed segments of a dream can nevertheless exhibit the logic of causality. In *Un Chien andalou* the prologue metaphor acts as such a dependent clause positing the initial condition of castration-division-absence that the principal clause of the subsequent figures—and the diegesis that flows out of these figures—attempts to deny.

Still more may be said about the principal clause of the final metaphoric series ending with the androgyne. The androgyne herself is a dominantly feminine version of the contradictory gender traits of the dominantly masculine cyclist. Her feminine skirt is countered by short hair, angular body, and tailored jacket, just as the cyclist's suit and tie are countered by feminine frills. The cyclist and androgyne are also linked by their mutual possession of the diagonally striped box, which in one instance contains a necktie and in another becomes the receptacle for the severed hand. In the first instance the box appears to let out its secret: the necktie as substitute phallus and fetish working to deny a feared castration. In the second instance it functions as the container for the countersecret: the receptacle for the severed hand, which because it is once again a reminder of castration must be hidden away.

Taken together these figures establish a symmetrical pattern of assertion and denial, the basic terms of which are *presence* and *absence*. The prologue metaphor of cutting posits a gap-split-absence, which the metonymy of the fetish garments attempts to disavow.

[38] "'No' seems not to exist so far as dreams are concerned. . . . Dreams represent any element by its wishful contrary so there is no way of deciding at a first glance whether any element that admits of a contrary is present in the dream-thoughts as a positive or a negative." *Interpretation of Dreams*, p. 353.

The hole in the hand posits a similar gap-split-absence, which the following series of metaphorically similar shapes even less successfully disavows. The desire of the text thus mirrors the desire of the (male) subject. It seeks perpetually and impossibly to fill in, cover over, and to otherwise deny an original loss. If castration is one meaning of the prologue metaphor, it is itself, as Lacan has said, also a metaphor for difference, for the fundamental lack-in-being that marks the entrance into the Symbolic and structures desire.

Thus the intense figural activity of this first part of the film offers a conscious imitation of the rhetorical form of the discourse of the unconscious. The dream work carried out by condensation and displacement in actual dreams is closely imitated in *Un Chien andalou* by the Surrealist use of metaphor and metonymy in which the meaning of the text is generated entirely through its figures. Only by putting off the initial impulse to interpret these figures on the micro-level of their relation to the immediate diegetic situation have we been able to discover the latent text consisting of the repeated assertion-denial of castration in the context of awakening sexual desire. These Surrealist figures intentionally frustrate our attempts at interpretation based on the relation of the figure to the diegesis that surrounds it, because the discourse of this film is carried out by and large on the level of its figures. This is the final reason for the disturbed hierarchy between diegesis and figure noted earlier. The desire expressed by this film cannot be directly named or diegetically presented: it can only be generated by a hidden discourse, which like the discourse of the unconscious in dreams, Freudian slips, or bungled actions disturbs and rearranges the memory traces, logical speech, and action of our daily lives.

*Sexual Pursuit.* When the cyclist observes the death of the androgyne on the street below, his response is mounting excitement (captured beautifully by his breath fogging the window through which he gazes). This excitement immediately becomes overt sexual desire for the woman who has been observing the scene below with him. Until this point his relations with her have been mostly filial and passive. Suddenly, in direct response to the death of the androgyne, he is on the verge of raping her. One interpretation of his reaction would be to see the death of the androgyne as at least a temporary resolution of the castration fear and the fetishistic impulses this fear engenders. This resolution allows a progression toward desire for the opposite sex. From this point on, the woman is no longer a mother substitute, whose absence of a penis is a source of disturbance to the male child; now she has become a woman, whose difference becomes the object of his desire—his first act is to grab for her breasts.

In the second half of this film, the intensely Surrealistic figurations examined above give way to more conventional symbols. Desire here becomes a conscious pursuit of a concrete love-object. But it should be clear from the preceding analysis that this love-object is herself nothing but another substitute for the fundamental lack-in-being posited by the castration metaphor of the prologue.

Turning from the window from which he has witnessed the death of the androgyne, the cyclist begins a comic cat-and-mouse pursuit of the woman. On the sound track a jaunty Argentine tango alternates with the ponderous and passionate *Liebestod* from Wagner's *Tristan und Isolde*.

Momentarily catching the woman, the cyclist caresses her breasts over her clothes. A dissolve reveals the same hands caressing entirely nude breasts. A close-up of the cyclist's face shows that he, too, has undergone a transformation. His face is contorted, his eyes roll up so that the pupils are no longer visible, and from the side of his mouth drips a bloody drool. This transformation begins a pattern of association linking passion with the paroxysms of violence and death. This is a frequent association in a great many of Buñuel's films, in which sexual desire is never beautiful but always that which dirties, mutilates, or profanes its object and subject. In most cases this excessive passion represents the pursuit of an impossible and absolute union that death alone can finally offer.

In the love-death scene in question, when the cyclist begins to caress the woman's breasts, his passion immediately evokes a reaction that approximates death: his eyes roll up into his head and drool drips from his mouth. Love and death are inextricably connected, because only the transgression and separation of death can accomplish the ultimate union of love. Bataille points out that in French *orgasm* is often referred to as a *petite mort* (little death), a brief

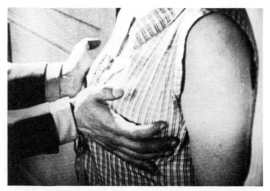

1. The cyclist caresses the woman's breasts over her dress.

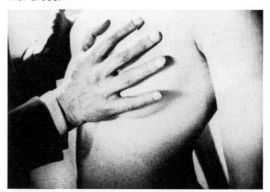

2. The breasts are suddenly nude.

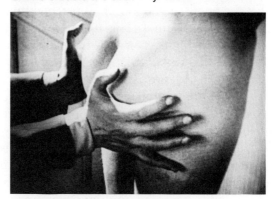

3. The breasts become buttocks.

moment in which an individual transgresses the separate discontinuities of daily life to dissolve into continuity with the rest of the universe. He also notes that such eroticism can place the very existence of human consciousness in question.[39] *Un Chien andalou* is precisely such a questioning of the self and of the illusion of the unity of the self through eroticism. Unlike the Wagnerian *Liebestod*, this love-death is not a romantic affirmation of the transcendent power of love that finds its ultimate fulfillment in death. The Wagnerian references, like the similar references in *L'Age d'or*, are ironic, as the musical alternation between the ponderous and passionate *Liebestod* and the jaunty Argentine tango suggests.[40] Where Wagner's *Liebestod* is a transcendent unity, Buñuel and Dalí emphasize the impossibility of ultimate consummation. Just as masculine signifiers evoke feminine signifiers, so also desire evokes death. For Buñuel and Dalí it is the process of the movement between these poles that holds our attention, not their transcendent merging.

The cyclist's passion begins when he caresses the woman's breasts through her clothes. On a dissolve the breasts are suddenly nude; then they are clothed again. In a repeat of this sequence, when the hands caress the alternately clothed and nude breasts, the mounds of flesh turn out to be not breasts but buttocks. The switch from breasts to buttocks comprises a movement from sexual orthodoxy to relative perversion—a transgression that obviously heightens the cyclist's passion. It is also a transgression that presents a similar flux of male and female signifiers observed in the first part of the film.

The breasts belong to the woman's body and the buttocks seem to also. But in the context of being caressed and substituted for breasts, these buttocks tend to suggest the perversion of a normal male desire for *different* body parts (breasts or vagina) into an abnormal male desire for *similar* body parts (buttocks or penis). Whether the buttocks are male or female, we tend to read them as yet another variation on the frequent assertion-denial of sexual difference begun by the figural castration of the prologue.

At this point the woman runs away. The cyclist chases her around

[39] George S. Bataille, *Erotisme* (Paris: Editions de minuit, 1957), p. 34.
[40] At the film's first public screening, Buñuel stood behind the screen with a record player. In 1960 this same music was placed on the soundtrack of the film.

the room and across the bed. Grabbing a tennis racket that is hanging on the wall, she fends the cyclist off. Against such resistance the
cyclist has recourse to more subtle stratagems, sublimating his ener-
getic desire into a more socially acceptable form. Retreating a bit he
casts about for some alternative. Finding two ropes on the floor he
grabs them and resumes his movement toward the woman pulling a
rope over each shoulder, evidently pleased to have found "the solution." The frame does not immediately reveal just what is attached
to the ropes, although it is clear that the weight must be enormous.

Even before we know what the cyclist is pulling, the action of
pulling alone is a fairly clear imitation of the process of sublimation.
The energy for one (sexual) purpose is channeled into another; direct movement toward the woman is balanced by the weight on the
other end of the ropes. Subsequent shots of what he pulls reveal the
various forms taken by his sublimation: ropes and corks at the beginning suggest the accoutrements of fishing and the notion of en-
trapment. Next the two Marist brothers dragged along by the ropes
seem to represent the smug piety of religious sanctions, the religious
weight and authority that impedes and transforms the cyclist's initial
desire. The same can be said of the two grand pianos which follow,
except that this sublimation is cultural. On top of it all, mocking
these religious and cultural pretensions is the dead, rotting flesh of
two asses, one on top of each piano. Their exposed teeth are an
echo of the pianos' keyboards, and their blinded, oozing eye-sockets
are a reminder of the prologue eye-cutting as well as a prefiguration
of the gouged eye-sockets of both man and woman in the final tableau. The rotting asses are a reminder that the ultimate end of all
desire can only be death and decay. Thus the castration of the prologue blinding gives way in these later blindings to the general symbolic meaning of death. Here sex and death begin to approach each
other in a different way. The asses' blinded eyes signify an absence of
desire. Associated with death, they are an ironic mockery of the
cyclist's sexual energy, and their dead weight slows him down to the
extent that the woman manages to slip away into the next room.

The next room is exactly the same as the one she has just left,
down to the last detail of a tennis racket and sailor hat hanging on
the wall. Indeed, everything that takes place in this scene is a kind of
repetition or doubling of what has come before, from the repetition

The cyclist pulls pianos and rotting donkey carcasses toward the object of his desire.

of the room itself to the repetition of the hole-with-ants in the hand, to the appearance of an actual double who knocks on the door. As the woman escapes into the next room and closes the door against her pursuer, his wrist is caught in the door. In a prolonged and agonizing struggle, the pressure of the door grotesquely squeezes the ants out of the hole that has suddenly reappeared in his hand. The cyclist on the other side of the door reacts in agony. The escape to another identical room, along with the return of the previous image of ants-and-hole in hand suggests a regression to a former state, as the subsequent rediscovery of the cyclist dressed in his frills on the bed seems to affirm.

Certainly the trauma of a hand caught in a door is analogous to the vulnerability to castration of an erect penis. This is especially so in the context of the earlier metaphoric series begun by the same image of the hole in the hand. But while the first appearance of the hole and ants emphasized the fear that women have *undergone* castration, the excruciation of this same hand caught in a door emphasizes the more present and direct agony of *undergoing* dismemberment. From the apparent danger of this aggressive acting-out of sexual desire, the cyclist regresses back to a fear of castration, resulting in a return to the fetish-attachments of the beginning of the film. As the woman is still engaged in her struggle to close the door against her pursuer, she glances around and sees that "he" is now lying on the bed in his former frills, the striped box around his neck. Once again the cyclist resorts to the infantile attempt to cover over the possibility of sexual difference through disavowal by the fetish.

At this juncture a stranger wearing a hat rings the doorbell. The stranger quickly enters the room, imperiously orders the cyclist off the bed, roughly pulls off his frills and box. Then, going to the window, he throws them all out one by one. During this entire sequence the stranger's back is to the camera; we never see his face. He places the cyclist face-to-the-wall with hands out to form a cross. Thus far the stranger's actions have indicated an authoritarian role—either father or teacher. These functions correspond with Freud's concept of the super-ego, a censuring agent of self-observation that measures the self against a social ideal.

As the stranger turns around, we discover that he is the cyclist's double. This resemblance confirms the interpretation of the dou-

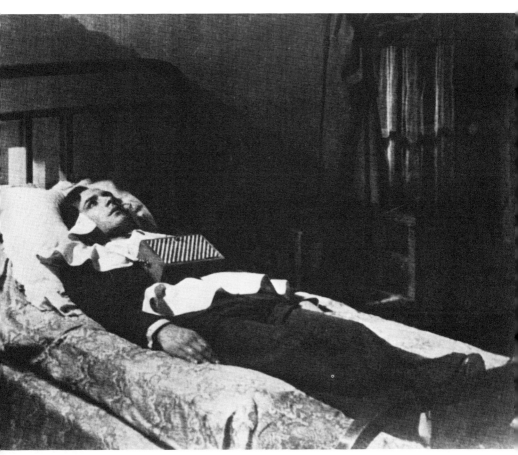

The cyclist reverts to his former frills in the adjacent room.

ble's function as super-ego—another, idealized, aspect of the self.[41]
But the stranger is something else as well. When he rips off the
fetish garments and throws the box and its cord out the window, he
becomes a threat to the cyclist's tenuous sexual equilibrium. It is as
if the cyclist has retreated to this infantile stage to protect himself
against the stranger's feared punishment: castration.

But immediately the stranger's aspect changes. When he turns to
face the camera for the first time in a slow-motion shot with a
gauze-effect, his assertive manner gives way to a gentle sadness, as if
overwhelmed and dismayed by the spectacle of what, by virtue of
his resemblance to the cyclist, we now see to be his own youth. He
walks over to a school child's desk that has suddenly appeared in the
center of the room, picks up two books, and clasps them to his chest
in a manner reminiscent of the way in which the androgyne clasped
the box to her chest just before she was hit by a car. He puts a book
in each of the cyclist's hands and moves away.

Suddenly the books become revolvers.[42] Now it is the super-ego's
turn to raise his hands, a tremendously hurt and martyred expression on his face. When the cyclist shoots, the super-ego begins his
slow-motion fall in the room and ends it outside in the meadow. As
he completes his fall, his hand grazes the length of the naked back
of a woman seated in the meadow. Again a moment of extreme agony coincides with a moment of sensual bliss. The lyrical beauty of
the nude woman seated in the meadow, whose image slowly disappears after the super-ego has fallen, combines with the paroxysm of
his death and the final gesture of grasping for, but never possessing,
a fleeting image of desire: another instance of the interdependence
of passion and death.

The death of the super-ego double marks an important phase in
the successive stages of psycho-sexual development thus far portrayed. With this death and the funeral procession that follows it,
the film for once lets a passion play itself out. In the only restful
moment in the entire film, the claustrophobic and intense enigmas

---

[41] Kelman refers to the super-ego function of this personage in "The Other Side of Realism," p. 115. Durgnat refers to the stranger as an authority figure in *Luis Buñuel*, p. 33.

[42] The books-into-revolver theme is typical of Surrealist images. André Breton, in his second manifesto (*Manifestoes of Surrealism*, p. 125), had written that the simplest Surrealist act
would be to go out on the street and shoot at random at a crowd.

of the male-female sexual games give way here to a kind of irrelevant dénouement—a man dies in a field, and a group of strangers discover and carry off his body in a series of increasingly "epic" long shots, at the end of which they all disappear. The funereal commemoration this death receives marks it as a significant loss. Though the death of the super-ego frees the cyclist from the social forces that have attempted to sublimate his sexual energy, it also leaves him insufficiently socialized and, as far as the woman is concerned, irrelevant. At this point the focus of the film begins to move away from the desires and fantasies of the male and increasingly toward those of the female.

After the funeral procession we return once again to the room. The woman enters slowly, leans against the door, and looks intently at the opposite wall. The wall is blank. A second shot of the same wall reveals a small black spot. A closer shot reveals that the spot is actually a moth with a death's head on its back. A close-up of the death's head alone completes the series. As in many of the previous instances of metaphoric formulation, the death's head is an extremely formal variation of round shapes evolving out of a character's subjective glance. This, however, is not a metaphor but, rather, a conventional symbol of death.

Suddenly the cyclist appears in the room as well. In a rapid movement he puts his hand over his mouth and takes it away. His mouth has disappeared. The woman looks at him disdainfully. As if to assert her own possession of an oral orifice, she rouges her lips defiantly. In the next shot of the man, a tuft of hair "grows" where his mouth once was. This last outrage seems to have a desired shock effect upon the woman, who, looking with surprise at her underarm, discovers that the hair is gone; it has moved to the cyclist's face. Scornfully she sticks out her tongue at the man—a second assertion of her possession of an oral orifice—and leaves the room forever.

This particularly enigmatic scene can be understood only in relation to all the slicings, dismemberments, and holes that have preceded it and of which it is a direct reversal. Up until this point, physical mutilation has functioned as, among other things, a symbol of psychic interiority. Penetration of the flesh has corresponded to an analogous penetration of ordinarily repressed realms of the unconscious. Now, however, this final appearance of the cyclist closes

1. The cyclist.
2. The cyclist places his hand over his mouth.
3. His mouth disappears.
4. A tuft of hair appears where his mouth was.
5. The woman discovers her underarm hair missing.

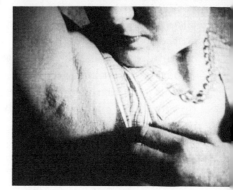

and seals the flesh, not the grotesque wounds generated throughout the film, but a perfectly natural orifice: the mouth. It then covers this newly closed orifice with alien underarm hair.

Thus the last moments of the film seal and cover the interiority that the beginning of the film so grotesquely opened. Unnatural cutting is followed by equally unnatural closing. Though an epilogue follows, this final scene between the cyclist and the woman truly ends the revelation of psychic interiority begun by the prologue. Once the literal and figural openings have been sealed, nothing more can pass between them.

This reversal of cutting images also brings an end to the accompanying castration theme, but it does so in a peculiar way. When the underarm hair appears on the space that was once the cyclist's mouth, the effect of this triangular patch of hair is rather startlingly that of a misplaced patch of pubic hair.[43] Since the hair has sprouted over a *sealed* orifice, we know that it cannot conceal female genitalia. But neither does it cover male genitalia, for there is no protruding phallus. This particular displacement of body parts contradicts all previous instances of the assertion of masculine and/or feminine sexual traits. It represents the decidedly neutral absence of *any* sexual signifiers, even through it provides their natural context (pubic hair). In other words, displaced hair sets up an expectation for the signifiers of sexuality, which the sealed mouth denies. In this context the protrusion of the woman's tongue connotes a bit more than the usual disdain. Like her previous lip rouging it asserts her own possession of orifices (and thus of gender) and the man's pathetic lack (of gender, virility). Her tongue is a phallic protrusion that he can no longer emulate.

The woman now leaves the cyclist. The role of the woman, which began passively, now becomes active. Up until this point, events have tended to happen *to* her. Her role has been that of an object responding to the cyclist's initiatives: maternally to his bicycle fall and fearfully to his sexual advances. Now, in the face of his lack of initiative, she asserts her own desire to pursue the new man on

[43] In a 1934 canvas that later appeared on the cover of André Breton's *Qu'est-ce que le Surréalisme?* (Brussels: R. Henriquez, 1934), René Magritte created a similar figure. Entitled *Le Viol*, it is a portrait of a woman in which breasts take the place of eyes, a navel is the nose, and a triangle of pubic hair is the mouth.

the beach. But, although the woman's own desires now come into focus for the first time, these desires are not of the repressed, unconscious variety that have dominated the rest of the film. Even when she does find and win over the new man, this new relationship serves only as a comment on the deterioration of the former. This happens in the following way.

Before the woman leaves the room, she opens the door and waves to someone off-screen while a breeze blows her hair. In the next shot a new man in golf clothes turns around to face her. From the Parisian apartment she steps immediately onto the beach. The man in golf clothes at first shows her his watch as if to reproach her for tardiness, but he soon succumbs to her charms. In a close-up we see the side of the woman's face on the left of the frame, and the man's hand and watch horizontally on the right. This shot echoes the first part of the prologue in which a close-up of the woman's face and another male hand figured prominently. Smiling, the woman puts her hand over the watch and pulls the man's hand down out of the frame. When she does this, a horizontal white fence in the background bisects her face at exactly eye level, recalling the same visual motifs that culminated in the prologue's eye-cutting. But this man's hand holds no razor and the fence that bisects the eye leads to no cutting. Here the latent meanings that underlay the initial cutting metaphor—castration, fear, and denial; psychic interiority; filmic creation—have been exhausted.

The subsequent discovery on the beach of the broken and abandoned box, cord, and frills functions similarly; but here it is through a metonymy placed in paradigm, much like the pince-nez in *Potemkin*. The single image of the box and frills evokes the cyclist with whom it was associated earlier. But the added feature of deterioration of the box and frills comments metaphorically on the reduced status of the cyclist in the woman's affections, on the present absence of any desire. The useless box is kicked away by the new man, while the woman picks up the frills and cord. She laughingly gives them to the man, who throws them away one by one, in a manner that recalls the similar gesture of the super-ego double when he threw these objects out the window.

These paradigmatic evocations of previous metaphors and metonymies function much more traditionally than their initial formulation in earlier parts of the film. Unlike these earlier figures, they do not generate the diegesis but only comment contrastingly upon previous developments, primarily upon the wearing down of desire that once generated so much of the discourse. As the new man walks along the beach with the woman, the banality of the final "happy ending" of united lovers rings false. It has no traditional integrating effect because the rest of the film has not functioned on this level.

The final tableau, with the words "in the springtime" written at the top of the frame and the new man and woman buried up to their chests in sand, blinded and devoured by insects, further mocks the happy ending. This frozen image of the putrefying carcasses of the two characters is one of final exhaustion, a remarkable precursor of Beckett's similar stage image fifty years later in *Happy Days*.[44] But here it is the unnatural stillness of the image that is significant. The effect is of a painted tableau with real people stuck in the sand like dead flowers. The tableau effect gives none of the violence of the previous surreal images in spite of the fact that the two figures have hollowed eye-sockets and are eaten by insects.[45] Rather, it is a worn-down, exhausted image of death that includes the previous element of blindness/castration as well as a new suggestion of return to the womb in the half burial[46] that resembles the corpse planted in a garden in Eliot's *Waste Land*.[47]

The title "in the springtime" is also an ironic mockery of rebirth, fertility, and energy (another resemblance to Eliot's *Waste Land*). What purports to be a beginning is really an end. Just as the beginning images (preceded by the fairy-tale "once upon a time") opened the semantic paradigm "romance" through the insistence of moon, balcony, man, and woman and then subverted this paradigm

[44] Samuel Beckett, *Oh, les beaux jours* (Paris: Editions de minuit, 1963); id., *Happy Days* (London: Faber & Faber, 1962).

[45] I should add that, although these details are indicated in the scenario, I have yet to see a print in which they are very noticeable. The eyes simply look dark and hollow. Neither is it very clear that the man in the tableau is the man from the beach, although the scenario so indicates.

[46] In his essay "The Uncanny," Freud notes that dreams of burial often express a desire to return to the womb. *Complete Psychological Works*, 17:217–52.

[47] "Stetson! You sho were with me in the ships of Mylae / That corpse you planted last year in your garden, / Has it begun to sprout? Will it bloom this year?" T. S. Eliot, *Selected Poems* (New York: Harcourt, Brace & World, 1964), p. 53.

through the metaphor of the eye-cutting, so the final image of the man and woman united on the beach opens up a similar semantic paradigm of "happy ending to romance," which the content of the final tableau disrupts. Such are the tensions that structure the entire film. From a metaphoric blindness that is also a figure for a new kind of sight, the film moves to the final blindness of death, from which no further vision ensues.

*Secondary Revision.* Throughout much of *Un Chien andalou* there is rather scrupulous attention to the classic rules of film editing and *mise en scène.* Early in the film, when the woman leaves her apartment to run downstairs, the filmic transition is careful to show a sample of every step of her journey, across the room, down the steps, and out the door to the street. But these details are established only so that, at a later point in the film, when she leaves the apartment for good, the abruptness of the transition from Parisian apartment to seaside will be felt.

These transgressions of filmic conventions modeled on the distortions of the unconscious in dreams or fantasies register as such only if the laws transgressed are first established. In other words, a process at work in this film tries to satisfy our conscious expectations of intelligibility. But this intelligibility is only a semblance analogous to another agency of dream formation, which Freud has described as secondary revision.[48]

As Freud defines it, *secondary revision* is contemporaneous with the process of dream formation. It is a form of censorship that covers up the illogicality of dreams. Freud compares it with the false semblance of coherence encountered in the enigmatic inscriptions that entertained the readers of a popular journal of his day. These inscriptions were "intended to make the reader believe that a certain sentence—for the sake of contrast, a sentence in dialect and as scurilous as possible—is a Latin inscription. For this purpose the letters contained in the words are torn out of their combination into syllables and arranged in a new order. Here and there a genuine Latin word appears."[49] To read the real text the reader must actually

[48] Freud, *Interpretation of Dreams*, p. 539.
[49] Ibid.

disregard the semblance of Latin, looking only at the letters and not at their ostensible arrangement. In a similar way *Un Chien andalou* creates the illusion of obeying the codes of filmic narrativity. But, like the spurious Latin text of Freud's example, it does so only to transgress them.

This process is a further refinement of the way Surrealist film imitates what Artaud calls the "mechanics" of the dream—its textual procedures. As in the early screenplays of Apollinaire, Desnos, and Artaud, the quality of surreality is not achieved by the "liberation" of pure imagination. It is achieved rather through the tension between the categories of the Imaginary and Symbolic. Thus, if the transgressions of the Imaginary are to be felt, it is necessary for the film to first set up certain diegetic expectations, which the intrusion of the Imaginary then transgresses. Secondary revision is thus ultimately a set-up for an eventual rupture of the very codes it pretends to obey. This rupture occurs either through the eventual nonobservance of the diegetic code itself (as when the woman exits from Parisian apartment to the seashore with no transition) or through the disturbed hierarchy between diegesis and figure occurring at significant points throughout the film.

*Physical Violence/Textual Violence.* I have already shown the very subtle ways in which the relations between figure and diegesis are transgressed in this film, but I have not yet commented on the way in which this textual violence is also connected with a very physical violence. Violence is not as gratuitous an element in this film as at first appears. Physical violence is used as a catalyst for even more radical forms of textual violence, to cue a textual progression to a greater interiority of vision (or envision). This envision could be more usefully rechristened *Mindscreen* after Bruce Kawin's book of the same name.[50] Mindscreen is a filmic visual field that presents itself as the product of a mind. Often associated with self-reflexive works, it is a concept developed to explain a general textual subjectivity that is not confined to the more limited notion of subjective camera and point of view (which imitate the activity of a character's physical eye). Mindscreen can thus be used to describe the visual

[50] Bruce Kawin, *Mindscreen* (Princeton: Princeton University Press, 1978).

workings of film texts in which there is no fictionalized character whose mind is visualized—works in which the text itself projects the workings of a mind. This occurs in films as diverse as *The Cabinet of Dr. Caligari*, *Persona*, and *Un Chien andalou*.

We have seen how the physical violence of the eye-cutting of the prologue opens up a literal and figural gap out of which the rest of the film's exploration of unconscious sexual fantasy spills, just as the gelatinous fluid spills out of the eye. This is the first pattern-setting instance of an act of physical violence that triggers the textual violence of mindscreen. In this initial instance the mindscreen is the whole balance of the film considered as an unconscious reaction to the fear of castration.

But within this basic structure are many smaller repetitions of the progression from physical violence to mindscreen. If the overwhelming violence of the prologue triggers the mindscreen of the rest of the film, subsequent moments of violence trigger localized progressions to mindscreen that can be read as the subjective fantasies and unconscious projections of individuals within the initial mindscreen: mindscreens within mindscreens.[51] Thus the violence of the mutilated hand (another gap) leads to a metaphoric progression that is a mindscreen for the flux of male and female signifiers. Or a violence to eyes and face in the breast-caressing scene triggers another mindscreen of the nude breasts that become buttocks. And, finally, the more conventional murder of the super-ego leads to another mindscreen in the image of the nude woman seated in the field.

Physical violence on the Symbolic level of the diegesis consistently leads to a new level of textual violence—the rupture of the diegesis and a progression to Imaginary fantasy. Thus, even when physical violence does not lead to a specifically metaphoric elaboration as it does in the prologue metaphor or the mutilated-hand series of metaphors, the effect is quite similar: physical violence on the diegetic level triggers a textual violence that moves the film to a different level of discourse altogether. Each of these new levels or mindscreens entails a visual elaboration of the opposition between male and female signifiers. Both the violence *in* the diegesis and the

---

[51] Buñuel develops this procedure extensively in his later films—*Belle de jour*, *The Discreet Charm of the Bourgeoisie*.

violent rupture *of* the diegesis are ways in which the film overcomes the censorship usually imposed on sexual obsessions. It is therefore another way in which the diegetic codes (and sexual taboos) of the Symbolic are transformed by the workings of the Imaginary.

But if, as we have seen, *Un Chien andalou* is about sexual desire (and the accompanying fear of castration), it is not about a love affair whose consummation is thwarted by the intervention of society. I state this because, even though some critics who have dealt with the film proclaim the enigmatic presence of unconscious meanings, they still tend to read it in terms of a love affair that is never consummated due to moral and social circumstances.[52] In fact, to speak of sexual consummation at all in this film is misleading. *Un Chien andalou* focuses on the unconscious oppositions that structure sexual desire rather than on a psychological love affair that either is, or is not, consummated.

The principal oppositions that structure sexual desire in the film are, in their most abstract and schematic form, male-female, love-death, and sight-blindness. These oppositions are in continual flux in many different and complex ways throughout the film, finally coming to rest in complete stasis at the end. For example, the assertion of passion in the scene in which the cyclist caresses the woman's breasts leads directly to an apparent contradiction of this passion in the death throes that follows. A similar, though reverse order, pattern occurs during the love-death of the super-ego. In this instance murder leads to a passionate caress as his dying hand grazes the naked woman's back. Finally, in the frozen tableau of the two dead lovers buried up to their chests in sand, love and death coincide.

Sexual desire manifests itself in this context as an energy that transgresses and dissolves the constituted forms of social life. But only insofar as these forms *are* constituted can transgression have value. Because transgression is forbidden, it is by definition a violence to the established order. This quality of violent transgression marks Buñuel's portrayal of sexual desire in all his most Surrealist films. These transgressions are the search for an impossible unity that only death can finally offer. Thus death, violations, and mutila-

---

[52] "Man is not free to approach the woman he loves. He carries around with him a whole load of moral and social circumstances." Buache, *Cinema of Luis Buñuel*, p. 12.

tion express a complicity with the very law that forbids them. Love evokes death and death evokes love in a fascinating structure of opposition. Sight and blindness are opposed in similar ways.

If *Un Chien andalou* pushes these transgressions to their limit, it does not do so to negate one or the other pole. Death does not negate love, neither does blindness negate sight. As in a dream, negation and contradiction do not exist. As Freud observed above, there is no "no" in dreams.[53] The film does not assert or deny any one truth about desire; it simply reveals the opposing elements that structure it and the rhetorical figures that enact it.

[53] Freud, *Interpretation of Dreams*, p. 353.

1. A cyclist appears on a deserted Paris street.

2. The woman places the cyclist's frills on the bed and adds the box.

3. The severed hand is prodded with the stick.

4. The cyclist and woman observe the scene in the street below.

5. The policeman puts the hand in the box.

6. The policeman admonishes the androgyne.

# CHAPTER THREE

# L'Age d'or

L'Age d'or (The Golden Age), 1930

Production: Le Vicomte de Noailles.
Director: Luis Buñuel.
Script: Luis Buñuel, Salvador Dalí.
Photography: Albert Duverger.
Design: Pierre Schilzneck.
Editor: Luis Buñuel.
Music: Luis Buñuel: montage of extracts from Mozart, Beethoven, Mendelssohn, Debussy, Wagner; the final pasodoble by Georges van Parys.
Assistant directors: Jacques B. Brunius, Claude Heyman.
Leading Players: Lya Lys (The Woman), Gaston Modot (The Man), Caridad de Labaerdesque, Lionel Salem, Max Ernst (The Bandit Chief), Madame Noizet, Liorens Artigas, Duchange, Ibanez, Pierre Prévert (Péman, a bandit), Pancho Cossio, Valentine Hugo, Marie Berthe Ernst, Jacques B. Brunius, Simone Cottance, Paul Eluard, Mañuel Angeles Ortiz, Juan Esplandio, Pedro Flores, Juan Castane, Joaquin Roa, Pruna, Xaume de Maravilles.
60 minutes. Black and white.

## L'AGE D'OR AND ITS MYTH

L'Age d'or[1] is almost universally considered the one uncontested masterpiece of Surrealist film, a success not only as a work of art and

---

[1] Most accounts give Buñuel primary credit for this film. Although Dalí and Buñuel wrote the scenario together, Dalí later claimed in his autobiography that he had nothing to do with the shooting and that he was terribly disappointed at the outcome of the final film. Buñuel had evidently changed much of the original work before shooting. Francisco Aranda, whose biography Luis Buñuel confirms this relative nonparticipation of Dalí, quotes Buñuel, "Dali had nothing to do with the filming, and I put his name alongside mine on the titles out of friendship," ibid., p. 69.

as one of the first innovative uses of sound in the French film,[2] but also as a revolutionary assault on the viewer. Perhaps no other film in the history of the medium has enjoyed so much critical success because of the enemies it made. Ado Kyrou tells how, in the same year that Eisenstein's *The General Line* was banned in France, *L'Age d'or* became the issue in a political battle between left- and right-wing forces.[3]

During a public projection of the film at Studio 28 in Paris, a planned demonstration broke out at that moment in the film when a reliquary is placed in a gutter beside a car. At the sight of this display of anti-Christian sentiment, demonstrators, construing that such sentiment could only come from Jews, began shouting, "Death to the Jews." They let off smoke bombs in the theater; ripped apart canvases by Dalí, Ernst, Man Ray, Miró, and Tanguy in the lobby; cut telephone wires; and, finally, in a gesture that could only emphasize its own futility, threw ink on the screen. These members of the Anti-Semitic and Patriotic Leagues then began a campaign in the right-wing papers to ban the film, protesting its immorality and Bolshevism and claiming that the incidents in the theater had arisen spontaneously. Complaints to the police succeeded in suppressing two scenes involving bishops. Another right-wing press campaign succeeded in banning the film in its entirety. But it also succeeded in making *L'Age d'or* the first Surrealist film to actually carry out the revolutionary aims of Surrealism. The film became a cause. *L'Humanité, Le Quotidien,* and other left-wing journals took up its defense. The Surrealists, who had already issued an eloquent manifesto for the film signed by (among others) Aragon, Breton, Crevel, Dalí, Eluard, and even Tristan Tzara, also published a *Questionnaire* asking if religious propaganda should not be censored along with political propaganda. In short, *L'Age d'or*, especially when fi-

[2] Aranda notes that the soundtrack of the film as a whole remains the most important of early sound film. "Not until Pudovkin's *Deserter* was the richness of the sound language in Buñuel's film surpassed," ibid., p. 83. Aranda's point is that, whether aware of it or not, Buñuel was putting into practice the theory of image-sound counterpoint put forth by Eisenstein, Pudovkin, and Alexandrov in their 1928 manifesto on the sound film. Eisenstein, *Film Form*, pp. 257–60. This theory was based on the idea of using music and other sounds as nonsynchronous counterpoint rather than redundant accompaniment to the visuals.

[3] Kyrou, *Luis Buñuel*, pp. 29–33; id., *Le Surréalisme au cinéma*, pp. 223–26.

nally banned by the police, became a cause célèbre, and Buñuel became the cinematic equivalent of the *poète maudit*.[4]

Even today, owing partly to the fact that it has not been in commercial circulation since it was banned in 1930,[5] *L'Age d'or* retains its reputation as a revolutionary assault on bourgeois values—to the extent that it is still difficult to sort out the film's real impact from that of its myth. Most critics, including the Surrealists themselves—have privileged it as the one masterpiece of Surrealist film. In doing so they have tended to praise *L'Age d'or* at the expense of *Un Chien andalou*, favoring the later film for its more explicit emphasis on societal ills.

This split in the reaction to these two classics of Surrealist film roughly corresponds with a split that had taken place within the Surrealist movement itself. Some Surrealists wanted to pursue the "aesthetic" experiments already begun, others wanted to place this new aesthetic in the service of the revolution. *L'Age d'or* is clearly the product of this latter, politically more militant phase of Surrealism—a phase that coincided with the new publication of the aptly titled journal, *Le Surréalisme au service de la révolution*.[6]

Most favorable critics saw the film's presentation of the superficiality of high society as the beginning of a new social dimension in Surrealist film. This satirical view of high society and religion, combined with a seemingly favorable presentation of a disruptive and irreverent passion, seemed the beginning of a new socially satiric vein in Surrealist art. Although it is certainly true that this vein has thrived in much of Luis Buñuel's subsequent work, the problem with such a view is that it again comes uncomfortably close to reas-

---

[4] Note, for example, the terms of Kyrou's panegyric: "*Ce film gênait, il était donc nécessaire. . . . L'Age d'or eut le courage de montrer les possibilitiés du cinéma, capable comme Les Chants de maldoror ou comme Une Saison en enfer, de révéler l'homme à lui-même.*" Kryou, *Luis Buñuel*, p. 33.

[5] Although the film is no longer officially banned, in the past the Vicomte de Noailles, who financed and owns it, has not permitted commercial showings. For many years only the Museum of Modern Art and the Cinémathèque Français were allowed to show the film legally. However, just this year even this de facto ban appears to have been lifted. A distributor, Corinth Films, will now rent the film in both 16 and 35 mm. at rather exorbitant rates.

[6] The first issue of *Le Surréalisme au service de la révolution* contained the text of a telegram to Moscow proclaiming the Surrealist group's willingness to follow the directives of the Third International in the event of a war between imperialist nations and the Soviets. Maurice Nadeau, *Histoire du surréalisme* (Paris: Seuil, 1964), p. 134.

serting a false dichotomy between form and content. According to this dichotomy *Un Chien andalou* falls in critical esteem because of its supposedly formal preoccupations, whereas *L'Age d'or* rises because of its socially critical content. Such a reductive dichotomy fails to account for much that is truly revolutionary in either film, e.g., the latent content of *Un Chien andalou* and the revolutionary form of *L'Age d'or*. In this scheme *L'Age d'or* receives praise for mimetic qualities that must inevitably detract from its Surrealism. Freddy Buache, for example, calls the film "the most exhaustive catalogue of oppressions ever compiled for the screen."[7]

In fact *L'Age d'or* is very much a continuation of the Surrealist exploration of the structure of desire begun in *Un Chien andalou;* it is simply given a different elaboration and emphasis in the later film.[8] Where *Un Chien andalou* is a questioning through erotic desire of the unconscious and illusory unity of the self, *L'Age d'or* is a questioning of society and of the illusory unity of the social body, once more through the disruptive force of erotic desire. Similarly, where *Un Chien andalou* is psychoanalytic in its use of both the subject matter and form of unconscious discourse, *L'Age d'or* is anthropological, drawing upon anthropology's detached, comparative, and scientific study of myths, ceremonies, and social organization. In neither case, however, is the film actually doing the work of psychoanalysis or anthropology. What the films do instead is imitate a form of discourse—a dream in *Chien,* a myth in *L'Age d'or*—informed by the discoveries of each discipline. Thus both films portray an interest in dream and myth that anticipates the structuralist approach to these phenomena.

Neither is it possible to say that *L'Age d'or* has dispensed with the oneiric qualities of the earlier film. Just as Freud could not have arrived at the anthropological insights of his later works, *Totem and Taboo* and *Civilization and Its Discontents,* without first elaborating the topology of the unconscious begun in the *Interpretation of Dreams,* so also Buñuel and Dalí could not have arrived at the innovations of *L'Age d'or* without first passing through the dreamlike procedures of *Un Chien andalou.*

Thus, although *L'Age d'or* has been correctly read by most critics

[7] Buache, *Cinema of Luis Buñuel*, p. 15.
[8] Ken Kellman explores some of these relations in *The Essential Cinema*, pp. 118–19.

as indicative of a new social dimension in Surrealism in general, these themes do not account for much that is truly revolutionary in the film—for its dreamlike associations of condensation and displacement. And these associations are all the more effective precisely because of the film's deceptive appearance of conventional diegesis. Synopses of the film usually stress its character as a love story: Gaston Modot's pursuit of Lya Lys in a bizarre society that, whatever other strange practices it might be able to accommodate, cannot accommodate the union of the two lovers. But most critics forget that this story occupies only two out of the film's five distinct sections. Much of the significance of the film is to be found in the relations among these fragmented sections. Part of my own objective in the analysis of this film will be to articulate the relation between these sections.

*Secondary Revision, Again.* Although *L'Age d'or* presents fragments of discernible stories, these stories are a further development of the secondary-revision[9] process discussed in chapter 2. That discussion shows how *Un Chien andalou* often conforms superficially with certain rules of cinematic diegesis. It offers, in other words, a semblance of narrative coherence that can be compared with the secondary revision of dreams, in which the radical incoherence of the dream is covered up by a superficial and false appearance of intelligibility. Of course, intelligibility in any kind of text is a very relative thing. But even among Surrealist films, some appear more intelligible than others; *The Seashell and the Clergyman* is superficially less intelligible than *Un Chien andalou*, for example.[10]

As shown in chapter 1, part of the development of Surrealist film, from the early scenarios through *The Seashell and the Clergyman* on to *Un Chien andalou*, has related to the problem of the extent to which the film can take on the actual incoherence of a dream without this incoherence becoming a sign in itself—that is, without its gaining a certain paradoxical coherence. This happens when the

---

[9] Freud, *Interpretation of Dreams*, p. 539.

[10] This may well be a factor in the failure of the Germaine Dulac version of Artaud's scenario. For, even though Artaud was able to persuade Dulac to remove the label *dream* from the opening credits, the extreme incoherence of the film encouraged audiences to read it as if it were an authentic transcription of an Artaud dream.

alert spectator learns to "crack the code" in a totally superficial way, reading an unfamiliar procedure or an unlikely succession of images as the signifiers of "dreamlike-ness" or "avant-garde-ness."[11] This is essentially what occurred when, much to Buñuel and Dalí's amazement, *Un Chien andalou* was praised by the same audiences that applauded the avant-garde essays of Gance, Epstein, and l'Herbier.

Buñuel's preface to the published scenario of the film complains bitterly of just this phenomenon. He lamented, "What can I do with audiences who find *beautiful* or *poetic* what is really a desperate and passionate call to murder!"[12] What he can and did do, of course, was to make another film in which this understanding of "beauty" and "poetry" was replaced by a nonunderstanding that forces the audience to look again. Buñuel understood that the relationship between an audience and a text changes constantly. To keep his work from rigidifying into the generic sign of dreamlikeness, he gave his next film—in a manner analogous to the dream's secondary revision—a greater appearance of narrative coherence. But, as in secondary revision, this coherence is only a superficial cover for a very profound break with narrative form.

*L'Age d'or* begins quite straightforwardly with an apparent documentary on scorpions, moves to narration of an attempted assault by a group of bandits and to another of the founding of a city, then to two lovers kept apart by that city, and finally ending with one of the Marquis de Sade's favorite characters leaving the scene of an orgy—except that this character looks like Jesus Christ.

Although the radical dreamlike discontinuities of *Un Chien andalou* are much less in evidence, audiences, at first reassured by the clarity of each narrative, soon find themselves struggling to relate one incomplete narrative to another. As in a dream, it is the rupture of the discourse that betrays the presence of another, latent, discourse underlying the first. These ruptures are found in the space between the fictive universe of each section, in the gaps that sepa-

---

[11] Christian Metz points out with regard to avant-garde film that the aware public knows it is proper to both understand and not understand at the same time—that, in fact, to not understand is often the best way to understand. "The Fiction Film and Its Spectator," pp. 88–89.

[12] Introduction to the published scenario of *Un Chien andalou*, in *La Révolution surréaliste* 12 (December 15, 1929): 33. The translation is mine.

rate the documentary on scorpions from the narrative about bandits, the founding of a city, and the end of an orgy. It is with a special eye to these gaps that I offer the following summary of the film.

Since *L'Age d'or* has been seen by considerably fewer viewers than *Un Chien andalou* and since published versions of the scenario differ in important ways from the final film, I will give here a fairly extensive summary of the film's five sections, detailing individual shots whenever it seems necessary. The episode titles and numbers are my own and are provided to facilitate future reference. Short commentaries following each episode point out the parallels and transitions between sections. They are meant only as preliminaries to the analysis that will follow.

*Episode 1: Documentary on Scorpions.* This section begins with a written title in the manner of silent documentaries informing us that scorpions belong to a class of arachnids found in the warm regions of the ancient world. (Mendelssohn's *Fingal's Cave* accompanies the entire scorpion episode.) Three scorpions crawl in the cracks of a very rocky terrain. A man's hands place two scorpions in a box. Title: "The tail is formed by a series of five prismatic sections."[13] Close-up of the five sections of a scorpion's tail. Extreme close-up in iris of one of these sections. Title: "The pincers resemble the large pincers of the crayfish; they are organs of warfare and information." A second iris shows a close-up of two pincers. Two scorpions are seen fighting. They separate. Title: "The tail ends in a sixth vesicle containing the venom. A curved sharp stinger injects the poison into the puncture." More shots of scorpions fighting against a rocky background. Title: "A lover of darkness, he makes his home under the rocks to escape the glare of the sun." A scorpion digs under a rock. Title: "Not very sociable, he ejects the intruder who troubles his solitude." A scorpion is twice repulsed from another's cavelike residence. Title: "What lightning speed, and what

[13] All translations from the film are my own. They are based on a 35mm copy viewed at the British Film Institute.

virtuosity in the attack! In spite of its fury even the rat succumbs to its blows!" A rat is stung on the nose. After much nose-rubbing it dies. (The music comes to an end. Silence.)

Comment: One important feature of this short documentary on scorpions is the dominance of the written titles, which constantly inform and control our view of the scorpions even before we see them. These titles are a mixture of detached scientism ("class of arachnid") and the most blatant anthropomorphism ("lover of darkness," "not very sociable"). A tension arises between the natural images of the scorpions themselves and the two discourses—scientific and anthropomorphic—that comment upon them.

*Episode 2: The Bandits.* This section is linked temporally with the first by the opening title "A few hours later." Fade in to a barren and rocky cliff, where a ragged bandit, leaning on a rifle, keeps watch over the ocean. (Music of Mozart's *Ave Verum* swells.) The bandit looks down to some rocks below, where he sees four seated bishops beside the sea muttering a mysterious liturgy from books on their laps. The bishop's crooks remind us of the scorpions' pincers. The bandit leaves his rocky perch to begin a long trek back to a dilapidated hut. He stumbles over rocks many times along the way. Like the scorpions he moves among rocks, but in contrast with their "lightning rapidity," his movements are slow and painful; once he falls flat on his face.

Inside the hut a group of bandits await him. They are apparently weakened and demented by hunger, living amid a strange array of knives, guns, ropes, crutches, and pitchforks. (The music is now Beethoven's *Fifth Symphony*). In the center of the room two bandits stand facing each other with raised pitchforks locked in a strange and lethargic contest that recalls the close-up of the scorpion's two pincers. A young bandit (Pierre Prévert) with bandaged head and bare legs lies on a mat winding rope onto a wooden spool. A bandit with a knife (Max Ernst) seems to be the leader. He orders an end to the pitchfork contest and prevents another bandit from opening the door. He opens it himself to allow the bandit from the cliff, who has returned exhausted, to enter.

Upon hearing that the "Majorcans are already here," the leader orders his band to arms. They form rank in a motley troupe and march out of the hut, all except Prévert, the young man with the bandaged head. Asked why he doesn't leave, he replies, "I'm fagged out." The leader answers, "We are too, and yet we go." "Yes, yes," the young bandit replies, "but you have accordions, hippopotami, keys, climbing leaders and . . . paint brushes." This last word—*pinceaux*—recalls the *pinces*, or pincers, of the scorpions of the previous section, as well as the pincerlike crooks of the bishops.

The bandits begin a trek to the sea, to meet the Majorcans. (Debussy's *La Mer* accompanies their tired steps.) One by one they fall under the scorching sun along the way, until finally only the leader continues on to the spot where the original sentinel spied the Majorcans. He looks back to discover that he alone of all the bandits has arrived. He gazes out at the sea in exhaustion. (*La Mer* and the sounds of the sea end together.) Fade out.

Comment: The similarities between the bandits and scorpions are readily apparent. Both are indigenous creatures living in rocky, barren terrain. Both have organs of warfare and information—the scorpions have pincers, and the robbers have guns, knives, pitchforks, ropes, and the sentinel (an organ of information) who keeps watch. Both are "not very sociable," quarreling among themselves and ejecting (or trying to eject) the intruder who threatens their turf. The difference, of course, is that whereas the scorpions are swift and effective in ejecting the intruder and killing the adversary, the bandits are lethargic and ineffective. Everything in their behavior aims at violent assault, but this violence aborts due to a simple failure of energy. Also, while the strangeness of the scorpion is anthropomorphized through written titles, the robbers, who *are* human, have practices and objects (the pitchfork ritual, the "hippopotami," and "the climbing leader") that are as strange as those of the scorpions. No commentary explains their behavior to us. There is also a much greater ambivalence in our attitude toward the bandits: we are not sure whether they are the aggressors or the victims of the mysterious Majorcans.

*Episode 3: The Founding of Imperial Rome.* Close to the shore, in the vicinity of the four bishops, to the tune again of Mozart's *Ave Verum*, a fleet of small boats approaches the rocky coast. A crowd of dignitaries—priests, nuns, civilians in formal dress, and soldiers—

The bishops are reduced to skeletons.

disembarks and makes its way over the rocky terrain toward the bishops. Pausing before them, they pay their respects. The bishops are where they were during the bandit sequence, but now they are reduced to skeletons. More boats disembark. In a long shot this enormous crowd recalls the movements of the scorpions and bandits over the rocky land.

After the crowd has paid its respects to the remains of the four bishops, an extremely short man with a very large mustache—apparently the governor—clears his throat, text in hand, in preparation for an oration. As he opens his mouth to speak, wild and indecent cries are heard from the rear of the crowd. Heads turn to discover a man and woman rolling together in the mud, in an advanced state of sexual abandon, piercing the air with their shrill cries of pleasure. The crowd forms a circle around them.[14] The man begins kissing the woman's neck. He has worked his way down to her breasts by the time the offended crowd pulls the two apart. The woman is forcibly led off, followed by two pious-looking nuns. She looks back yearningly at her lover. He grovels in the mud in despair at losing her, then he ecstatically bites his lower lip.

A fast dissolve shows the same woman in a medium shot seated on a toilet—the chain and handle of the toilet dangle at screen right. Her breast heaves and her mouth opens and closes in an expression of infinite desire. Another shot shows the toilet bowl with no one on it and a long piece of unraveled toilet paper that has caught fire at its end. The sound of a flushing toilet is heard as the next shot reveals a big bubbling mass of what could be lava but, within the context, one suspects might be feces.

The man, played with half-comic earnestness by Gaston Modot, still in the mud, nearly smiles at this apparent vision. The crowd roughly marches him off, the governor's speech begins, and a dog barks. Suddenly the man breaks away from his captors for the sole purpose of kicking the barking dog, then again to squash a beetle. He is recaptured and led off on both occasions.

The governor's speech is long and pompous. The little pile of mortar ceremoniously laid by the governor as the foundation for a new civilization looks suspiciously like a turd. As the mortar is laid,

[14] This is reminiscent of the crowd that forms a circle around the similarly indecent spectacle of the androgyne with the severed hand in *Un Chien andalou*.

116

a title informs us "In the year of Our Lord, 1930, on the place occupied by the remains of the four Majorcans, was placed this first
foundation stone for the city of. . . ." A second title appears, "IM-
PERIAL ROME."

Comment: Here, I mark the end of the "Founding of Imperial
Rome" section and the beginning of a new section. I make a break
between the two because, although the man (Modot) and the
woman (Lya Lys) appear in both, they function differently in each.
In the first they are coupled until the new civilization is founded.
One of the premises of its founding seems to be their separation. In
the following section, "Scenes from Roman Life," they are separated, constantly seeking to reunite; but when finally left alone to do
so, they cannot.

*Episode 4: Scenes from Roman Life.* We are suddenly in the twentieth century. Typical tourist shots of the modern Vatican follow the
title "IMPERIAL ROME." But these views soon change to more
eccentric shots of handwritten notes left on doors, banal street
scenes, traffic jams, and buildings that suddenly collapse. The title
"Picturesque and diverse aspects of the big city" is followed by the
most banal of city scenes, by a man kicking a violin along a side-
walk, and by another man who balances a stone on his head in imitation of a statue that does the same.

Modot, now in handcuffs, is dragged along a city street, against a
background of window ads, by two plainclothes policemen. An ad
for a women's hand-cream product called "Leda" catches his attention. In close-up it shows a woman's right hand, with the two middle fingers together, displayed against a black background with the
slogan *blanche et précieuse*. In a fast dissolve this photographed
hand becomes a real one—now with a bracelet and ring—which
rubs its two middle fingers onanistically into the black cloth of the
background. Gradually all the other elements of the ad disappear,
leaving only the woman's hand moving in what now appears to be
short hair. Modot, on the street, spies a sandwich-board ad for
women's silk stockings composed of a woman's stockinged leg and
another slogan. This is followed by a third ad—a hairdresser's window display—consisting of the profile of a woman's head voluptuously thrown back. Another quick dissolve reveals a live female

head in a similar position. It is the woman of the "Founding of Imperial Rome" section (played by Lya Lys). A reverse traveling shot reveals her entire body lounging on a sofa. Her left hand hangs limp at her side, her right hand rests on the black material of her skirt, at crotch level, in a position and with a background similar to that of the hand in the hand-cream ad (the bracelet and ring are the same). The inference, of course, is that the previous shots of the hand rubbing the cloth and hair belong to this woman, who has just left off masturbating. Cut to Modot, who stands on the street as if he has witnessed this scene. He again bites his lower lip ecstatically.

Lys, still on the sofa, sits up lethargically, adjusts her skirt and walks off. A long shot reveals an elegant room. She enters another such room, where her mother is reading a magazine. As Lys thumbs through a book near her mother, we see that a large bandage is now on the third finger of her right hand—presumably the same finger we saw earlier rubbing first the cloth then the hair. When the mother questions her about it, she replies that she has had a sore finger for eight days. She then launches into a long, inane speech describing her efforts to help her father obtain musicians for the party to be held that evening. The details of the speech recall motifs from the previous two sections: "There are already four Majorcans. The smallest of them sang like the others and had a little mustache." The mother interrupts to tell her to get ready for the party, "The Majorcans will arrive at nine."

Lys returns to her bedroom, where she shoos a cow off her bed more in exasperation than in surprise. Even though the cow leaves the room, the sound of its bell is heard ringing throughout the rest of the scene. In what follows, the spaces and sounds appropriate to the two lovers merge with a third space and sound imagined by Lys and emanating from the mirror of her dressing table. Since this scene is important to the analysis in the later part of this chapter, I will describe it here in some detail.

Lys sits down at the dressing table and absently begins buffing her nails (the bandage is now gone from her finger). Cut to Modot as he is still being led along the street. (The cowbell continues to be heard.) Cut to Lys now with the finger bandage back on. She puts her hands over her breasts. Cut back to Modot as a dog barks at him from behind the fence. Modot bites his lower lip passionately, while

Lys lounges on sofa, right hand at crotch level.

the dog's barking mixes with the sound of the cowbell. Cut to Lys who smiles and then bites her lower lip. The sounds of cowbell and barking continue. Modot is again led off. Cut to Lys in a side view before her mirror; a strong wind blows her hair. The sound of the wind mixes with the barking and the cowbell. Cut to a close-up of her dresser mirror with a flower pot to its left. Instead of Lys's reflection, the mirror reveals rapidly moving clouds in a windy sky. The wind emanating from the mirror blows the flowers in the flower pot.

Thus the mirror ceases to reflect what is in front of it, but only partially; for at the same time, at the very bottom of the mirror, we see reflections of the little glass vials that sit along Lys's dressing table. The next shot shows Lys in profile as she stares straight into the mirror. (Wind, barking, and cowbell sounds continue and gain in intensity.) From this angle we can't see what the mirror reflects. Cut to Lys from behind her head as she still stares into the mirror so that the back of her head totally obstructs our view of what would be her reflection. The remaining visible parts of the mirror still show clouds and sky, but just around the edges of Lys's hair it is possible to detect not only the hair itself still blowing in the wind, but what looks like its reflection in the mirror. Cut to Lys in profile again. She rests her head against the (now hard) surface of the mirror even as the wind continues to blow her hair and as we see part of her reflection. Thus the mirror alternately reflects, doesn't reflect, and only partially reflects what is placed before it.

A fade out takes us back to Modot still on the street. He has finally had enough. He explains to his two captors that he is an "important personage," while a flashback shows the ceremonious awarding of the documents for his important mission by the "International Assembly of Good Works." Cut back to the street. Modot completes his explanation, hails a taxi and leaves the two policemen dumbfounded in the street. Before getting into the cab, he maliciously knocks over a blind man on the street. Fade out.

Title: "Just outside Rome, in their magnificent villa, the Marquis and Marquise of X . . . prepare to receive their guests." Guests in furs and top hats arrive in limousines. In the salon the formally attired Marquis (Lys's father) greets his guests, brushing absently at several flies that swarm stubbornly around his face. A reliquary is placed on the ground beside a car that has just pulled up outside.

Among the guests inside the villa is the little man with the large mustache who laid the foundation mortar in the previous section. A cart filled with drinking farmhands moves noisily through the rooms, knocking over tables as it goes. The guests take no notice. Outside the gamekeeper plays affectionately with his Mongoloid son. Inside Lys onanistically rubs her same finger (now without bandage) above her breasts. Cut to a servant who echoes this masturbatory gesture in the process of polishing a carafe. As this same servant prepares to serve drinks, a maid runs out of the kitchen screaming, followed by billows of smoke and shooting flames. No one pays much attention. Outside the gamekeeper begins to roll a cigarette. His son playfully knocks it out of his hand, then runs off into a field, waving back at his father. The gamekeeper grabs his gun and shoots the boy, who falls like a rabbit. Inside the guests have heard the shot. They move out onto the balcony to see what has happened. Below, the gamekeeper makes gestures that explain his son's disruption of his cigarette rolling. His explanation seems acceptable to all.

Inside Lys continues brooding, until Modot, in a tuxedo, arrives dragging behind him a dress identical to the one she is wearing. He casually tosses the dress into a chair where it obediently sits as if someone were inside it and in a position that resembles Lys's own position in her chair. As the two lovers catch sight of each other, they radiate with joy, oblivious to everyone else in the room. They bite their lower lips in what has by now become a signal of their passion, but are careful not to get too close lest they be observed. The Marquise (Lys's mother) engages Modot in polite conversation, while he continues sneaking glances at Lys. When the Marquise accidentally spills wine on his suit, Modot brutally slaps her across the face. Lys can barely contain her delight at the affront to her mother. Modot is ordered out of the house, but he sneaks back behind a curtain to arrange a surreptitious rendezvous with Lys in the garden. Once again, they signal their longing for one another across the crowded room.

Outside they finally meet to walk arm in arm down the garden path. Cut to a terrace adjacent to the garden, where musicians prepare to give a concert as guests take their seats below. (Sounds of the orchestra warming up.) In the garden Modot and Lys walk arm in

121

arm toward some chairs; they are somewhat awkwardly intertwined. Cut to more orchestra preparations. In the garden Modot and Lys have fallen out of their chairs in their eagerness to embrace. They sit again facing each other. Modot has an end of her dress in his mouth and Lys has all four fingers of his right hand in hers. Modot then puts her four fingers in his mouth as well. Each sucks greedily on the other's fingers, teeth bared. (Birds are heard chirping.) Lys leans back voluptuously in her chair. Modot's fist begins to stroke the side of her face. Lys is ecstatic. But when Modot turns over his fist to stroke her face with the back of his hand, we see that it is not a fist but a hand without fingers.

On the terrace the conductor taps his baton about to begin. Cut to Modot and Lys, who are about to kiss. The conductor raises his hands and begins the first note. (Music continues.) Cut to the lovers. Modot pauses, surprised at the sound, and turns to look in the direction of the orchestra. Lys, who is eager to resume their embrace, lurches toward him at the very moment he turns his head; their heads collide. They rub the sore spots, then reach for each other again. Modot lifts Lys off her chair but can't support her weight. Both drop to the ground awkwardly, where more of the same continues. Again in their chairs, they finally manage a kiss. During this kiss, at the first recognizable phrase of the *Liebestod* from *Tristan*, Modot's glance happens to fall on the naked toes of a statue whose feet are at eye-level close by. He pulls back from Lys to stare at the statue's foot. Lys looks dejected, as Modot can't tear his eyes away from the foot.

At this point, three monks run quickly across a nearby bridge. A fourth monk pauses midway to spy on the lovers below, then runs back the way he came. Modot finally pulls himself away from the foot. Tenderly and sadly he caresses Lys, then puts his hand to his forehead in a gesture of despair. She reaches up to him. Picking her up again he finds a place to put her on the ground and lies down nearly on top of her. (This last movement is a wonderful combination of the passionate and the ridiculous.)

Cut to a general shot of the orchestra and audience. Insert of one of the monks from the bridge playing the violin. Back to the lovers still on the ground touching the full length of their bodies. A butler interrupts their embrace with a message for Modot: he is wanted on

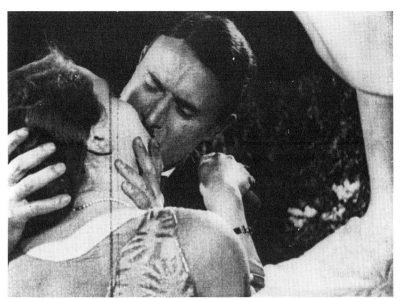

Modot and Lys kiss in the garden before Modot spots the statue foot to the right of the frame.

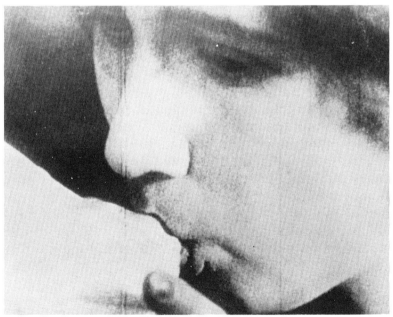

When Modot leaves, Lys begins to suck the statue's toe.

the phone. Modot angrily follows the butler back to the villa. The abandoned Lys, propped up against the statue with her face near the foot, watches him leave. Without taking her eyes off him, she touches the statue's toe with her mouth, begins licking it with her tongue, and—finally giving the toe her full attention—sucks it avidly. This sucking continues for some time, with several intercuts to the orchestra as it continues playing the passionate strains of the *Tristan Liebestod*. Fade out.

Inside Modot is on the phone with the minister who earlier had entrusted him with his mission. The minister hurls epithets: he has ignored his mission; he is responsible for the death of many honorable men, innocent women, and children. Modot is unconcerned. In despair the minister shoots himself and falls inexplicably to the ceiling. Modot tears the phone out of the wall and returns to the garden.

Reunited the lovers have a resurgence of passion. But just as Modot separates Lys's legs—her dress trembles convulsively between her legs as he does so—their passion turns to tenderness. Closing her legs, Modot mutely signals his love to Lys as he did once before from behind the curtain. Without opening their mouths the lovers speak intimate words of tender affection to one another. Now it is as if they are in bed together, hovering on the edge of sleep. He whispers, is she sleepy? She whispers back that she was falling asleep. He asks if she is cold. She replies that she felt as if she was falling. Throughout this interiorized dialogue, in which the lovers seem to speak with their eyes, Lys's hair has become gray. She rests her head comfortably on his shoulder. Intercuts of the orchestra still playing. Once again the lovers' passion builds. Lys bites her lip, while her voice from offscreen cries out, "I've waited for you so long. What joy! What joy to have murdered our children!" Modot's left eye now pours out blood that smears over his face as he murmurs in the voice of Paul Eluard, "*Mon amour, mon amour, mon amour!*"

Several views of the conductor and orchestra follow. Suddenly in mid-note the conductor comes to a stop, his hands still raised. With both hands he grasps his forehead and staggers down the steps from the podium toward the garden. The music has stopped; the audience murmurs. Still holding his head, he walks down the same

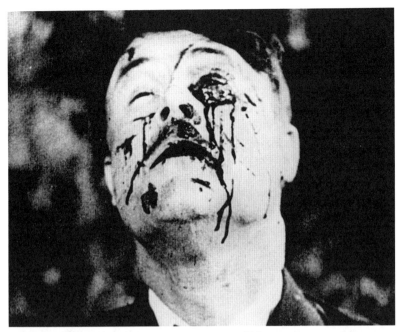

Modot's left eye spurts blood as he murmurs, "*Mon amour, mon amour, mon amour!*"

Modot grabs his head as the conductor did before him and staggers off.

garden path the lovers used before. The crunch of his footsteps on the gravel is the only sound heard. He walks to a spot near Modot and Lys, where he stands swaying, still holding his head, not seeing the lovers. Lys suddenly spies him. With a gasp of recognition, she runs over to embrace him. They kiss passionately.

The abandoned Modot stands up angrily. In his haste he smashes his head against a hanging flower pot. Now it is his turn to grab his head and stagger off, retracing the conductor's steps back up the garden path. (A loud drum roll begins with the blow on Modot's head and continues throughout most of the rest of this section as well as the next.) Fade out.

Modot enters Lys's bedroom still holding his head. In despair and anger he throws himself on her bed and begins tearing apart her pillow. Grabbing a handful of feathers he looks at them for the first time; then he casts about for something to do with them. Seizing a statue, he is torn between the possibility of doing something with it or with the feathers. Then, grabbing an enormous plow that has suddenly appeared, he wields it phallically about the room, feathers still in hand. But he is still not sure what form his pent-up animosity should take. Sighting a window he finally has an idea. From outside the window we observe the following items as they are thrown out: a burning pine tree, a live bishop, the plow, a spear, and a wooden giraffe that lands incongruously in the sea with a big splash. Finally the feathers are slowly let out. The scene ends on a close-up of the feathers.

Comment: This long fourth section is usually presented as the real center of the film. For the moment I would like simply to point out its thematic relation to the previous sections. Beginning with episode 1, Documentary on Scorpions, violence is presented as a natural instinct, although the anthropomorphic commentary tries to color it differently. With episode 2, The Bandits, violence still seems to be a functional reflex necessary for survival. Its failure in this section spells their doom. In section 3, The Founding of Imperial Rome, violence ceases to be useful for survival. Here a self-establishing social order attempts to outlaw the unseemly and violent aspects of the lovers' passion and, in the process, institutionalizes its own violent urges (kicking Modot and dragging him off to prison) and sublimates the unconsummated passion of the lovers into vio-

Modot rips apart the pillow to release his frustrated passion.

Modot grabs an enormous plow and wields it phallically about the room.

lent aggression upon helpless victims—a dog, a beetle, and a blind man.

The present section is a further elaboration of the consequences of the institutionalization of violence in section 3. Here the lovers' passion becomes a function of their separation. The more they are kept apart the more they yearn for one another and the more their original passion is twisted into random acts of violent aggression (the assault on the blind man, the slap on the Marquise's face). But once the lovers are together, their passion lacks the force to bring them to the kind of wild sexual abandon exhibited in the mud during the founding of Rome ceremony. They can only fantasize a violent ecstasy (Modot's bloody face, his mutilated fingers, the joy of murdering their children), which comically they cannot execute. For all its violence, Modot's sublimation of frustrated sexual energy through the phallic objects thrown out the window is also a patently ridiculous ritual that threatens no one, least of all the social order that has thwarted his passion.[15] More ridiculous than the earlier dog-kicking and beetle-squashing, it is not clear whether the unwieldy plow, spear, bishop, and giraffe are substitute releases for Modot's phallic drives. What *is* clear is that violence itself has become a substitute for sexual release, as the final episode reveals.

*Episode 5: The Duc de Blangy*[16] *and Jesus Christ.* The transition to this final section does not follow the previous patterns of temporal or spatial linkage. Instead, to the sound of the same drum roll that accompanied Modot's frenzied activity in the bedroom, an upward-moving, crawling title informs us:

> At the exact moment when these feathers, torn out by his furious hands, covered the ground at the foot of the window, at this very moment, as we said, but very far away, the survivors of the Château de Selliny were departing, on their return to Paris.

A shot of the white feathers is followed by snow-covered ground.

[15] As in *Un Chien andalou,* the interest in this scene lies in the process of inventing the appropriate sublimation of sexual energy. Just as Batcheff pulls a piano charged with an unlikely collection of people, animals, and objects, so Modot seizes upon a similarly unlikely hodgepodge. Both protagonists create their own comic-ritual enactment of sexual sublimation.

[16] The film titles spell the duke's name *Blangy;* de Sade's text spells it *Blangis.* I have maintained the film's spelling.

Tilt up to discover an obvious model of a castle high on a distant, snowy mountain top. The titles resume:

> To celebrate the most bestial of orgies, four famous and utter scoundrels had locked themselves up in an impregnable castle for one hundred and twenty days. These scoundrels have no law but their depravity; they are libertines with no God, no principles, no religion, the least criminal among them is sullied by more evil than you can name; in his eyes the life of a woman—what am I saying? of one woman, of all the women in the world—is as unimportant as the destruction of a fly. They had taken with them to the château, solely to serve their filthy designs, eight marvelous girls, eight splendid adolescents, and, so that their already jaded imaginations should be continually stimulated, they had also brought with them four depraved women whose stories incessantly fed the criminal lust of the four monsters.

Cut to a close view of the castle door. The titles conclude:

> Here now is the exit, from the Château de Selliny, of the survivors of these criminal orgies. The four organizers and leaders. The Duc de Blangy:

The castle door opens slowly. But instead of an eighteenth-century, depraved nobleman, we see a bearded, long-haired figure in a biblical robe looking unmistakably like Jesus Christ. Exhausted and dazed, he blinks at the brightness of the snowy outdoors, looks slowly back at the castle, then moves forward. He crosses the drawbridge from the castle with arms crossed piously over his chest. Three other men file out. They are in the expected eighteenth-century dress and look even more exhausted.

When all have reached the other side of the bridge, a young girl with long hair comes to the door and faints. Blood drips from a wound near her breast. Christ/Blangy slowly recrosses the drawbridge, one arm outstretched toward the girl, picks her up protectively, and while slowly glancing over his shoulder at his companions, leads her back into the castle. The door shuts behind them. While the camera pauses on the door, there is a moment's silence, followed by a blood-curdling scream.

Again Christ/Blangy emerges from the castle, and again he walks slowly across the drawbridge, eyes to heaven, tears in his eyes. Inex-

plicably he is now missing his beard. He passes his three companions, who are now headed back into the castle. (End of drum roll.)
A final shot shows a wooden cross leaning in a snowstorm. From it
hangs what could be either Christ's beard or the scalp of the long-
haired girl. This last shot is accompanied by a few bars of a gay little
tune.
   End of film.

   Comment: The reference to the Duc de Blangy and to the one
hundred twenty days is from de Sade's *120 Journées de Sodome*.[17]
Buñuel has chosen to present the duke and his three libertine companions at a moment that does not occur in de Sade's (incomplete)
text—at the moment of their exit from the castle where their sadistic
orgies have taken place. Rather than seeing the duke and his companions in the throes of their violent orgies, we see them at the end,
exhausted, barely able to hobble out of the castle in a moment of
comically sheepish satiety. This satiety is in extreme contrast with
the lovers' inability to satisfy themselves in the previous two sections. Thus, a violence that began with the natural reflexes of a
scorpion and continued through the frustrated assault of the bandits
and the frustrated eroticism of the two principal characters in sections 3 and 4 is finally sated in the final section by murder. It is
murder, not sexual fulfillment, that the film has been leading up to
all along. Murder moves to the foreground, in an explicitly sadistic
context, to replace the sought after sexual fulfillment. As in *Un
Chien andalou*, the final discontinuity of death displaces erotic
passion.


### *L'AGE D'OR* AS MYTH


*L'Age d'or* tells of the origins and final disintegration of the modern
world through the conflation of this world with the ancient Golden
Age of myth. As a result of this conflation, when the Majorcans
found the imperial city of Rome, they are already in modern dress,
paying homage to Christian martyrs. Subsequent views of the city

[17] Donatien Alphonse François Sade, *Oeuvres complètes* 16 vols. (Paris: Cercle du livre
précieux, 1966), vols. 13, 14.

reveal it to be completely modern. But, while *L'Age d'or* conflates the vision of ancient and modern in the mock-mythic presentation of the founding of Imperial Rome (as well as in the subsequent decay of this civilization in the scenes from Roman life and, finally, in the even stronger fusion of Jesus Christ with the Duc de Blangy), it also provides a peculiar sense of the movement of human history through time, beginning with primitive forms of life and "progressing" to increasingly complex social systems. Thus the first section begins with the nonhuman and antisocial world of scorpions; the second moves to the barely human and still primitive society of bandits; the third moves to the founding of a full-blown civilization; the fourth to a later view of the picturesque sights and mores of that civilization; and the fifth to a perverse travesty of social organization in de Sade's antisociety of the Château of Selliny, where the rules and regulations are perverted reversals of the rules and regulations of "normal" society.

The final sequence of the exit of Christ/Blangy from the scene of bestial orgies is the most condensed of all the film's sections—the final expression of a pseudomythical vision of violence that has been insidiously developing throughout the entire film. Thus, while retaining an often contradictory temporal specificity, the film also achieves an effect of mythic time.[18] This mythic time, the "Golden Age" of the title, is posited as the etiology for the way things are today: primitive scorpions and bandits, the founding of Rome and decadent scenes from Roman life, the time of Christ and the time of de Sade all suggest a mock-mythic explanation for the historical dilemmas we find ourselves in today.

Beginning in the first section with the scorpion sting that kills the rat and ending with the murder-torture of the young girl by the Christ/Blangy figure, each of the film's five sections culminates in acts of violence. But while the violence is constant, its meaning constantly changes with the many shifts of cultural context in each section. Thus in the first section violence is the perfectly natural reflex of a scorpion pitted against a rat. In the second section, violence is a human attribute that has already evolved to a rudimentary level of technology: the bandits are armed with knives, guns, and

---

[18] Mircea Eliade refers to this atemporal time of myth as *illo tempore*. *Myth and Reality* (New York: Harper & Row, 1963), p. 11.

other more curious implements. Like that of the scorpions, their violence is territorial, directed against the intruding Majorcans, who in this episode are bishops. But the bandits lack the strength to carry out their violent intentions. During their long trek to the sea, they change mysteriously from aggressors to victims. Unlike the scorpions, they fail to eject those who have come to "trouble their solitude."

Thus far violence has been portrayed as a simple necessity of self-preservation. In the third section, with the founding of a complex social order, violence changes its function. Again we see the bishops, but rather than invading aggressors, they are now victims. They are the martyred forefathers, the church vanguard that has tamed the new land, and the newly arrived colonists pay respects to their remains.

Now that the new social order is established, violence that does not receive social sanction becomes a threat to the community and is punished by the community's own self-sanctioned violence. This happens in the case of the lovers. The interesting twist here is that violence is manifested *as* sexual behavior. The lovers are not simply yearning to unite; they are interrupted in a union that is a veritable orgy of violent shrieks and convulsive movements that the society, at the very moment of its inception, experiences as a disruption and threat to its own stability. Rolling in the mud like animals, the lovers recall the primitive behavior of the scorpions and bandits. Their disruptive sexual violence elicits the sanctioned violence of the crowd that brutally kicks Modot and wrenches the lovers apart.[19] At this point the frustration of the lovers' sexual urges leads to a further and more gratuitous violence: Modot kicks a dog and squashes a beetle in the film's first instance of the sublimation of sexual drive. Thus the "pure" functional violence of survival in the first two sections gives way to increasingly gratuitous acts of violence that are displaced forms of sexual gratification in the last three sections.

The fourth section, "Scenes from Roman Life," is a more de-

---

[19] This scene recalls a similar moment in *Un Chien andalou* when the crowd forms a circle around the androgyne, who pokes the severed hand with a stick; at the sight of the severed hand, the crowd becomes violent. A policeman then forces the androgyne to conceal the hand in the diagonally striped box. In the present scene the violent reaction of the crowd as it watches a similarly indecent exposure calls for a similar repression in the violent separation of the lovers.

tailed exploration of this displaced sexual energy. Much has been written about the *amour fou* of Modot and Lys's relationship, but too often the fundamental fact of their impotence has been ignored.[20] In the scene in the garden, for example, the possibility of finally satisfying the lovers' desire has the paradoxical effect of dampening it. Only the imagination of murder revives it; for this murder of the love-object preserves the desire for the love-object by placing it forever outside the satisfaction that ends all desire. Although impotent in the flesh, Modot and Lys are able to bring their imagined selves to an ecstatic pitch, conjuring images of their own mutilation and the assassination of their future children. The orchestra conductor simply intrudes upon these imaginary flights of fancy designed to preserve desire itself. An enfeebled Modot, once the aggressor and intruder himself, now fails (like the bandits) to repel the intruder, as he exchanges places with the orchestra conductor, walking down the garden path. His sexual drive is displaced—this time onto the random objects of Lys's bedroom.

By the fifth and final section, violent aggression replaces the sex act altogether. The torture-murder of the adolescent girl behind the castle door is the final perversion of a violence that once functioned as a simple means of survival.

Thus Buñuel begins with a nonhuman and natural use of violence and progresses to increasingly complex social orders in which violence becomes a substitute release for the taboo of sexual union. A key factor in the film's relating of sex and violence is, as in *Un Chien andalou*, the establishment of an opposition between law and its transgression. But the difference between these two films is that in *L'Age d'or* this process becomes much more explicit; we are actually shown, for example, a ceremony akin to the founding of social law. The unsanctioned copulation of the couple represents the antisocial disorder against which the founders' authority is established.

From this point on, neither sex nor violence can be a simple biological function. The desire for each is paradoxically dependent

---

[20] Ado Kyrou, in *Le Surréalisme au cinéma*, writes that the lovers are revealed to themselves through love and that they desperately defend this love by their indifference, scorn, and hate of society (p. 218). Freddy Buache writes, "Buñuel demonstrates how love is able to destroy established order, and why it is vital to do so if there is to be any hope of founding a form of humanism that is truly the measure of man." *Cinema of Luis Buñuel*, p. 24.

upon the law that forbids them. Thus not only are sex and violence related in a way that reveals their complicity, both are also revealed as violations that are profoundly in complicity with the interdictions set up by the law.[21] A closer look at the parallel structure of sections 3 and 4 should help elucidate these relations between law and transgression.

Both sections 3 ("The Founding of Imperial Rome") and 4 ("Scenes from Roman Life") present elaborate arrivals of the Majorcans. In section 3 the Majorcans are the crowds of colonists who arrive in boats; in section 4 they are the crowds of guests who arrive in cars at the villa of the Marquis. In both sections, the Majorcans arrive to attend a ceremony: the ceremony of the founding and the ceremony of the party and concert. The first ceremony presents the origins of a civilization, the second an elaboration of that civilization's cultural practices and social rituals. In the latter section this civilization seems to be in a relatively late and decadent period. Although many of the cultural practices of this society are familiar, certain elements—the flies on the Marquis's face, the farm cart that moves through the elegant salon, the gamekeeper who kills his son in a fit of pique—invert the usual expectations of social behavior, giving the film its distanced, anthropological tone.

In both sections the lovers are separated by a society whose values of patriotism, family, and class are threatened by the urgency of the lovers' desire. But in the earlier section, it is the violent eruption of the lovers' passion that interrupts the ceremony of the founding, whereas in the later section it is the ceremony—first the music, then the conductor himself—that interrupts the lovers. In the earlier section civilization appears to emerge from sublimation. Sexual energies are directed onto substitute objects and images—the dog and beetle, the image of Lys on the toilet—while in the later section the lovers have become so dependent on these substitute objects and images that they are incapable of carrying out their original intention. Fetish objects—the dress Modot brings to the party, the statue's

---

[21] These films—especially *The Milky Way* (1969), *The Discreet Charm of the Bourgeoisie* (1972), and *The Phantom of Liberty* (1974)—are characterized by precisely this quality of a displaced, surreal, metonymy rather than the surreal metaphor of the prologue to *Un Chien andalou*.

foot, and the phallic objects tossed out the window—have come to replace the original object of desire.

In this fourth section the lovers have become dependent on the law that separates them. They need it to fuel their desire. Without the institution of this law, they are impotent. Thus the parallels between sections 3 and 4 set off the differences between the raw passion of the lovers' first attempted union and the culturally mediated, fetishized passion of their second attempted union.

The final—Christ/Blangy—section is the culmination of all the previous displacements of sexual energy. In this section pure, violent aggression replaces the sexual urges of the lovers. From the innocent violence of the scorpion's destruction of a rat, we move to the sadistic violence of the victimization of a young girl and to the culmination of the interdependence of sex and violence, murderer and victim, that runs throughout the film.

## INTERDICTION AND TRANSGRESSION

In the first section of the film a scorpion kills its natural victim. In section 2 the bandits begin as aggressors, their potential victims the Majorcans. But by the end of the sequence, the roles have shifted; the bandits cease to be aggressors, and by the beginning of section 3 it is clear that the new wave of Majorcans have intruded upon the territory of the bandits. Now the Majorcans are the aggressors and the bandits are the victims. In the mythologizing eyes of the new civilization founded on the bandits' soil, the bishops become the martyred heroes of the Majorcan conquest and the cornerstone of a new Christian civilization. They embody the paradox of this civilization's need for martyrs and its accompanying dependence upon the violence that kills them. Thus, the bishops change from potential victims to aggressors, then back to victims in a very short lapse of screen time: the aggressors of one section become in the next, like Clytemnestra from one play to the next in the *Oresteia*, the martyrs upon whose memory a new civilization is founded.

Late in section 3 the opposition of murderer and victim gives way to the more abstract but similar opposition of interdiction and transgression as elaborated in the sexual desire of the two lovers. We have already seen how the desire of the lovers becomes increasingly a function of the law transgressed by their passion. Much of the fascination of *L'Age d'or* derives from the way the dependence of sexual desire on the transgression of the law echoes the earlier violent relation between murderers and victims. In the fourth section, what increasingly excites the lovers are images of their own mutilation and the "joy" of having murdered their children, for murder is the ultimate transgression of the law.

While the early sections of the film offer a rapid fluctuation between the roles of murderer and victim, pointing out the paradox of a Christian civilization's need for martyrs and for transgressors who kill them, the final section condenses the roles of murderer and victim, sadist and masochist, transgressor and martyr into one person: Christ/Blangy. The point of this condensation is to discover the hidden similarities that underlie the differences: that the function of Christ is to be murdered although innocent and the function of de Sade's Blangy is to murder the innocent. Their combination in a single person proclaims the complicity of one with the other. It is this final, surreal union of complicity between murderer and victim that structures the entire film.

The film ends with an even further condensation of the complicity between murderer and victim, transgressor and martyr in the image of the leaning cross with tufts of long hair, like scalps, hanging from it. Just as earlier we were given an image of the flesh-and-blood bishops, who were then reduced to skeletons and even later evoked by a reliquary, so also here the flesh-and-blood figure of Christ/Blangy is subsequently evoked by the iconographic shorthand of cross/scalps. The cross is, of course, the traditional icon of Christianity; more specifically, it is the place of the torture-murder of the figurehead of that religion, the scene of the murder-transgression on which the whole religion is based. As the icon of the Christian tradition, it stands precisely for the interdiction of the very murder upon which it is itself based; and the scalps that hang from it are a mocking reminder of the paradox of this tradition. Thus, even though the scalps on the cross, like the condensation of the Duc de Blangy with Jesus Christ, are sacrilegious in the extreme, they do

136

not simply mock the sanctity of Christianity; instead, they show that sanctity itself is in complicity with the sacrilege that opposes it.

Similarly, the lovers themselves are not privileged examples of a passion that exists outside the civilization that stands in the way of their union. Their passion, as we have seen, is very much a product of that civilization. Rather than using the lovers to exalt any impossible amour fou, Buñuel shows us that sexual desire, too, is a product of the interdependence of law and transgression. And sexual violence—as in the garden, the bedroom scene, and the final torture-murder—is an ultimate transgression of the law, a transgression that eternally preserves the desirability of the love-object.

## DIEGESIS AND FIGURE

In L'Age d'or each separate section seems to exist both as a diegesis in its own right and in figural relation to the rest of the film. The beginning documentary on scorpions functions both as a presentation of a particular representation of "reality"—in this case a "real-life" naturalist documentary—and as a figural comment on the theme of violence that runs through the film. In this last sense especially, the anthropomorphic comments on scorpion behavior— their lack of sociability, "lightning attack," ejection of intruders— become figural analogues to the antisocial violence of the lovers and Christ/Blangy and, by contrast, to the slowness of the bandits, who fail to eject the intruding Majorcans. These similarities and differences function in much the same way as metaphors; through them the text momentarily moves away from the diegesis to a connotative comment upon it, becoming components in a rhetorical construct that compares the violence of one species with the violence of another.

However, the shift here, from the diegetic to the figural level, is not momentary. It is sustained in a complex way through all five sections of the film. In sections 3 and 4, for example, similar instances of *coitus interruptus* function to reveal the difference between the raw passion of the lovers' first encounter in the mud and the culturally mediated, fetishized passion of their last encounter in the garden. As in *Un Chien andalou*, the figures dominate and generate the diegesis. But, unlike the earlier film, the "figures" of *L'Age d'or* are both figure and diegesis at the same time. To see how this is so, it will help to look more closely at the transitions between sections.

For the most part these transitions are based on spatial or temporal continuities but rarely on both at the same time. For example, the transition between the scorpion documentary and the bandit narrative occurs through a written title indicating "A few hours later." Yet there is no diegetic relation of action between this documentary and the following narrative, although there is at least a potential spatial link between the two sections in the similar rocky soil against which both scorpions and bandits move.

The next transition—from bandit sequence to the founding of imperial Rome—offers a clear continuity of space in the rocky perch of the bishops that occurs in both sections. But the temporal order is strangely discontinuous: in the bandit sequence the bishops are alive and chanting; in the next sequence they are dessicated bones. Thus spatial continuity mixes with temporal discontinuity in the transition between sections 2 and 3. In contrast, the transition between section 3, the founding of Rome, and section 4, scenes from Roman life, offers temporal continuity—Modot is discovered still in his mud-splattered suit and in the custody of the police—but spatial discontinuity—rather than on the rocky seacoast, it is set in a large modern metropolis.

Thus far the various sections of the film have been linked on the basis of partial, and sometimes even contradictory, elements of space and time. These partial contiguities in space and time often link very separate diegeses. When placed in relation to each other, these diegeses begin to behave figuratively through spatial and temporal contiguities that can be compared with the contiguities that underlie metonymic figures in more conventional films. In other words, the rationale for the association between one section and another is not initially felt by the viewer to be based on the metaphoric similarities or contrasts between them but, rather, on these peculiarly displaced and partial metonymies.

As we saw in chapter 2, metonymies are figural associations based on contiguity rather than similarity of the referents. Unlike metaphor, metonymy does not engage the spectator in a jarring leap from the diegetic to the figural plane because the vehicle of the association—the pince-nez of the ship's doctor in *Potemkin*, for example, which stands for the doctor after his death—arises out of the diegesis through the previous contiguity of pince-nez and doctor. Thus a typical metonymy preserves the dominance of diegesis and tenor over figure and vehicle.

In *L'Age d'or* metonymic associations behave differently. In this film, large, discontinuous segments of apparent diegesis are associated only by partial spatial or temporal contiguities (for example, the spatial connections that displace the incomplete bandit episode onto the founding of Rome episode). Since each discontinuous segment of diegesis remains in suspension, we are forced, as in the classic structure of the metaphor, to seek a motive for the association in the similarities or differences of the successive segments of diegesis. Thus the Surrealist metonymy of *L'Age d'or* treats each new diegetic segment as if it were the metaphoric vehicle to the tenor of the previous segment. But the contiguous, metonymic nature of the association does not force an abrupt leap to a connotative plane the way most metaphors do.

In *L'Age d'or*, figure and diegesis coexist more fully. Without blatantly breaking with the illusion of diegetic space and time, *L'Age d'or*'s large metonymic units preserve an apparent realism; thus the shock of the Surrealist metaphor gives way here to a more subtle displacement. And, even though these metonymies arise out of the diegesis, they do not serve the diegesis in the way more normal metaphors and metonymies do. Once again, the hierarchy between diegesis and figure has been disturbed; this time the disturbance arises out of a distortion of realistic procedures.

Even though this metonymic practice is not consistent throughout *L'Age d'or*—we will see in a moment that the final transition is entirely metaphoric—it is important in light of the subsequent development of Buñuel's later Surrealist work, in particular *The Phantom of Liberty* discussed in the next chapter, which has appropriated many of the qualities of this earlier film.

The last transition of the film—from the scene in which Modot tears apart Lys's bedroom to the departure from the château—differs from the previous transitions. The written titles inform us that when

Modot drops the feathers from Lys's pillow, "at this very moment
. . . but very far away the survivors of the Château de Selliny were
departing, on their return to Paris." These titles establish a chrono-
logically impossible link between three distinct moments in time:
the moment in 1930 when Modot drops the feathers, the fictional
eighteenth-century moment of the exit of de Sade's survivors from
the scene of their orgy, and the first century moment of the life of
Jesus Christ. So obviously false a synchronicity destroys the already
tenuous contiguities of time and place that have so far operated in
the film. Here the Surrealist metonymic links of only partially contiguous spaces and times give way to a blatantly extradiegetic and
metaphoric condensation of three different moments.

Thus, in its final section, *L'Age d'or* reverts to the Surrealist metaphoric procedure of discovering similarities between very disparate
elements—between Modot, Blangy, and Christ. Here, as in *Un
Chien andalou*, the initial motive for such a comparison arises from
a seemingly irrelevant, formal similarity—falling feathers and falling snow.

When D. W. Griffith ends *The Birth of a Nation* with his nondiegetic metaphor of Christ instituting the City of God in place of
the warring states of the Union, he shifts his text to an extradiegetic
realm in order to make a metaphoric comment on the South's hope
for achieving a new "justice." The metaphoric shift to Christ gives
Griffith a way to comment in an abstract and "universal" way on his
story of the South. In *L'Age d'or*, however, Buñuel's metaphoric
shift to Christ/Blangy is not a way to abstract and universalize the
concreteness of the preceding diegesis.

*L'Age d'or*'s final metaphor is more abstract and more intellectual
than Griffith's because, ironically, it develops its metaphor in the
concrete and denotative manner of a diegesis. Christ/Blangy is not
just brought in momentarily to shed light connotatively on a preceding story of violence and sex; Christ/Blangy is also there diegetically to present yet another example of aggression and sexuality. In
this respect Buñuel's Christ/Blangy resembles another of Griffith's
visions of Christ: the story of Christ that intercuts with three other
historically different stories in *Intolerance*. But, while *Intolerance*
intercuts its four thematically similar stories, it keeps their diegetic
worlds completely separate; each separate diegesis could be recut to

run continuously. The four parallel stories are presented as universally constant themes of human intolerance, each separate diegesis reflecting metaphorically upon the others. The semantic field of one sequence is not restructured by each subsequent section; they are all more or less synonymous. In *L'Age d'or*, however, the semantic field is constantly restructured. Scorpions, bandits, bishop's bones, lovers, and Christ/Blangy all belong to separate kinds of discourse (naturalistic documentary, action narrative, Christian hagiography, and pornography).

Thus in *L'Age d'or* the shifts from one section to the next are not extradiegetic rhetorical commentaries that momentarily abstract concrete elements of the diegesis as in the metaphoric vision of Christ at the end of *Birth of a Nation*. But neither are they shifts from one autonomous diegesis to another as in *Intolerance*, where the repetition of similar themes in different concrete diegetic form functions as a cumulative metaphoric abstraction of each separate diegesis. The relation between figure and diegesis in this film is something altogether different. While preserving the concrete qualities of diegesis, the film never completely draws us into the "reality" of its imaginary world. And while it does offer highly abstract conceptualizations through its figural procedures, these conceptualizations evolve in dynamic ways that are similar to the plot developments of the diegeses.

Where Eisenstein constructs his text through conflicts in the microunit of the shot, Buñuel constructs his through the larger level of the conflicts between his five sections. Each of these sections is also a partial imitation of a certain recognizable discourse: naturalist documentary, action narrative, epic tale, anthropological documentary, and the long-winded descriptive enumerations of the "divine Marquis." But each of these distinct discourses is also distorted or undercut in some way. The scorpion documentary is overly anthropomorphic. The action narrative of the bandits is played out at a lethargic pace. The epic ceremoniousness of the founding of Rome is undercut by the ridiculous appearance of the governor (and the turdlike mortar laid on the cornerstone). The documentary scenes from Roman life present both the most inconsequential and inexplicable sights. And, finally, Jesus Christ replaces the anticipated view of de Sade's most degenerate libertine.

Thus, not only is each discourse different from the others, but each departs significantly from the rules of the genre it is supposedly imitating. The result is a collage effect in which the different parts—usually taken "raw" from the real world—are themselves inauthentic. Audiences are never allowed to "take in" the presentation of an already existing, fictional world. Instead they become active participants in the dynamic construction of this world. Reality is never given but always made.

The visual presentation of sex and violence in *L'Age d'or* is a particularly good example of the way in which Buñuel intellectually constructs even these most seductively realistic of film images. For the most part Buñuel does not actually represent either sex or violence, even though most of his film is about both. Typically he makes us infer a particularly erotic sequence, as in the masturbation scene, which is not really a scene at all but a series of obscure hints that we reinterpret after the fact to have been a scene. Similarly, the murder-torture of the young girl in section 5 takes place behind the closed castle door. All we perceive is her scream offscreen. Or, if the film does show an erotic or violent action, it is either comic or grotesque, as in the garden love-scene, which is a little of both; or it is acted out by nonhuman characters for whom the laws of civilization do not apply, as with the rat and scorpion. Thus Buñuel precludes audience identification with the seductive images of sex (as in *Last Tango in Paris*) and violence (as in any Peckinpah),[22] so that he can get on with the task of understanding just how these cultural signifieds mean.

But if Buñuel subverts his audience's tendencies to be seduced by the diegetic "reality" of the image, it is still this image that fascinates him, not as a source of identification, but as a process that structures

---

[22] Peckinpah's *The Wild Bunch* offers a particularly apt contrast to *L'Age d'or*, especially since it too begins with an apparently unrelated section on scorpions. Before the real violence begins with a robbery of a western town, the film shows a group of children on the outskirts of town setting fire to a nest of scorpions. The children's malicious violence is directed toward animals that are themselves regarded as malicious. This violence to scorpions is a metaphor for the treachery perpetrated upon the outlaws in the rest of the film. But Peckinpah's particular use of violence has us identify with either its victims or its perpetrators. We squirm as the scorpions burn, just as we squirm when the outlaws become the victims of law-and-order overkill. Buñuel's murderers and victims are not prone to this kind of identification. The presence of scorpions at the beginning of both films points out the differences between the function of violence in each.

the very desires of which the film speaks. The next section looks closely at the role of the image in structuring this desire.

## THE FALSE MIRROR

Chapter 1 shows that much of the Surrealists' fascination with the film image derived from its similarity to the image-discourse of dreams, to the ability of the unconscious to "think" in images. This chapter also shows that the Surrealists' interest in film arose not from the power of motion photography to create an illusion of diegetic time and space, but from the power of the image to structure this time and space into radically different forms. The Surrealists delighted in the differences between the film image and the "reality" it supposedly reflects. In remarkably Lacanian terms, they focused on the misrecognition (*méconnaissance*) of the image—its endless paradox of believable falsehood. To do this, Surrealist film frequently exposes the illusions of diegesis—the false representative powers of the iconic sign. I have tried to show that it does this most successfully, not by eliminating diegesis altogether, but by altering the relation of diegesis to other elements within the film. Thus as early as Apollinaire's *La Bréhatine* (in which images of a Breton girl's life become inextricably linked with imaginary images created by the novelist who inspires himself from her story) and continuing through the disturbed hierarchy of metaphor and diegesis in *Un Chien andalou* and the fragmentation of multiple diegetic elements in *L'Age d'or*, the misrecognitions of an Imaginary identification with the diegetic image have, one way or another, been exposed.

In their efforts to reveal both the seductive power and the fundamental falseness of the image, Surrealist artists have often employed mirrors in their works. René Magritte's work in particular is filled with mirrors—as well as windows and canvases that are often given mirrorlike functions—which either do not reflect what is placed before them or do so in partial and bizarre ways. One such painting, ironically entitled *La Réproduction interdite* (Not To Be Reproduced) shows a man standing with his back to us before a mirror so that we see both his back and his reflection in the mirror. His reflection in the mirror ought to show his face and chest; instead it shows the same rear view of the back of his head that we already see in front of the mirror. In other words, the mirror reflects precisely the part of the man that it (and he) cannot see but we, looking at the "reflection" of the painting, do see. It is hard to say which reflection lies, that of the mirror or that of the canvas. But since mirrors reflect only what is *seen* and since the only thing seen here is the back of the man, which *we* see, the painted mirror does not lie at all. On the contrary, it exposes the lie painted mirrors have perpetrated for centuries, that they are a kind of eye that sees what we know is not there but is only posited through our tenacious faith in the representation of reality. Clearly, it is the difference between the mirror image and the reality it reflects that interests Magritte. As in much Surrealist art, this difference illustrates the very enigma of signification.[23] It shows that the world of objects can never really be covered by the signifiers that claim to represent them. But, also, since a mirror is most often the means of reflecting images of the self, it becomes the locus of a further enigma: the apprehension of the self which precedes language and to which Lacan gives special emphasis in his mirror stage.

As outlined in chapter 1, the mirror stage is the key moment in the early formation of the self. Mythically, it occurs when the child looks into the mirror and sees its own image reflected in much the same way it sees the images of others. The identification with this image allows an initial placing of the self in the world. It is the child's first experience of the self, an experience made possible only through the identification with the self as an Other. This image of the subject as object makes possible the first stage in the construction of the ego. "I" does not exist prior to its construction through the identification with the Other.

Lacan also shows that the mirror stage and, in fact, the whole category of the Imaginary is a narcissistic misrecognition of the unity of the self. The child believes that the image with which it identifies is a unified subject, when in fact this unity is prematurely assumed. The child does not yet have a place in Symbolic relations; it cannot yet manipulate the Symbolic forms of *difference* inherent

---

[23] In an untitled short work on dreams, Paul Eluard writes, "I am captivated, truly captivated by the reality of a mirror that does not reflect my appearance," *Le Surréalisme au service de la révolution* 1 (July 1930): 2.

in language's distinction between, for example, *he* and *she*. It can only identify with the Other, unaware of any difference, believing in the illusion of unity. At this early stage the child is caught in the trap of the mirror, in its seductive misrecognition of unity.

Even after the child masters language to enter the world of difference—Lacan's category of the Symbolic—important relations are still dominated by the Imaginary. Sexual and love relations in particular are crystallized by its function. In Freud's theory of love, for example, the loved object is the equivalent of the "ego-ideal," which is itself a substitute for an earlier narcissistic phase, when the child was its own ideal ego.[24] Desire for the loved one is simply an extension of the process of identification with an ideal self begun in the mirror stage. This means, as Lacan has pointed out, that narcissism is not simply a relation between the individual and his or her own body but a relation with the self that is mediated (like the mirror stage) by the relation to an object.[25] This understanding of how love relationships are structured by the projected image of an ideal self can help us appreciate the importance of the mirror—and the mirrorlike advertising posters—that crystallizes the lovers' desire in *L'Age d'or*.

These two related episodes in the fourth section of the film (see description on pp. 128–37) have been frequently cited as examples of filmic Surrealism par excellence.[26] Such praise usually emphasizes the way in which these mirror images work to overcome the distance between the two lovers and thus to achieve the triumph of amour fou in the face of an indifferent world. But what is especially interesting in these episodes is not so much that the lovers overcome, for the moment, the obstacles that separate them, but the Imaginary mechanisms of their union. These mechanisms are: (1) the erotic-narcissistic images of female body parts designed to instill

[24] Freud, "Group Psychology and the Analysis of the Ego," *Complete Psychological Works*, 18:67.

[25] Lacan, "La Bascule du désir," *Le Seminaire*, vol. 1, *Les Ecrits techniques de Freud*, p. 188.

[26] Freddy Buache writes, for example, "Love refuses to accept space and time: it fills the universe and plunges it into eternity" (*Cinema of Luis Buñuel*, p. 18). Raymond Durgnat, who refers to the scene before the mirror as "one of the intensest moments of erotic longing ever shown on the screen," says that Modot's visions of Lys are achieved by his ability to see through "the commercialized eroticism of the posters to his *anima*" (*Luis Buñuel*, p. 41).

a desire in the consumer-viewer for a given brand of hand cream, silk stocking, or hair style that lead to what may be the first depiction of masturbation in the history of film; and (2) the equally erotic-narcissistic image of Lys buffing her nails before a mirror, using this mirror as access to her erotic fantasies.

The narcissistic elements of each episode are readily apparent. The poster and window ads in section 4 that trigger Modot's fantasies of Lys masturbating feature the usual narcissism of all advertising images hawking products to enhance female desirability. When a woman buys a product whose image she has admired on the body of another woman, she buys a false image of herself as desirable; only because the product is on this other woman does it seem desirable. Thus what really occurs is the creation of a sense of lack in one's self that the product purports to fill. In these visually manipulative ads a desired image of the self is mediated by the Other in much the same way it is mediated in the mirror stage. When Modot sees these advertising images, he uses them to conjure up further images of the woman he desires: one image of desirability engenders another.

The narcissism already implicit in the window ads becomes increasingly explicit in the images of Lys that Modot conjures, to the point of becoming blatantly onanistic. Yet, surprisingly, none of this is actually shown. The first suggestion of masturbation occurs when the female hand of the hand-cream ad comes alive and begins rubbing the black cloth of the background with two fingers. But even when the black cloth is suddenly replaced by hair, the nature of the gesture is not immediately apparent. Nor is it clear whose hand this is. When a subsequent window display of the image of a woman's head transforms into Lys's head, we recognize that it is her image that Modot has been conjuring, using the public display of feminine desirability to trigger his own private fantasy. When the camera tracks back to reveal the whole woman lying on a sofa with legs spread and right hand resting over the black material of her skirt (see photo p. 119), the previous hand movement is finally understood; all the advertising images of hand, leg, and head have been part of Modot's imaginative efforts to conjure up a total image of the object of his desire. This imagined object of desire, we now understand,

146

had just completed the onanistic hand movement glimpsed earlier.

Thus Modot's masturbatory fantasies of Lys are presented only through fragmentary images of the female body triggered by the narcissistic imaginary relation to the advertising posters. Our understanding of the masturbatory nature of Modot's fantasy only comes to us indirectly; it is further complicated by the fact that what begins as the subjective fantasy of a character suddenly—as the camera pulls back to show Lys in her room—leads into the primary diegesis of the film: Lys is actually there and continues to be so throughout a good portion of the film; her masturbation is not just a product of Modot's imagination. Thus the film confuses the plane of the real with the plane of the imaginary. More significantly, it introduces this plane of the "real" woman through the plane of the imaginary. It also shows that the real woman is both desirable and desiring as a result of the merging of her own narcissistic pleasure and her lover's fantasies of this pleasure. Like the metaphors in *Un Chien andalou*, the peculiar distortions of this sequence arise from the rhetorical violence of repression. Sexual desire asserts itself in both films indirectly, as a kind of violent wrenching of more normal modes of discourse.

The second mechanism by which the lovers overcome the distance that separates them is even more narcissistic. When Lys sits before her mirror buffing her nails with the same right hand that we saw in the Leda ad (the middle finger of this hand had been mysteriously bandaged in the previous scene with her mother), she continues a more acceptable variation of the masturbatory gesture Modot had earlier imagined her performing. Already in that earlier scene the distinction between what is imagined by Modot and what is really taking place has been blurred. Just as Modot's fantasy of Lys masturbating soon became the diegetic focus of the film when the camera pulled back to show Lys in her bedroom and then continued to locate the action of the film in this new space, so now reality and imagination blur again through the vehicle of the mirror. Lys looks into her mirror, but the angle is such that we don't yet see what is reflected in it. A cut-away shows Modot still being led down a street somewhere in the city. Back to Lys, her finger once again bandaged, who puts her hands over her breasts. Another shot of Modot shows a dog barking at him from inside a fence. The cowbells first heard ringing in Lys's room continue in the following shot of Modot, along with the sound of the dog barking. In the next shot, again in Lys's room, the sound of cowbell and barking continue. These two overlapping sounds—the dog sound associated spatially with Modot and the cow sound associated spatially with Lys—seem to overcome the space separating the two lovers. But it is the third sound and the third space issuing from the mirror in the following shot that finally makes their union complete.

In profile we see Lys looking into her mirror. A wind from the mirror blows her hair. The sound of the wind mixes with that of the dog bark and cowbell. The next shot is a close-up of the mirror alone. But instead of Lys's reflection, we see clouds racing across a wind-blown sky. Yet, at the bottom of the mirror, the glass vials of the dressing table on which the mirror sits are also reflected. In other words, the mirror reflects both Lys's room and a place far away associated with neither Lys nor Modot, but whose sound mingles with both their sounds. Like the sea breeze that wafts into the Parisian apartment to blow the woman's hair in *Un Chien andalou*, this wind ushers in a realm far away from the worlds of the two lovers, suggesting the potential space of their union, a union once again suggested by a narcissistic image. For what Lys seeks in her mirror is ultimately to possess herself in the image and the place of another. The mirror allows her to project images of herself onto other places and other selves. This false mirror is her private movie screen and, like most movie screens, it offers an escape to another world that is really a way of possessing oneself as another in the elsewhere of another world. This becomes obvious in the following sequence.

Lys is seen from behind, staring directly into the mirror, obsessed with her reflection but seeing this reflection as part of another space. We could assume that what she sees is simply the cloudy sky, except that the back of her head obstructs our view of what would normally be her reflection. The remaining visible parts of the mirror do show clouds and sky. Around the edges of her hair we see not only the hair itself but its haloed reflection in the mirror. So, although we cannot see her reflected face, we infer that she sees it transposed to the distant and desirable space of the cloudy sky.

This is what the narcissism of the advertising images and the onanism of Modot's fantasies have been leading up to all along: the paradox of the longing for another revealed as a means of possessing oneself. Thus the real innovation of Buñuel's film does not lie in the hackneyed triumph of love over the space that separates the lovers, but in the way in which the image of the self fuels the flames of Lys's passion. Each lover finds his or her identity reflected in the eyes of the other used as a mirror of the self.[27] The desire for the other can never be fully satisfied, as the love scene in the garden amply demonstrates. For while the absent image excites, the present flesh disappoints.

In the garden the lovers' flesh is all too comically present. It gets in the way of the very desires the image, in all its glorious absence, had ignited. Not until Modot leaves the garden when called to the phone does Lys begin to show anything like the passion she had demonstrated before her mirror. Significantly also, this newly aroused passion finds its stimulus in a statue, whose cold, stone foot arouses Lys to more erotic excitement than did Modot's warm flesh. Like the poster ads that excited Modot to conjure up further onanistic images of his absent lover, the statue's toe is an onanistic substitute for the absent lover's penis that, as a fetish substitute, has

---

[27] This sequence is the cinematic analogue to Louis Aragon's poem "Contre-Chant" (quoted by Lacan in *Four Fundamental Concepts of Psychoanalysis*, pp. 17, 79), in which the poet-lover compares his function with that of a mirror:

*Vainement ton image arrive à ma recontre*
*Et ne m'entre ou je suis qui seulement la montre*
*Toi te tournant vers moi tu ne saurais trouver*
*Au mur de mon regard que ton ombre revée*

*Je suis ce malheureux comparable aux miroirs*
*Qui peuvent reflechir mais ne peuvent pas voir*
*Comme eux mon oeil est vide et comme eux habité*
*De l'absence de toi qui fait sa cécité*

(In vain your image comes to meet me and does
Not enter me where I am who only shows it
Turning toward me you can find on the wall of
My gaze only your dreamt-of shadow.

I am that wretch comparable with mirrors
That can reflect but cannot see
Like them my eye is empty and like them inhabited
By your absence which makes them blind.)

more power to excite than the real thing. (It is also the first in a long line of foot fetishes in Buñuel's films, from *L'Age d'or* through *El, Viridiana* and *Le Journal d'une femme de chambre*.[28])

When Modot returns to the garden, the lovers finally manage to achieve a form of union. But once more they do so only by collectively imagining themselves to be in another space and time. We see them sitting together in the garden, but the words they speak, like the clouds that moved across the sky in the mirror, come from a completely different, imagined, place—not from their mouths. They simultaneously appear to speak and listen to their own imagined conversation. Whispering sleepily and intimately, they attend to each other's comforts. Lys's hair has suddenly become gray. Excited by this mutual fantasy, their passion mounts. A gray-haired Lys bites her lower lip as her voice offscreen cries, "What joy to have murdered our children!" Modot responds with his famous *"Mon amour, mon amour, mon amour!"* while blood pours over his face.

Spurred on by the mounting intensities of the *Tristan Liebestod* played by the orchestra on the adjacent terrace, the lovers' passion soars to new heights as they move toward their own love-deaths. Looking into each other's eyes, they find mirror-escapes to a realm of absolute passion, where desire is infinitely prolonged in death and the discontinuities of daily life dissolve into continuity with the universe. But like *Un Chien andalou*, the film does not actually recreate the transcendence of the Wagnerian *Liebestod*. Like its predecessor, *L'Age d'or* is not interested in transporting its audience via identification with the lovers to the realm of infinite desire on the other side of the mirror. It is much more interested in revealing the narcissistic relation to the fake image that structures this desire.

[28] Fetish attachments, as we have already seen in ch. 2, are ways of covering suspected lacks (originally the suspected lack of a penis in a woman). But the important feature of any fetish is the way in which a metonymically related object can be invested with all the desirability of the love object. In this sense the fetish relation is similar to the specular relation of the mirror-stage, in which the subject desires and identifies with a false image of itself. In both cases the subject misrecognizes—through recourse to a substitute object—the true nature of its desire.

# CHAPTER FOUR

# Contemporary Surrealism:
# Buñuel's *The Phantom of Liberty* and
# *That Obscure Object of Desire*

NEARLY ALL of the thirty-two films Luis Buñuel has directed over his long and productive career have had unmistakable surrealist touches. But, of all these films, only *Un Chien andalou* (1929) and *L'Age d'or* (1930) were made under the direct influence of the Surrealist movement and outside the constraints of the commercial industry.[1] In Buñuel's later work, especially in the middle period of his Mexican films, these constraints tempered the pure Surrealism characteristic of his first two films. As a result, all Buñuel's commercially financed films up to *The Exterminating Angel* tend toward coherent narratives, often based on novels, and participate to a large extent in the realism typical of that genre. Of course, even the most conventional of the Mexican films reveals an occasional bizarre juxtaposition or incongruous desire that intrudes upon the smooth surface of social relations (e.g., dream-sequences, subjective fantasies in *Robinson Crusoe* and *Los Olvidados*, foot fetishes in *El*, macabre eroticism in *The Criminal Life of Archibaldo de la Cruz*). But only with his late films, beginning with *The Exterminating Angel* (1962), did Buñuel begin to regain anything like the authorial freedom he had with the privately produced films of his first Surrealist period, and only in this period has he returned to Surrealism proper. It is to these late films that I would now like to turn—specifically to Buñuel's two most recent films, *The Phantom of Liberty* (1974) and *That Obscure Object of Desire* (1977)—for an understanding of the contemporary evolution of Surrealist film.

Quite naturally, much of the criticism of Buñuel's late style has

---

[1] *Las Hurdes*, a Surrealist documentary about a remote and miserably poor section of Spain, was made in 1932 with funds provided by Ramon Acin, who had recently won a lottery. The film was made just after Buñuel had separated from the Paris Surrealist group.

aimed at the identification of the increasingly familiar Surrealist "touches" that disturb the smooth surface of the bourgeois milieu so often depicted in his films. Critics compare, for example, the incongruity of *The Exterminating Angel's* bear-in-the-dining-room with the similar incongruity of the cart of workers that lumbers through the dining room in *L'Age d'or*. Such critics nod knowingly at these scenes, exclaiming that the old master has done it again, though just what "it" is has not always been clear. One thing that it appears to be is an increasingly indulgent satire of the foibles of the bourgeoisie by inopportune intrusions of crude animal needs, healthy doses of anarchy, and an occasional logical contradiction to keep viewers on their toes. This view, which represents a revision of the more traditional understanding of the old Surrealist rage, has been especially dominant since the release of *The Discreet Charm of the Bourgeoisie* in 1972. Led by Pauline Kael and Penelope Gilliatt of the *New Yorker*, many critics now regard Buñuel as the Hitchcock of Surrealism—a venerated master totally in command of his medium and for whom the art of filmic manipulation has become a delightful form of play. The earlier myth of Buñuel the murderous Surrealist iconoclast has given way to a new myth of Buñuel the mellowing Surrealist master. Thus Kael can write: "All the gloom, the cruelty, the outraged idealist's harshness seemed to have been transcended, and it was his humor that remained—that, and his movie-making technique, which magically became almost weightless, yet with a story-teller's energy, uncomplicated, without fuss or pressure."[2]

But Kael's emphasis on the new lightness of tone and on the knowing enjoyment of surface in Buñuel's late films has its limitations. It can lead to an ultimately superficial understanding of the continuing Surrealist enterprise, as if, relieved of the need to enter into and grapple with the structure of these works, we too can float along on the surface, smug and indulgent in our condescension, toward "the discreet charm of the bourgeoisie," chuckling knowingly at what Kael calls the shaggy-dog stories of a film like *The Phantom of Liberty*.[3] But Buñuel's films and, indeed, all Surrealist films are

[2] Pauline Kael, "The Cutting Light," *New Yorker*, December 19, 1977, pp. 128–30. This is from Kael's review of *That Obscure Object of Desire*.

[3] Id., "Taking a Chance," ibid., October 28, 1974, pp. 71–72.

more than shaggy-dog stories. To read Buñuel's late films in this way is really no different than the superficially knowing response of the avant-garde audiences who so readily absorbed the shocks of *Un Chien andalou* by reading it as an imitation of a dream.

Ultimately there is something lacking in both the myth of the raging Surrealist anarchist and that of the mellow, bemused observer of social foibles. Kael seems to confuse the new Buñuelian slickness and surface prettiness with a morally indulgent acceptance of something very akin to the "human condition." But it is important to realize that the very smoothness Kael describes is a rhetorical strategy that no more signals a new-found indulgence for the world and its creatures than it does a contrary misanthropy. As we have seen throughout this study, these kinds of essentialist statements say very little about the actual form and meaning of Surrealist film. If Buñuel's late-period Surrealist films have a slick prettiness, a sunny glamour, and an apparent storyteller's delight his early- and middle-period films do not have, it is because these qualities—like the similar qualities in late Hitchcock—have the rhetorical function of reassuring the spectator at the very sight of his or her unease. The slicker and sunnier the films appear on the surface, the more complex and troubling they can often be underneath. This is not to deny the humor and playfulness of these late films but to stress, once again, the futility of the conventional wisdom that regards all Surrealist film as either the rage or the winks of an anarchist.

Though very different from one another, *That Obscure Object of Desire* and *The Phantom of Liberty* represent a return to and a further development of the initial Surrealist enterprise begun with *Un Chien andalou* and *L'Age d'or*. In fact, these two films seem to me to represent the most recent permutations of the two primary poles of Buñuelian Surrealism running through the director's work and typified by these two early Surrealist works. These poles are: (1) the psychoanalytic discourse of unconscious desire as represented by the dreamlike images of *Un Chien andalou* and (2) the broader, more distanced, anthropological discourse on the myths that animate social and political groups as represented by *L'Age d'or*.

The psychoanalytic pole usually concerns a claustrophobic presentation of an obsessive desire that often culminates in a battle of wills. In the case of *Un Chien andalou*, unconscious desire is itself the subject of the film. In the case of the other narrative films of Buñuel's middle period—*El, Archibaldo, Journal d'une femme de chambre* and *Simon of the Desert*—the obsessive acts of abnormally desiring subjects become the focus. Then, with the films of his late period—*Belle de jour, Tristana*, and *That Obscure Object of Desire*—Buñuel returns, in very different ways, to a radically Surrealist presentation of unconscious desire.

The anthropological pole, on the other hand, opens up the problematic of desire to a much larger social field. The films in this group are episodic in structure, contain large casts of characters, include strong veins of social satire, and comprise a variety of styles of discourse. This pole begins with *L'Age d'or*, includes the Surrealist documentary *Las Hurdes*, continues with more traditional narratives like *Los Olividados, Subida al Cielo* or *The Young One*, and then returns to its Surrealist source with *The Exterminating Angel, The Milky Way, The Discreet Charm of the Bourgeoisie*, and, finally, *The Phantom of Liberty*.

These two poles are in no way mutually exclusive throughout the Buñuel œuvre. If I sort them out here, it is because it seems to me that *The Phantom of Liberty* can best be understood in terms of its sweeping, episodic, anthropological and metonymic structural affinity with *L'Age d'or*, whereas *That Obscure Object of Desire* can best be understood in terms of its obsessively narrow focus, metaphoric structure, and parody of psychoanalytic discourse—all of which have an affinity with *Un Chien andalou*.

### THE PHANTOM OF LIBERTY

*Le Fantôme de la liberté*, 1974.

Production: Serge Silberman, Twentieth-Century Fox.
Director: Luis Buñuel.
Script: Luis Buñuel, Jean-Claude Carrière.
Photography: Edmund Richard.
Leading Players: Jean-Claude Brialy, Monica Vitti, Milena Vukotic, Adriana Asti, Julian Bertheau, Michel Piccoli, Michel Lonsdale, François Maistre, Muni, Bernard Verley.
Color. 103 minutes.

Probably because it was somewhat overshadowed by the substantial commercial and critical success of the earlier *Discreet Charm* (1972), *The Phantom of Liberty* has not received anything like the attention it deserves.[4] Only Susan Suleiman, in a recent article, has stressed the radically metonymic structure of this perpetually suspended and interrupted nonnarrative.[5] Suleiman notes that the entire film is composed of a combination of contiguous narrative sequences, which although smoothly connected do not constitute a true story. What happens, she explains, is that each of the film's narrative sequences is displaced by another that interrupts the linear progress of the first and then is itself interrupted by yet another.

Although I do not fully agree with Suleiman's delimitation of each sequence or with her tendency to conflate the paradigmatic and syntactic axes of language with the metaphoric and metonymic axes of rhetoric, her analysis of the narrative structure of the film— and the "principle of infinite suspension" which makes the film even *more* linear than a normal narrative—is very illuminating. But where Suleiman concentrates on the narrative incoherence achieved by this exaggerated linearity, my own analysis will concentrate on the latent figural association these self-subverting segments build.

*The Phantom of Liberty* is in many ways an extreme instance of the kind of incomplete narrative segments that compose *L'Age d'or*, except that, where *L'Age d'or* is organized into five distinct diegetic segments, each of which grows in an aberrant and only partially continuous way out of the previous one, *Phantom*'s segments are much more numerous (I count 8, Suleiman counts 12) and seem to grow more continuously out of one another. For example, we saw in chapter 3 how the diegetic action of the bandits' trek to meet the Majorcans simply petered out as the bandits collapsed one by one on the way to their destination. Yet the following sequence—"The Founding of Imperial Rome"—continues partial diegetic elements from the earlier segment, combining spatial continuity with a temporal discontinuity that interrupts the primary action of one sequence with a new action in the next.

---

[4] Pauline Kael dismisses it, as mentioned earlier, as a series of shaggy-dog stories.

[5] Susan Suleiman, "Freedom and Necessity: Narrative Structure in *The Phantom of Liberty*," *Quarterly Review of Film Studies* 3 (Summer 1978): 277–95.

In *The Phantom of Liberty*, the viewer receives an even greater sense of discontinuity, in spite of the fact that each diegetic segment of the film is almost perfectly continuous, both spatially and temporally, with the next. Here the transitions from segment to segment are so excessively continuous that they often take place within the same shot—as, for example, when the camera simply follows the trajectory of a minor character from one narrative segment to the next. The smoothness of transition achieved by the avoidance of editing and the continuous presence of a "linking" character momentarily covers the fact that the narrative has radically abandoned its original direction.

*The Phantom of Liberty* thus proceeds by fits and starts. Almost no story is allowed to run its course before it is interrupted. Beginnings of stories proliferate, each loaded with the enigmatic promise of letters to be opened, fatal diseases that will take their toll, love affairs to be consummated. With utter whimsicality the narrative shrinks from any predictable development, from the pursuit of any single narrative thread. And yet each new story, which appears to the viewer as an evasion of the predictable progression of the former, repeats, teasingly, partial elements—themes, similar animals, phrases—from earlier episodes, slyly suggesting that the liberty we seem to experience on the level of the diegesis is, like the liberty of the film's title, only a phantom.

In the following discussion I will label the different sequences by the name of the character who appears most continuously in it (this is not always the same character who performs the transition, though it often is). Contrary to Suleiman, I simplify the narrative breakdown by considering as one episode any complex of narrative acts that occurs under the auspices of a single character, even if this character seems to take on an entirely new role.[6]

*Episode 1: The Napoleonic Captain.* The red letters of the credits appear over the dark, rich colors of Goya's painting *The Execu-*

---

[6] Thus I consider the Legendre segment to continue when that character moves from his role of patient-dying-of-cancer to father-of-missing-daughter, whereas Suleiman considers these two separate sections. I do this both to simplify and to place the focus of my analysis of the transitions between *truly* discontinuous narrative segments (i.e., there is no real transition between M. Legendre's above-mentioned roles, but there is a radical transition displacement between the Foucauld and nurse segments).

*The Executions of May 3, 1808*, by Francisco José de Goya.

*tions of May* 3, 1808, which shows Napoleonic soldiers executing a group of Spanish patriots. Sounds of gunshot are heard over the painting. The opening scene then brings this same painting to life as a very similar execution scene is reenacted. But this time we repeatedly hear the gun shots and the prisoners' enigmatic cry, *Vivan las caenas!* Translated literally from the Spanish this means Long live chains! although a subtitle in the French print of the film translates the phrase as "*A bas la liberté!*" ("Down with liberty!").

Although a cry of defiance to the occupying French army, *Vivan las caenas!* is shouted at the forces of revolution—at the Napoleonic army "freeing" Europe from the tyrannies of monarchy and church (among those executed is a priest, played by Buñuel himself). Exactly what we are to make of this scene and cry remains problematic at this point. Only one thing is certain: there is no obvious or easy division between the forces of tyranny and the forces of freedom. The Napoleonic army typically represents the forces of liberation, while the Spanish loyalists typically represent the tyranny of king and church; yet in this case the presumed forces of liberation, the Napoleonic soldiers, oppress the presumed forces of tyranny, the Spanish loyalists. Perhaps the cry Long live chains! ironically means that the Spanish loyalists prefer the chains of monarchy to the "liberty" that here executes them. At any rate, one effect of this cry is to make freedom and tyranny appear as very relative forces. Not only is one person's freedom another's enslavement, but the Spanish patriots who cry Long live chains! (or Down with liberty!) may also acknowledge a truth inherent in any defiance of oppression: that the dream of freedom depends on the very existence of slavery; because there are chains, we desire to be set free. Much of the rest of the film will explore the ramifications of this paradox, though not exclusively in political terms, as the second half of this first section shows.

As the executions continue, a young captain in the Napoleonic army, whose camp has been set up inside the church of Toledo, gets drunk on the wine used for the service. He spies a lovely statue of Doña Elvira while kneeling in prayer above that same woman's tomb. As the gun shots continue outside, the captain leans to kiss the statue. Suddenly the arm of the adjacent statue of Doña Elvira's husband comes down hard on the captain's head, knocking him out cold. As soon as the captain receives this unexpected blow from a supposedly inanimate statue, a woman's voice continues the narration of this story, explaining that with this blow the captain resolved to exhume Doña Elvira's body and to "have" her in his bed.

Late at night in the same Toledo church, as the woman's voice continues to narrate the event, we see the raised and opened tomb of Doña Elvira. The captain rests his sword on the hands of the adjacent knight and leans forward to pull back the sheet covering the body. The corpse of the young woman is as fresh and beautiful as the day she died. As the captain once again approaches her lips, the scene changes abruptly from this dark historical moment of the past to a sunny public park somewhere in Paris in the present day.

Two women are seated on a park bench. One of them is reading a description of Doña Elvira's body to the other. She is the narrator whose voice we heard in the previous scene. Evidently the scene we have just witnessed was merely a story read by her to another woman. The first woman continues reading, stumbling over the word *paraphernalia*, which, the second woman pedantically explains, refers to a woman's personal property.

In this first fragment of narrative, one recognizes a familiar presentation of the nature of desire: the captain's illicit desire for the dead body of the woman buried in the tomb, who herself belongs to a similar story of illicit passion and vengeful statues, is spurred on by the male statue's jealous gesture of prohibition. In fact, the story breaks off at a moment of intense suspense that leaves us wondering not only whether the captain will succeed in his desire to make love to a corpse, but also whether the knight will once again succeed in thwarting this desire. But, ironically, the captain is an oppressor whose law gives rise to the Spanish patriots' desire for freedom in the first part of this story and a revolutionary lover who transgresses moral and religious law in the second half of the story. The political position of the Spanish patriots is thus similar to the erotic position of the French captain: just as the Spanish patriots' desire for freedom arises from the tyranny of the French army and the impossibility of ever achieving liberty as an absolute condition, so the French captain's desire for the Spanish beauty is spurred on by the gesture of prohibition enacted by the knight's statue and the ultimate impossibility of ever possessing a corpse. In both cases what seems impossibly out of reach is most desired.

Improbably, however, the captain's desire for the beautiful corpse seems nearly attainable. At least it is not thwarted by any impediment within this particular story. Rather, it is the narrative process that intervenes, placing this first story within the frame of another, which teasingly interrupts the first at the greatest moment of erotic suspense. Thus narration itself takes on a dimension of erotic tease that will continue throughout much of the film, slyly equating the movement to the end of the story with a sexual movement to climax of the character within the story.

*Episode 2: The Foucauld Family.* The women on the park bench belong to a new story that has now interrupted and subsumed the first, but neither of these women figures prominently in it. One of them functions simply as a link between the two narratives: the invisible narrator in the first is a minor character in the second. As we shall soon learn, this woman is the maid of the Foucauld family. In another part of the park her charge, Véronique Foucauld, encounters a perverse-looking man who delightedly shows her and her friend what we assume to be obscene post cards. At home that evening Véronique shows the post cards to her parents, who in outrage fire the maid.

But, when alone, the Foucauld parents become sexually excited as they glance through the offending cards. In the chaos of their mounting passion, a card falls to reveal for the first time that the pictures are nothing more than typical views of Paris monuments. This incident introduces the first in a long series of taboo reversals at work in the film. In these reversals a normally innocent object or act takes on the negative marks of a cultural taboo. These reversals emphasize the apparently arbitrary nature of these positive or negative marks as they occur in any given culture. Thus the Foucaulds are sexually aroused by the post cards simply because they are taboo and not because of any intrinsically erotic content. In this way transgression itself becomes erotically charged.

Later that night Mr. Foucauld, who cannot sleep, watches as a rooster, a figure in black, a postman who hands him a letter, and an

The Foucauld parents, Jean Claude Brialy and Monica Vitti, look at their daughter's dirty postcards.

ostrich troop through his bedroom. Disturbed by these seemingly real visions, he visits a doctor the next day. To prove to the doctor that he was not seeing things, Mr. Foucauld shows him the letter delivered by the postman. As the doctor begins to open the letter, a nurse suddenly interrupts to hand him another communication, a telegram informing the nurse of her father's illness. She asks for time off immediately to visit her father. Rather than returning to Mr. Foucauld and his problem, we now follow the nurse on her way to the country to visit her father.

The device of the two written missives, the letter from Foucauld's dream and the telegram from the nurse's father, emphasizes the moment of narrative juncture. The doctor's decision to open the nurse's missive before his patient's is also the decision to displace the Foucauld story by that of the nurse, leaving us in permanent suspense as to the content of the dream letter. For the second time in the film, a mysterious and suspenseful narrative turn of events is interrupted by a story that seems comparatively ordinary and banal.

*Episode 3: The Nurse.* On her way to visit her father, the nurse encounters a group of military men in tanks incongruously hunting foxes. They inform her that the road ahead is washed out and that she would do well to stay at a nearby inn. This arrival at the inn is a detour in the nurse's itinerary, which is itself a detour from the previous story. What is fascinating at this point in the film is the way physical trajectory—the nurse's trip—has been translated into narrative trajectory, as if the restless generative force that propels the film's narrative cannot resist the impulse to follow a physical movement, even—or especially—if that movement leads us away from the primary story. This process is repeated frequently throughout the film and is powerfully emphasized in the following scene.

After all the hotel guests, including the nurse, have retired to their rooms, there is a quiet moment in which the shot remains fixed on the dark landing of the stairs leading to the hallway adjoining the rooms of the various guests. The moment is pregnant with possibilities, as if the camera were hesitating as to which new narrative thread to pursue among so many contiguous lives. The very fact that we do not immediately pursue any one of these threads makes us all the more aware of this moment of narrative freedom, which by not entering into any one story maintains the potential of them all. This potential is then realized in the elaborate orchestration of chance encounters that follows.

Observing from the polite distance of the landing, we view the various trajectories of the guests as they go to their rooms and then back and forth to the hallway bathroom. A monk goes to the bathroom door, finds it occupied and returns to his room. Immediately afterward, a flamenco dancer (in French referred to as an "*andalouse*") exits from the bathroom and enters her own room. Through the open door we observe a flamenco guitarist, who plays as she begins to dance. Another door opens and a tall gentleman, apparently disturbed by the noise, goes to the flamenco dancer's door, closes it, returns to his own room, and closes the door. Then another monk mounts the stairs and enters a room. A different door opens, another monk comes out carrying a small, portable altar; he goes to a different room and knocks. A cut to the interior of the room abandons the camera's polite distance on the landing encompassing the potential for narrative to pursue a specific narrative possibility. The narrative pursued is the same one we just left: the monk has knocked on the nurse's door.

Each opening of a door represents a distinctly new narrative possibility. Each closing of a door without entering into the world behind it, represents a temporary deferment of that possibility.[7] Eventually, however, in spite of the apparent decision to pursue one of the many narrative possibilities, all the characters we have glimpsed in this hallway (with the exception of the flamenco dancer and guitarist), plus several others we have not yet seen, converge in one room to pursue, in an orgy of fortuitous linkings, nearly all of these possibilities at once.

The monk who arrived at the nurse's door proposes an impromptu prayer meeting for her sick father. After he and his three brothers have performed this function, they politely invite themselves to a game of cards with the nurse. As time passes their game becomes an intense late-night session of poker, in which the monks and nurse gamble for religious medals, while the innkeeper serves

---

[7] Marsha Kinder notes that this hallway offers the perfect visualization of the whims of the storyteller, who can choose either to follow a character into a room or not. "The Tyranny of Convention in *The Phantom of Liberty*," *Film Quarterly* 28 (Summer 1975): 25.

The nurse and monks gamble for religious medals.

The nephew makes insistent advances toward his timid maiden aunt.

them drinks. Downstairs more guests arrive. The innkeeper shows a young student and his gray-haired aunt to their room. The nephew makes insistent advances toward his timid maiden aunt, who finally agrees to let him look but not touch. In a gesture that recalls the Napoleonic captain's removal of the sheet covering Doña Elvira's corpse, he pulls off the sheet that had covered her naked body. Like Doña Elvira, she has the magically preserved body—if not the face—of a young woman. After an unsuccessful attempt to force himself upon her, the nephew runs out onto the landing. In this now familiar locus of intersection, he encounters the tall gentleman glimpsed earlier. This gentleman invites the nephew to his room, where his lovely roommate serves them drinks. As this latest chance encounter and narrative detour gets underway, the nurse knocks on the gentleman's door to borrow matches, and soon the two parties— monks, nurse, and innkeeper; tall gentleman, roommate, and nephew—are all gathered in the tall gentleman's room to "cele- brate," the gentleman says, "the chance that has brought us together in this place."

As the festivities reach their climax, they are suddenly interrupted by a sado-masochistic drama performed by the tall gentleman and his roommate: he sprawls on the bed in black leather pants with no bottoms while his roommate, also in black leather, whips his ex- posed buttocks. It appears that this display was the reason for the tall gentleman's hospitality. The party rapidly disperses after this abrupt "climax." Back in the hallway each character quickly returns to his or her own room. The nephew, upon entering his room, finds his aunt now willing to accept his caresses. The camera cuts from the embracing couple to the embers of the fire in the dining room downstairs, where several stuffed animals are displayed. The glass eyes of a stuffed fox—the animal the soldiers in their tanks had been hunting—shine in the dying embers of the fire.

The next morning the nurse comes down to the same dining room ready to continue her journey. A strange man politely requests a lift to the town of Argenton. She agrees and they drive off together. At Argenton the man gets out and thanks the nurse, who drives off. But the camera stays with the man, who moves off on foot. Once again we veer away from one story and into another, and once again this veering away is represented by the physical trajectory of a newly introduced character. We never know whether the nurse finally reached her father.

The above episode is among the richest in the film. The many intersecting stories, each of which reveals a hidden passion, become the narrative equivalent of Lautréamont's famous anticipation of the Surrealist figure's ability to combine the most unlikely images. Here, the most unlikely characters are brought together in equally arbitrary juxtapositions and in contexts that bring out surprising qualities. The pious monks, who arrive in the nurse's apartment with their rosaries, medals, and icons to pray for the nurse's father, are soon using these same objects as tokens of exchange as they gamble, drink, smoke, and even make suggestive remarks to the nurse, who is herself similarly transformed. The prim maiden aunt finally invites her nephew into her bed, and the tall gentleman transforms himself into a howling masochist. One climax follows another as the various characters return to their proper rooms. Only the nurse's story—the primary motivation for all the other converging narratives—fails to end.

*Episode 4: The Professor.* The stranger to whom the nurse had given a lift enters a school for gendarmes, where he is a professor. His student-gendarmes behave like school boys, singing, dancing, and even shooting their guns in an excess of high spirits. The professor establishes order, but minor rebellions—tacks on his seat, a paper cut-out attached to his back, not to mention frequent calls to duty that leave him with only two students in the end—punctuate his ensuing lecture.

The subject of the lecture, law and transgression, is strangely akin to the theme of many of the stories we have thus far witnessed. Citing Margaret Mead on the polygamous practices of the Melanesians, the professor points out that laws are pure conventions that vary from country to country. Thus, he states that polygamy, which is the law in some places, is prohibited. This rudimentary lesson in anthropology restates in pompously pedagogic terms the "lesson" we have already experienced (and will continue to experience) in other parts of the film, especially in the Foucauld episode of the "dirty"

167

postcards. In that episode the insertion of what Suleiman terms a *transgressive content* (the transgression of a cultural norm)[8]—the postcards that first offend and then sexually arouse the Foucauld parents—calls our attention to the fact that what a given culture agrees upon as morally pure or obscene has little to do with the intrinsic nature of values.

At the same time, however, the basic fact of opposition between positively and negatively marked poles, between the reversal of the positively marked cultural artifacts of monuments and the negatively marked photographs of the sexual act, emerges as significant. The reversal forces us to look at the structure of opposition itself. It also reveals another, even more typically Buñuelian, structure in the observation that the Foucauld parents are aroused by these forbidden "obscene" pictures of Paris monuments: desire arises from the mere fact of prohibition, regardless of its nature.

But if the professor stresses culturally determined social differences—polygamy in Melanesia and monogomy *chez nous*—he does so somewhat inconsistently to draw the moral lesson that the reversal of our own positively marked, social practices would be monstrous. To illustrate his point the professor tells a highly ambiguous tale from his own recent past containing just such a monstrous reversal.

In flashback we see the professor and his wife arriving for what appears to be a dinner party at the home of friends. But instead of sitting down to dine, the guests casually sit down on toilets around a low table strewn with magazines. During this party they make very bold explicit conversation concerning excrement but in embarrassment shush a child who complains of hunger. Soon the professor retires to a small cabinet in another part of the house, where he noisily and privately devours a half chicken and a bottle of Bordeaux.

The intent of the professor's tale seems to be to prove to his gendarme-students that a reversal of the positively marked and socially acceptable act of eating and the negatively marked and socially taboo act of defecating would indeed be monstrous. It is not clear, however, whether this is the moral that *we* perceive; since, for one

[8] Suleiman, "Freedom and Necessity," p. 291.

In the professor's story the guests seat themselves on toilets around a table.

thing, the professor himself behaves within his own exemplary tale as though public and social defecation were the norm. In a sense the lesson of the film differs from that of the professor, for the film has already prepared us for this kind of reversal. Having already witnessed the reversal of a positively marked content—Paris monuments—for the negatively marked dirty postcards, we are prepared to witness the contrary substitution of a negatively marked content—excrement—for the positively marked food. We are also better prepared to accept the arbitrary nature of the positive and negative marks of the oppositions, while the professor in his classroom remains culture-bound in his unacknowledged belief that polygamy is savage and monogamy is civilized, and by implication, that excrement is socially unacceptable and food is acceptable. In other words, there is a difference between the value system underlying the professor's reversal of eating and defecating, which seems intended to shock his students, and the *film's* reversal of these body functions.

The film's lesson has to do with the arbitrary nature of the opposition, while the professor's lesson has to do with the shocking effects of such a reversal and thus relies on a more absolute order of values. But the above is even further complicated by our encounter in the professor's own classroom with yet another taboo reversal in the behavior of the gendarmes. These guardians of the public order cavort like children, shooting guns in play and performing practical jokes on their teacher. They enact an inversion of social behavior similar to that illustrated by the professor's lesson, yet the professor himself seems unaware of this.

When the professor finishes his lecture, the last two students remaining in the classroom are called to duty as highway patrolmen. Once again we follow secondary characters into another story. And again this narrative shift is accomplished via the camera's decision to follow movement. But here the gendarmes function only as links between stories. They stop a speeding motorist on his way to a doctor's appointment in Paris, reprimand him, and—in keeping with the principle of where there is movement there goes the story—are immediately left behind, as the motorist and the story speed on.

*Episode 5: Legendre Family.* The motorist, M. Legendre, arrives at his doctor's office. After a casual consultation, the doctor informs

170

him that he has cancer of the lung and needs an immediate operation. The doctor offers him a cigarette with the news, with no visible
awareness of the irony of such an act. As if the doctor had insulted
him, M. Legendre slaps him across the face and returns home. At
home a new drama displaces the one just begun: Legendre's daughter has disappeared from school.[9] The parents rush to the school,
where we find that although the daughter is quite visibly there and
even says so herself, everyone else acts as though she is missing. So
the Legendre family, daughter in tow, visits the police commissioner
to report her missing.

*Episode 6: The Poet-killer.* After the Legendre family leaves the
commissioner, a sergeant, who had been reprimanded by the commissioner for not shining his shoes, goes to have them shined. (Like
the gendarmes who link sections 4 and 5, this sergeant commands
no story of his own.) His path crosses that of a man with glasses who
is also having his shoes shined. This man pets a dog, quotes the gos-
pel, and curses all those who mistreat animals. He is the poet-killer
(or so he is named by a narrator later in the film). We follow him
into an elevator up to the Montparnasse Tower, where he randomly
begins to shoot passersby in the street below with a telescopic rifle.

In the second manifesto of Surrealism André Breton wrote that
the *simplest* Surrealist act would be to go out into the street and fire
randomly into a crowd.[10] This statement has often been taken as an
expression of Surrealist anarchy, just as similar gestures in Buñuel's
films—the eye-cutting or revolver-wielding sequences of *Un Chien
andalou*, the wanton destruction of Lys's bedroom in *L'Age d'or*, the
above incident from *Phantom*, or the random terrorist acts in *Obscure Object*—have been misconstrued as the impassioned protest
of an inveterate Surrealist anarchist. But in all these cases it is
patently absurd to interpret random or gratuitous violence as having the political or moral endorsement of the Surrealist attitude.
(Breton himself was quick to add, in a footnote to his statement in
the manifesto, that what he had said was the *simplest* Surrealist act,
not the best or most appropriate.)

We should beware, then, of the temptation to identify the poet-

[9] See note 6 above.
[10] Breton, *Manifestoes of Surrealism*, p. 125.

killer with the filmmaker or to assume that the crazy murderer of the Montparnasse Tower represents a proper response to social or political wrongs. (The only injustice he seems to be aware of is cruelty to animals.) The poet-killer's act is simply a random gesture of violence that interrupts the daily routines of a multitude of different characters. Tried, found guilty, and sentenced to death, he is suddenly released from custody, a celebrated hero. For the first time in the film a story comes to an end, although this end amounts to a reversal of the anticipated outcome.

*Episode 5: The Legendre Family* (continued). As the killer signs autographs outside the courtroom, a narrator informs us in voice-over that during the trial of the poet-killer the search for the little Legendre girl had continued. In this way, we return to the story of section 5, picking up on it many months later. This is the only instance in the film of a transition via pure narration rather than the trajectory of a character. (The transition from the first to the second section was achieved by a narrator who was subsequently revealed to be a character.)

The conclusion to the resumed Legendre story offers a most predictable happy ending to the classic tale of a lost child. Yet in context of the film's consistently interrupted narrative, the predictable happy ending achieved by the finding of the lost child is itself a strange reversal. Having created a pattern of consistent rupture and reversal, the narrative disrupts this pattern with the use of direct narrative statement to return to a perfectly conventional ending: the police have found the little girl and she is reunited with her parents in the prefect's office. Yet even this conventional movement-to-completion is subverted by the fact that the little girl who is supposedly restored was never missing in the first place.

Like the episode of the poet-killer, this episode offers a similarly blatant reversal of expectation: the Legendre girl is clearly present, nevertheless she is declared missing; the poet-killer is clearly condemned, nevertheless he is set free. Both cases offer a variation of the taboo reversal discussed earlier, playing here with the very logic of cause and effect.

*Episode 7: The Two Prefects.* After restoring the little girl to her family, the prefect of police goes to a café, where a chance encounter with a woman in black who resembles his dead sister triggers another story. The prefect tells this woman about his sister. In a flashback we see the prefect in shirt sleeves wander into a room on a hot summer day; there his sister sits playing the piano in the nude, her large breasts swaying in time with the music. The prefect listens in deep contemplation. When the first piece is over, he requests a Brahms rhapsody, which his sister obligingly plays. Neither of them takes any note of her nakedness, although there is a relaxed air of tender intimacy between them. Back in the cafe the prefect sadly finishes this fond remembrance with the confidence that his sister died of a horrible disease in which excrement is expelled from the mouth.

This story within a story confronts us with a disturbing echo of the professor's earlier story within a story about the toilet party. Part of our enjoyment of that story was based upon our enlightened understanding of the reversal of two similar but opposed body functions— ingestion and excretion. This reversal nevertheless preserved the separation of the two opposing organs of mouth and anus. We could laugh at the reversal, even though the notion of a defecation party might seem distasteful because of our intellectual understanding that the social and public context of eating had been exchanged for the asocial and extremely private context of defecating. But just as we get comfortable with this notion, Buñuel jolts us with the present reference to the prefect's sister's mode of death. This death reverses the food/excrement opposition in a completely new way: rather than a simple reversal of the private/public social context of these two related body functions, it places excrement in the place of food. All our social conditioning against excreta, which the anthropological lesson of the professor had supposedly exposed, reemerges forcibly when excrement turns up not in the social context of the dining room but literally in the mouth.

Struck by the resemblance between the woman in black and his dead sister (both parts are played by Adriana Asti), the prefect invites the woman to the police ball. But he is interrupted by a telephone call from his dead sister, who invites him to meet her in the family crypt, where he will be able to discover "the true mystery of death." That night, in a torchlit scene that recalls, in both content and atmosphere, the Napoleonic captain's raising of Doña Elvira's tomb, the prefect approaches a coffin from which a long piece of hair trails. Beside the coffin hangs the telephone from which the deceased apparently made her call. As the prefect attempts to pry open the coffin, two policemen arrest him, ignoring his cries that he is their superior.

With this last twist in the prefect's story, the film doubles back on itself sharply. Up to this point it has merely teased us with occasional repetitions of minor details of plot or theme: M. Foucauld's visit to a doctor is echoed by M. Legendre's visit to a doctor, foxes crop up uncommonly often during the nurse's story, as do animals in general throughout the entire film (e.g., the poet-killer's reference to the "bastards who mistreat animals," the rooster and the ostrich that wander into M. Foucauld's bedroom, and the ostrich that reappears at the end of the film). Similar repetitions of the theme of illicit desire also occur, beginning with the Napoleonic captain's necrophilia, continuing through the dirty-postcard scene, the digression of the nephew and his aunt, and the sado-masochistic drama enacted by the tall gentleman and his roommate. But only when the prefect begins to pry open the lid of his sister's coffin do we see the extent to which the many diverse narrative and thematic threads have begun, if not to converge, at least to repeat one another in strangely displaced ways.

The prefect's attempt to keep a date with his dead sister by opening her coffin repeats the theme of illicit desire by building upon the transgressive content of her naked breasts in the earlier flashback episode. In other words, we now seem to recover the meaning of those naked breasts: the prefect has an incestuous desire for his sister, just as the nephew had for his aunt, who was also glimpsed naked. So, even though the prefect simply responds to a bizarre phone call, unconsciously he follows a deeper desire. The desire for his sister even more emphatically echoes the necrophilia of the Napoleonic captain, who was also interrupted in the act of opening a tomb.

All these episodes have in common the typical Surrealist pursuit of an infinitely desirable—because ultimately elusive—love object. In each case desire is enhanced by both the extreme difficulty of possession—Doña Elvira and the sister are both dead, the aunt is elderly and maiden—and by the conventional prohibitions against necrophilia and incest. Erotic desire emerges in direct proportion to the law that prohibits it. Thus, the dialectic between what the professor calls *"loi et délit"* (law and its transgression) establishes the lure of the phantom object of desire.

It is not at all surprising then that in two of these three cases of amour fou the love object is quite literally unobtainable, perhaps not even there at all.[11] In *L'Age d'or* the most intense moments of desire occur when the lover either substitutes a fetish object—statue toe or woman's dress—or imagines the loved one present. In *Phantom of Liberty* absence also engenders desire, not just in the usual sense of making the heart fonder, but in the more fundamental sense of the illusion of the original "lost object." Buñuel suggests that upon such illusions are based not only political ideals and erotic pursuits but human identity itself. As Lacan shows and as Surrealist art—whether by Desnos, Dalí, Buñuel, or Breton—illustrates, human identity is forged in the Imaginary lure of the mirror phase and through the subsequent alienation of the self in language. This alienation spells the death of the thing-in-itself to give birth to the desire for what can never be possessed.

The Napoleonic captain who desires a corpse, the nephew who desires his aunt, the masochist who desires to be whipped, the prefect who desires his dead sister are all situated in a system of moral law that prohibits what they desire. As each breaks this law, each simultaneously demonstrates a dependence upon the law that makes this transgression possible. But in this film, erotic desire is simply one aspect of a larger structure of animating illusions, including the notion of liberty itself. The film ends, not with this reprise of grave-robbing, but with yet another echo of the story of the Napoleonic captain.

As the prefect is about to open his sister's tomb, he is arrested by his own gendarmes and taken to the same commissioner who handled the Legendre case of the missing girl. On the wall of the com-

---

[11] After the prefect is taken away by the policemen, a subsequent shot of the coffin he had attempted to pry open shows neither the long hair nor the telephone on the wall that had appeared earlier in the scene. It would be possible to surmise, therefore, that the previous scene was the prefect's subjective fantasy, that is, if the film was the sort of narrative that permitted this kind of certainty.

missioner's office hangs a reproduction of Goya's *Executions of May 3*, which functions here as an elliptical reference to the political theme of the beginning episode. The commissioner explains to the prefect that he cannot possibly be the prefect. To prove his point he sends this supposedly false prefect (A) to the office of the supposedly true prefect (B). Prefect B receives Prefect A with the utmost cordiality. Instead of quarreling over which of them is real, the narrative drops the issue altogether, suddenly making room for the possibility of two prefects working in unison.

The two men chat like old friends, discussing the proper tactics to put down what appears to be a demonstration of young people planned for the zoo that noon. The important thing, B observes, is to keep the youths from attaining the cages of the animals, while A comments that it would not matter too much if an animal should be hit in the crossfire, since, "the life of one of our own men is more precious than that of a zebra."

At the zoo we see the animals in their cages. The two prefects arrive to direct a police charge against an offscreen force. Sounds of machine-gun fire and explosions are heard, along with voices crying the same *Vivan las caenas!* (Long live chains!) we heard at the beginning of the film. The final shot is a swish-pan ending in a close-up of a confused ostrich. The animal cranes its neck and darts its eyes wildly about in a manner similar to Goya's bug-eyed, stretch-necked Spanish prisoners at the moment of execution. As the sounds of slaughter and cries of *Vivan las caenas!* continue, the film ends.

*Permutations of Freedom.* These cries, coupled with the similarity between the ostrich and the patriots of the Goya painting, bring the film full circle—the swish-pan of the final shot emphasizing this circularity back to the political theme of the beginning. But now the terms of the original, political opposition of nationality (French vs. Spanish) have shifted to an opposition based on species (human vs. animal). Incongruous as this shift may seem, there is also a sense in which it is the natural and logical development of latent theme of animal revolt and repression running throughout the film. Hints of this repression have already appeared in the intrusion of the ostrich into M. Foucauld's bedroom, the fox-hunting soldiers encountered by the nurse, the disturbing glimmer of light in the glass eyes of the stuffed fox in the dining room of the inn, and the poet-killer's curse on the "bastards who mistreat animals." Finally, in this last scene, the bizarre way in which what appears to be a confrontation between youthful demonstrators and police becomes— through its zoo location, the apparent objective of freeing the animals, and the visual emphasis on the animals in their cages rather than on the demonstrating youths—a bizarre confrontation of animal and human. Once again the terms of an opposition have shifted.

It is tempting to read this final opposition of human repression and animal revolt as a Surrealist's championing of the "natural" animal in all of us.[12] I have tried to suggest elsewhere in this book, however, that such an approach to Surrealist film constitutes an overly crude and moralistic opposition between categories of good and bad—moral categories that no one would think of imposing on any other form of Surrealist art but nevertheless seem to plague the criticism of Surrealist film.[13]

I would suggest, instead, that the thrust of the oppositions occurring in this and many of Buñuel's other films has been to reveal the inevitable structure of the opposition between oppressor and transgressor, as well as the related shifting of the role any one character might play within this structure. Thus, the Napoleonic captain functions in two capacities: as oppressor of the Spanish patriots in the political section of his episode and as revolutionary transgressor in the later erotic section. Similarly, if we consider the division of the character of the prefect into two parts, we find that he also functions in two capacities, first in the role of erotic transgressor (Prefect A), then in the role of official authority repressing revolt (Prefects A and B).

The role of revolutionary and the role of lover are both transgressive, but significantly, revolutionary and lover do not converge in

---

[12] Marsha Kinder, in an otherwise excellent article, succumbs to this view when she writes, "Buñuel's anarchistic vision has remained constant. Man persists in denying his animal nature and creating a civilized code of laws and manners that only heightens his absurdity and intensifies his oppression." "The Tyrrany of Convention," p. 21.

[13] I refer especially to the works of Ado Kyrou, who may be partially forgiven, since Kryou pioneered the first critical appraisals of Surrealist film. Less forgivable, perhaps, is the more recent work of J. H. Matthews and Freddy Buache, both of whom tend to view Surrealism in film as a morally pure stance against all oppressive conventions, social, political, or aesthetic.

one person. Both captain and prefect are transgressors in one context and repressors in another—a fact that makes the moral purity of the clichéd anarcho-Surrealist position hard to maintain with respect to this film. It would seem that Buñuel "advocates" neither the moral right of revolution nor the moral purity of the lover. The actions of his characters are neither endorsed nor condemned. They are studied and contrasted, and structural similarities and differences are explored with an anthropological eye, allowing the terms of an opposition to challenge our own values. Thus, although we may naturally feel sympathy for the Spanish patriots at the beginning of the film, we are then asked to sympathize with the erotic desires of their oppressor in the continuation of that episode. Again, although we root for the victimized Spanish patriots at the beginning, we cannot so easily extend the same liberal and humanist sympathy toward the hippo, elephant, and ostrich at the end.

In this film, what begins as an apparent celebration of freedom and revolt—in political, erotic, and textual transgression—ends paradoxically as an illumination of the tyrannies that make the dream of freedom possible. The revolutionary's desire for freedom is just as much a phantom as the lovers' desire for the unpossessable women in the tomb or the narrative's desire to escape from narration. It is the force of opposition itself that animates all these desires. Because tyranny and slavery exist, there is a dream of freedom; because objects are beyond our reach, we desire them; and because stories have continuous linear movements, storytellers want to escape them. In each case the tyranny of law creates the desire for a phantom freedom. The phantom of liberty is born in the existence of chains. Thus the enigmatic cry of the film's beginning and end, *Vivan las caenas*, takes on a new meaning. These celebrated chains are what make the phantom of liberty possible. The more intensely we pursue this phantom, the more entangled we become within the structure of oppositions that give rise to this pursuit in the first place. We are as inextricably situated within this structure as we are within that of language itself.

It is no accident then that, although nearly everyone in this film is on the move either in vehicles or on foot, within their own stories and, more strikingly, within the restless trajectories that lead from one story to another, the cumulative effect of all movement is of paradoxical repetition and circularity, each episode fixed within the parameters of its oppositions. So, if in the first third of the film we experience the exhilarating liberty of so many bold thematic leaps, narrative displacements, and surprise reversals, this is only to lead us back in the end to the realization of the limits of freedom politically, erotically, and narratively.

The more we watch the more we become aware of patterns of repetition. The film begins and ends, for example, with scenes of political revolt and repression. It contains two visits to doctors, two scenes in which lovers pry open tombs, many sly references to animal revolt, and four references to Goya's painting *The Executions of May* 3, 1808. In a film in which narrative interruption and displacement has become a kind of rule, this repetition and linking of end and beginning is most striking. Not that the end completes anything that is begun in the first episode, but that it does emphasize the many permutations of revolt and repression, transgression and law that have been at issue throughout the film. Through the exploitation of the principle of contiguity underlying both displacement and metonymy, *The Phantom of Liberty* rearranges the originally presented themes of revolt and repression, transgression and law, displacing the political theme of revolt and repression of the first episode onto an entirely different context with the repression of animals at the zoo. Similarly, the illicit desire for an impossible love object contained in the grave-robbing of the first episode displaces, through the same inexorable link of spatially and temporally contiguous episodes, onto a final episode of illicit desire emphasizing incest as well as necrophilia.

*Surrealist Metonymy.* If we try to read *The Phantom of Liberty* as a linear narration proceeding from beginning to middle to end, we encounter continual frustration. But to say that this film sabotages its apparent linear structure does not mean that it sabotages all meaning as well. We have already seen that if *The Phantom of Liberty*'s multiple, discontinuous episodes do not allow a denotative reading as the diegetic illusion of a previously existing time and space, this is because they demand instead to be read in figural association with one another. Thus, we associate the Napoleonic captain of the first episode with prefects A and B of the last episode in their alternating roles as erotic transgressors or political oppressors, and thus we associate the cry of the executed Spanish patriots with the similar cry uttered in a different context at the zoo at the end of the film.

As in all rhetorical figures, Surrealist or otherwise, we measure similarity and difference between two terms in a movement that leads away from the denotative and toward a connotative plane of signification. But, unlike most classical rhetorical figuration, the usual relation between denotative diegesis and connotative figure is disturbed. Since *The Phantom of Liberty* has no continuous diegesis to begin with but only a pseudo-diegesis of noncontinuous events, we do not first take in a coherent denotative meaning and then proceed, as in most narrative film, to a connotative level. Instead, we are forced from the very beginning to seek significance at the (latent) connotative level of the figures alone.

We have seen repeatedly that this disturbed hierarchy between figure and diegesis is a familiar process in Surrealist film. Yet within this general phenomenon we can discern specific differences that point to the evolving nature of the figurative process. Audience familiarity with the famous eye-moon metaphor of *Un Chien andalou* has unfortunately placed a heavy burden of typicality upon a single metaphoric figuration. Part of the reason for this lies in the fact that this metaphor has often seemed a perfect filmic equivalent of the classic juxtaposition of disparate elements celebrated in Lautréamont's exemplary anticipation of the Surrealist figure—"the fortuitous encounter of an umbrella and sewing machine on a dissection table." Yet in many parts of *Un Chien andalou* and increasingly in the Surrealist films to follow, Surrealist metaphor gives way to Surrealist metonymy.

A case in point from *Un Chien andalou* (see p. 78) is the metaphoric series following the cyclist's view of the hole in his hand leading to several apparently metaphoric associations. This metaphor begins with the round hole in the hand and proceeds to the extradiegetic association of a round underarm patch of hair, a round sea urchin, and finally the round head on an androgynous figure playing with a round severed hand. The surprise here is that the final element of this series of formally similar shapes turns out also to be contiguously related to the beginning element in the series: a subsequent shot reveals that the androgyne and severed hand are spied on by the cyclist of the first shot in the series and that the two spaces are contiguous. Thus, what begins as an extradiegetic series of metaphors based on the similarity of shapes, ends as a surprise metonymy lending a retrospective and unsettling aura of reality to the figure by spatially "motivating" the association between the round objects in the contiguous space of room and street.

What is striking about the above figuration is that the association between the metaphoric series beginning with the hole in the hand appears to be doubly determined. Just as we become accustomed to the purely formal association of extradiegetic round shapes (in the style of the opening figure of eye and moon), we are given a final round shape that is also spatially contiguous to the first shape in the series and has, so it seems, a double motive for being there. Metaphoric similarity of the round shapes combines with a metonymic contiguity of the first and last shots in the series.

Thus, in spite of the fact that the most famous figure of Surrealist film—that of the moon and eye—is a striking example of an apparently "pure" extradiegetic association of similar shapes, there are many other instances, in this film and perhaps even in this figure, of underlying or outright metonymies.

Since pure metaphor consists of an association of elements that are rarely associated outside the signifying chain bringing them together, it often strikes the viewer, as Jean Mitry has pointed out, as a radical departure from the effect of reality which diegesis attempts to construct. Metonymy, on the other hand, with its basis in physical contiguity—e.g., the association of elements that are already physically related in the real world, as in Mitry's example of the pincenez and the ship's doctor from *Potemkin* (see p. 59)—necessarily gives the impression of greater realism.

In *L'Age d'or*, for example, we have already seen one possible result of the Surrealist exploitation of metonymy. In this film large, discontinuous segments of apparent diegesis flow into and out of one another through partially linked spatial or temporal contiguities, lending at least a superficial sense of realistic contiguity and coherence. In *L'Age d'or*, contrary to *Un Chien andalou*, we do not immediately experience each incomplete diegetic section as existing in figural relation to the next. We experience them initially as realistic but ultimately unsatisfying and interrupted fragments of diegesis. This experience creates a tension between the illusion of continuity typical of most narrative films and the actual discontinuity of space or time in each of these sections. Thus, without blatantly appearing to break with diegetic illusion, *L'Age d'or* nevertheless does so through a subtle process of displacement. Once again, though here in a different way, Surrealist film disturbs the usual hierarchy between figure and diegesis of the conventionally narrative film. But in this instance the disturbance arises from the parodic exaggeration of one aspect of the usual spatial or temporal contiguities that make up diegetic illusion.

Increasingly then, the Surrealist rhetorical strategy based on the shock of unlikely juxtaposition gives way to a process that exploits and ultimately subverts the realistic linear flow of most narrative film. In place of the shock of unlikely juxtaposition, we are presented with large segments of apparent diegesis, which, because each is interrupted by another diegesis, ultimately subvert their claim to representation. We are forced to look beyond the manifest discontinuities of the diegesis to discover a latent motive for the association of such disparate elements. This motive, which can only be established on the extended level of the entire text, constitutes the meaning of the figures. But, unlike the *Chien* metaphor, we arrive at this latent meaning through the paradoxically greater realism of the large metonymic unit. The original shock of the Surrealist juxtaposition thus becomes more subtle, catching us unaware, by seducing us into an apparent diegesis that gently displaces onto another, which itself displaces onto another.

As we see in *The Phantom of Liberty*, Surrealist film has increasingly cultivated these more subtle metonymies (or metaphors with metonymic features) as the vehicle of its latent meanings. Perhaps we can best appreciate the unique nature of this latest evolution of the Surrealist figure by comparison with a similarly discontinuous film whose large episodic segments also figuratively comment upon one another.

Max Ophuls's *La Ronde* (1950) is such an episodic work. The film depicts a series of love affairs, each of which links a roving partner from one affair with a new lover in the next. In this way the film moves from love affair to love affair, until finally the wandering

lover of the penultimate episode encounters the stationary lover of
the first, thus completing a circular trajectory, *la ronde* itself, sym-
bolized by the recurring extradiegetic metaphor of a carousel.

Ophuls's film is a bittersweet commentary upon the ever-renew-
able circle of love. As in *The Phantom of Liberty*, the link between
episodes is effected by a wandering character; and like *The Phantom
of Liberty*, the final episode returns—in the person of the first lover,
the whore who began it all—to its beginning. The discontinuity of
the episodic diegesis encourages the viewer to seek comparable features in the various stories of love. This process is facilitated by the
presence of the extradiegetic metaphor of the carousel, whose car-
nival atmosphere and circular movement becomes a statement on
the frivolity and futility of the "games" of love depicted in the diegesis. Each episode metaphorically invites comparison with every
other episode and with the more obvious extradiegetic metaphor of
the reappearing carousel. Thus the apparent variety of the many diegetic episodes reduces, metaphorically, to an essential statement
about the frivolity and circular futility of a love game in which variety itself becomes a form of redundancy: *plus ça change, plus c'est
la même chose.*

In the *Phantom of Liberty*, similarly episodic stories are linked by
wandering characters who continually break off and recommence a
new diegesis in entirely new directions. Both films use a wandering character to bridge the gap between diverse diegetic worlds,
metonymically motivating the metaphorical statement inherent in
the similarities and differences of each episode. But if metaphor
consists in the perception of similarity in dissimilars,[14] the special
nature of the Surrealist metaphor consists in the stubborn per-
sistence of dissimilarity within the most obvious similarity.

Near the end of *The Phantom of Liberty*, the prefect who begins
to pry open his sister's coffin performs an act almost exactly similar
to the Napoleonic captain who opens Doña Elvira's tomb in the first
episode. There is an equal similarity in the parallel moments of political revolt and repression, first in the execution of the Spanish patriots and then in the terrorization of the animals in the zoo. But in
both cases there is such a radical displacement of these elements of

[14] Paul Ricoeur, *The Rule of Metaphor*, trans. Robert Czerny (Toronto: University of
Toronto Press, 1977), p. 23.

similarity and such an extreme discontinuity of the diegetic segments in which they appear that the metaphoric statement typical of classical rhetorical figures cannot run its usual course.

The Surrealist figure does not permit the kind of essential connotative statement about the nature of the reality presented in the diegesis as Ophuls's *La Ronde*. In *La Ronde* the perception of similarity in difference leads us to reinterpret the rich variety of the many love affairs as the multiple manifestations of an essential erotic principle, the mechanism governing all the movements of the lovers. It thus becomes possible to make an abstract, essentializing statement about the nature of love as manifested in the reality of the diegesis—love is a game, a carousel, an eternal pursuit that perpetually renews itself with a new set of characters. In *The Phantom of Liberty*, however, the metaphoric statement seems to be about the diegetic action of political and erotic desires. But here similarity in the diegesis does not amount to the same kind of essential pronouncement about the nature of the diegesis, since the diegesis itself is displaced from moment to moment. Political and erotic desire cannot be reduced to the same kind of definitional statement of essential nature as in the classical metaphor. Variety persists in these Surrealist metaphors; it is not recovered by an abstract, all-encompassing connotative statement. Thus the extreme formal similarities within the displaced elements of diegesis point here to an altogether different figural structure. Ultimately what is "said" about erotic and political desire is not an enduring definitional truth but a simple delineation of structural opposition in the play of law and transgression. As we have seen before, the Surrealist figure resists immediate interpretation in order to call attention to its work *as* figure. Thus the figural statement diverges from the classic metaphor in its resistance to an immediate or local interpretation, in the latent quality of its metaphorical statement, and finally in its revelation of the oppositions that *structure* meaning instead of the *statement of* meaning itself.

In contrast with the metaphor of the prologue to *Un Chien andalou*, Surrealist metonymy has here transformed the stereotype of the Surrealist film figure from the pure extradiegetic metaphor and its shock effect of abrupt juxtaposition to a smoother, more continuous, pseudoconnectedness. Through Surrealist metonymy Buñuel has achieved a new smoothness of transition that appears to obey the codes of cinematic narrative but only to displace them in turn. In this very different way, Buñuel continues to achieve the same rupture with identification and with belief in the fictive unity of the work so typical of Surrealist film.

## THAT OBSCURE OBJECT OF DESIRE[15]

*Cet Obscur objet du désir,* 1977

Coproducers: Serge Silberman, First Artists.
Director: Luis Buñuel.
Script: Luis Buñuel and Jean-Claude Carrière, based on the novel *La Femme et le Pantin* by Pierre Loüys.
Photography: Edmund Richard.
Leading Players: Fernando Rey, Carole Bouquet, Angela Molina, Julien Bertheau, André Weber, Milena Vukotic, Pieral.
Color.

In *The Discreet Charm of the Bourgeoisie* Buñuel eroticized the desire for food, as a group of people were continually frustrated in their attempts to sit down together for a meal. In that film, oral frustration became a general metaphor for all the unsatisfied but perpetually renewable desires of an entire class. In *That Obscure Object of Desire* Buñuel further characterized the nature of the desire that has always been the focus of his most Surrealist work. This film relates the often comically frustrated attempts of an older man to "possess" an elusive younger woman. The film's narrative reduces this simple erotic quest to its crudest essentials, almost to the level of a dirty joke, as the aging possessor of the phallus embarks upon a ludicrous quest for the impossibly pure and virginal hymen. But this very reduction, this simplicity that strips each character of even the most rudimentary psychology, simultaneously reveals the truth of a desire born in the fundamental division of the human subject.

The basic situation is as follows. A (male) subject pursues an elu-

---

[15] "The object of desire, in the usual sense, is either a fantasy that is in reality the support of desire, or a lure." Lacan, *Four Fundamental Concepts of Psycho-Analysis*, pp. 103, 186.

sive (female) object. He is old, she is young. (Fernando Rey, who plays the man and has played similar roles in many other Buñuel films,[16] has come to represent the type of ultrasophisticated, self-assured bourgeois beset with incommodious desires.) He is obsessed, vulnerable, and comically sympathetic. She is mysterious, impenetrable, and elusive; and her ungraspable nature is emphasized by the fact that she is played alternately by two very dissimilar actresses.

Originally a turn-of-the-century novel by Pierre Loüys entitled *La Femme et le Pantin* (*The Woman and the Puppet*), this story of Concha Perez, the Spanish courtesan and femme fatale, has been filmed five times. It had been most notably adapted by Josef von Sternberg in 1935 in *The Devil Is a Woman* with Marlene Dietrich, then again in 1958 by Duvivier in *A Woman like Satan* with Brigitte Bardot. As the titles indicate, both of these film versions share the basic misogynist premise of the original novel. Although Buñuel's version updates the period and completely sabotages Loüys's misogyny, his version is also, curiously, the most faithful of the three, preserving much of the dialogue and many original scenes, including two infamous scenes that would have been impossible even for von Sternberg. In one the "hero" spends the night wrestling with an elaborate chastity belt, and in another Concha dances nude before tourists.

But Buñuel's fidelity to the letter of the novel in no way approaches the spirit of the Loüys original. In fact, the preservation of an anachronistic obsession with chastity into the last quarter of the twentieth century transforms this erotic quest into an almost intellectual abstraction. Buñuel need only nudge the original story in certain directions to suggest that Loüys's original tale of "the worst of women," hinging upon a rather dated dichotomy between virgin and whore, is really the fantasy of the desiring subject for an impossible and perpetually "obscure" object of desire.

The film begins with the apparent end of a tumultuous relationship. In a sunny picture-postcard Seville, Mathieu Fabert (Fernando Rey) buys a first-class ticket to Paris and returns home to his luxurious villa to pack. Once there he surveys the aftermath of a

[16] In *Viridiana* Rey plays Don Jaime, an old-fashioned Spanish hidalgo who falls passionately in love with his niece, a novice in a convent. In *Tristana* he plays a more liberal but similarly affected older man in love with his beautiful young ward.

violent altercation: a blood-stained pillow, high heeled shoes, and a pair of (wet) panties. On the state of the panties Mathieu's valet comments, "she must have been afraid." The valet then offers the first in a series of misogynist remarks that punctuates the film: "If you go with women, don't forget the stick." Thus the film begins (as it shall also end) with a focus on a woman's soiled and bloodied garment—the metonymic and fetishistic remainder of the absent object of desire.

On the way to the train station Mathieu observes an explosion that obliterates a chauffered limousine and its passenger, a man not unlike himself. His cool response is that of one used to such acts of terrorism. At the station the valet boards the second-class car and Mathieu enters the first-class compartment. A comic series of unlikely recognitions follows, emphasizing the homogeneity of this upper-class group. A mother and daughter already in the car immediately recognize Mathieu as their neighbor in Paris. They make polite conversation about the danger of plane hijackings until a middle-aged Frenchman enters the compartment. He, it turns out, is a judge who knows Mathieu's cousin, who is also a judge. Finally a middle-aged dwarf enters. Just as we begin to wonder how so obvious an anomaly can fit into the homogeneity of this group, the judge recognizes the dwarf from the bullfight. "Yes," the dwarf replies pertly, "impossible to mistake *me*."

As the passengers wait for the train to leave, a young woman with a bruised and bandaged face appears on the platform carrying a suitcase, anxiously looking for someone. Mathieu spies her before she sees him and, with a word to a porter, obtains a bucket of water that he then pours on the young woman's head as she attempts to climb on the moving train. With evident satisfaction he returns the bucket and settles back into his compartment, unaware that the woman has recovered from her dousing in time to climb onto a rear car.

Mathieu's fellow passengers are burning with curiosity to know the reason for the dousing, but they are too polite to ask about it. Finally the dwarf, who is a professor of psychology with a Sigmund Freud beard, politely requests the reason behind this strange action: "Since you are a gentleman you must have an excellent reason." Evidently pleased by such civilized understanding and interest, Mathieu agrees to tell his story, explaining that the woman he has just doused is "the worst of all women" and that the bucket of water was a far better fate than the death she deserved.

He then proceeds to tell the story of his passion for Concha Perez in a flashback that occupies the bulk of the film. This flashback story of the supposedly terminated affair will end when the train pulls into a Paris train station and Concha retaliates with a bucket of water poured over Mathieu's head.

With these crude slapstick devices Buñuel undercuts and frames the gloomy atmosphere of degenerate romanticism that pervades Loüys's original novel. In *La Femme et le Pantin* a once noble, middle-aged Spaniard, Don Mateo, recounts the tale of his destructive passion for Concha as a warning to a younger man who has become her suitor. At the end of Don Mateo's story the younger man goes to keep a rendezvous with Concha anyway, learning as he does that Don Mateo is as enthralled by her as ever. The novel's flashback structure allows Don Mateo to convince his friend (and the reader) that his affair with Concha is over, while the surprise ending outside Don Mateo's narration dramatically reveals that he is trapped in a never-ending cycle of self-debasing passion.

Von Sternberg's 1935 film version maintained the flashback structure, with the older man (Lionel Atwell) warning the younger (Caesar Romero) away from the woman they both desire, but it threw the emphasis onto the conflict between the two men. They fight a duel, and Concha eventually gives herself to Don Mateo, the emotionally devastated, wounded loser of the duel.

Buñuel's version dispenses with the warning to the younger suitor altogether. His Mathieu is no longer Spanish but an urbane Frenchman (played nevertheless by a Spanish actor) who tells his tale to a dwarf professor of psychology and a curious but essentially disinterested group of acquaintances seeking diversion on a long journey. In this new context Mathieu's story becomes less a misogynist warning against women and more an amusing parody of the dirty-story aspect of the analysand's cathartic purge. The Freudian dwarf listens to Mathieu's story with a smug, knowing air, occasionally interrupting to prove his superior knowledge and understanding of his "patient's" desires. But the putative catharsis of Mathieu's talking cure is based on the spurious notion that he has really begun to get Con-

Mathieu tells the story of his pursuit of Concha to sympathetic fellow passengers on the train.

cha out of his system, a notion that is totally undercut by her presence, unknown to Mathieu, on the same train.

The use of this train constitutes one of Buñuel's most inspired additions to the Loüys novel. As Mathieu tells the tale of his passion, he speeds through the countryside away from the nightmare of the past and Concha's native country, blissfully unaware that she is with him on the train, only a few cars behind. In this way the flashback story of his obsessive and perpetual movement *toward* the object of his desire is simultaneously countered by a contrary image of flight—the speeding train whose exteriors and interiors Buñuel playfully intercuts with Mathieu's flashback story—in which he is perpetually in motion *away* from this object. In neither motion does he make any real progress. The end of his journey simply lands him right back in the city where his story of desire began and in the company of the same woman, whom he can neither rid himself of nor possess. Only the film audience, which has seen Concha board the train, is aware that Mathieu, the pursuer in his own story, is simultaneously the pursued in the framing story. Pursuit and flight are equally futile, as both parties remain a fixed distance from one another no matter how far or fast they travel.[17] We shall see that this distance, this immutable separation between subject and object, is emblematic of the original separation or gap that engenders the impossible desire for union throughout the film.

But the train functions in another way as well. Just as Mathieu's story, told on the train, may be reduced to a crude phallic quest, so also the train itself may be viewed as in countless other films—perhaps most notably in Hitchcock's *North-by-Northwest*—as a metaphor for that quest. At the end of *North-by-Northwest*, Cary Grant and Eva Marie Saint are seen together in the sleeping car of a train, man and wife in the happy resolution of a long and harrowing journey-adventure. After they embrace, the final shot of the film shows an exterior of the speeding train entering a tunnel—a shot Hitchcock himself playfully claims as the only metaphor in the film. This is the classic form of the sexual metaphor in many films. Diegetic events leading up to the sexual act form the tenor (Grant and Saint

---

[17] Dave Kehr, in a review of the film, points out the irony of this fixed distance as well as the "raging phallic over-tones" of the train itself. "The Poetry of Paradox," *Chicago Reader*, March 31, 1978, p. 16.

embracing in the sleeping car, Grant lifting Saint up into the bunkbed in an initial movement toward coitus) followed, in a metaphor placed in syntagm, by a vehicle metaphorically completing the censored act (train entering tunnel) begun in the diegesis. But, while the phallicism of Hitchcock's train/tunnel metaphor offers a resolution to sexual tension, Buñuel's phallic metaphor only increases the sexual tension. Once again this occurs through tampering with the usual relation between figure and diegesis.

In this instance the tampering consists of the playful insertion of the train speeding through the tunnel as a literal interruption rather than a metaphoric completion of the diegetic action. In one flashback scene, for example, Mathieu and Concha are alone in her apartment. She sits on the couch with Mathieu, her legs spread invitingly, and puts a piece of candy in his mouth. As the moment becomes increasingly titillating, the sound of Mathieu's train is followed by a flash-forward to the interior of the train compartment where Mathieu and his fellow passengers are speeding in darkness through a tunnel. This tunnel and train might seem to function as a metaphor for the coitus he desires. But in fact the speeding train in the framing story functions to interrupt the phallic progress of Mathieu's narration of these events. For, although Mathieu tries, by shouting in the dark, to continue his narration of a scene that would presumably end in coitus, the noise and darkness of the tunnel are too much for him. He and his listeners are forced to sit in silence for the duration of the tunnel. Thus, the metaphor of the train hurtling through the dark tunnel functions as a teasing interruption—rather than completion à la *North-by-Northwest*—of the phallic progress of the diegesis, an interruption which offers an ironic displacement of the desired consummation. As we shall see, it is precisely this consummation—the true possession of the object of desire—that the film maintains is impossible.

Concha (Concepciòn) Perez is the "obscure object" of Mathieu's quest. She is everywhere and nowhere at the same time. Turning up first as Mathieu's maid, she disappears as soon as his advances become too insistent. When Mathieu later visits Switzerland, she turns up there as well, vaguely linked with activities of a terrorist group whose robberies and bombings seem to coincide with each of Mathieu's sexual advances toward Concha. Strangely, however,

Concha, Carole Bouquet, encased in her chastity belt, offers herself to Mathieu's gaze.

there is no political program to these terrorist acts. Mathieu's friend the judge characterizes the terrorists as gangsters and adventurers. Their primary function seems to be to taunt Mathieu with a revolutionary youth and virility he can never equal. At one point late in the film, a radio broadcast lists the acronyms of the terrorist groups as P.R.I.Q.U.E., R.U.T., and R.A.I.J.

The basic conceit of the film is that Concha exists for Mathieu as she was in the interrupted scene on the couch, legs spread and inviting, an image of infinite desirability precisely because she is just out of reach, to be seen but never touched, her will always a mystery. The pattern is repeated in scene after scene as Concha offers herself up to Mathieu's desiring gaze but always with some barrier between them—the bars of a window or gate, or the canvas material of an elaborate chastity belt. In one scene she stands at a barred window allowing Mathieu on the street outside to stroke her long hair. In another he is reduced to tears after a ten-minute struggle in bed with her chastity belt. In each of the above episodes particular emphasis is placed on the voyeuristic structure of Mathieu's desire. This is especially the case in three other scenes. In one Mathieu spies on Concha through a window above the door to her bedroom, in another he spies her through a window dancing the flamenco naked before a group of Japanese and American tourists, and in yet another he watches her through the iron bars of a gate making love to a young terrorist.

Mathieu's perpetual position as voyeur emphasizes the essential need for a distance or gap between subject and object for desire to come into play. This distance, which the real voyeur is always careful to maintain, is the very condition of desire. Christian Metz writes:

> The voyeur represents in space the fracture which forever separates him from the object; he represents his very dissatisfaction (which is precisely what he needs as a voyeur). . . . If it is true of all desire that it depends on the infinite pursuit of its absent object, voyeuristic desire, along with certain forms of sadism, is the only desire whose principle of distance symbolically and spatially evokes this fundamental rent." [18]

[18] "The Imaginary Signifier," *Screen*, 16:61.

Mathieu's perpetual position as voyeur emphasizes the essential need for distance between
subject and object for desire to come into play.

In a very radical sense *That Obscure Object of Desire* explores the Imaginary structure at the heart of the scopic drive—a passion *to see* that is based upon the fundamental absence or separation from the object one wishes to see. Nowhere is this so obvious as in the above-mentioned scene in which Mathieu, locked out of the villa he has bought Concha, looks at her through the iron bars of the gate as she gives herself to a young terrorist guitarist who has often been lurking about presumably enjoying the pleasures denied to Mathieu. Through the bars Concha cruelly confesses her disgust at Mathieu's advanced age. Then she invites him to stay and watch.

Although the presumed action of this scene takes place on the patio floor, where Concha undresses to lie with her lover, the camera never leaves Mathieu's face, framed by the bars of the gate that separates him from the scene of passion, to reveal the love-making itself. At one point Mathieu tears himself away from the bars to walk, stricken, out onto the street. But he returns, compelled to gaze unblinkingly at the scene before him. A prisoner of his passion, as the iron bars suggest,[19] his enthrallment depends upon being locked out. Like a child at the primal scene, he is separated from physical possession of the object of his desire and is thus eternally desirous of its possession.

This scene before the gate is a privileged representation of the nature of desire. It allows Mathieu to believe in the ability of the object to satisfy through his identification with the *imagined* satisfaction of a rival who takes his place. Thus the object of desire is possessed by another and on another scene—a scene whose very reality is undercut by the fact that the audience never sees it and, further, by Concha's later claim that the presumed love-making was only an act staged for Mathieu's benefit, designed to make him jealous. Since Mathieu himself had momentarily left the scene at the presumed moment of climax—when he returns Concha and the guitarist are getting dressed—this is indeed possible.

In this scene Mathieu witnesses a satisfaction that can only be imagined, a satisfaction that goes far beyond the purely physical

---

[19] Just prior to this scene, on his way to visit Concha, Mathieu had passed before a café named Las Cadenas (The Chains). This name comments upon the enslaving nature of his passion. It is also an allusion to the cry *Vivan las caenas!* in Buñuel's previous film, *The Phantom of Liberty*.

possession of the withheld portion of Concha's anatomy through an associated chain of signifiers extending back to the originally repressed "lost object" that motivates the desire of every human subject. For what Mathieu desires in this scene and throughout the film is not Concha herself or that mythically pure and untouched portion of her anatomy which seems so close and yet so far, but a form of *self*-possession that structurally repeats the mirror-stage apprehension of a mistaken unity of self and Other in the imaginary lure of the reflected image. This, I think, is one meaning of the random substitutions of the two actresses who play Concha. If Mathieu is blind to the individual characteristics of the two Conchas, if he treats them as one person, it is not only because he is interested in one part of a woman's anatomy and thus doesn't notice the difference, but also because she is totally the projection of his own subjective desire to fill the lack in his *own* being.

Since the Lacanian structure of the formation of the human subject emerges so forcefully in this film, I shall recall here some of its key notions. For Lacan the Symbolic comes as an intrusion and rupture of the Imaginary unity of the subject typified by the dual relations of the mirror stage. The Symbolic is an order of interconnected signs bound together by the relation of a given signifier to a given signified. This linguistic order mediates the relation to reality, forever distancing us from the immediate grasp of our own psychic truth. Using the binary oppositions of structural linguistics to show how the subject is situated in and created by language, Lacan stresses the disjunction between lived experience and the sign that replaces it, showing that the relation between signifier and signified at any one point in the flow of words is always tenuous. As Lacan writes, signifier and signified are two parallel flows connected by "anchoring points"[20] (the French *points de caption*, a metaphor drawn from the way an upholstery stud anchors only parts of the material and stuffing of a couch, leaving large quantities of the material floating freely). Thus discourse is always an enigmatic evasion of the real. Anika Lemaire points out in her book on Lacan:

> Each word in the sentence certainly acquires a meaning through the
> interrelational play between the elements of the sentence, but, at the

---

[20] "The Agency of the Letter in the Unconscious or Reason since Freud," *Ecrits*, ch. 2, pp. 146–78.

same time, this meaning is never fixed in a stable manner. The single word implies a series of references to the other words in the code, both synonyms and antonyms. . . . The anchoring point is mythical. The final signified for which one searches is radically excluded from thought as it concerns an incommensurable dimension, namely the Real.[21]

This final signified is the repressed lost object that gives rise to the unconscious.

As in the *fort/da* game played by Freud's grandchild, the reality of the thing itself—in this case the child's mother—is forever lost in the process of symbolization. Mediated by language, the human subject is divided from itself, the effect of the signifier alienates a self that can only be named in the discourse of the Other. It is this loss, both of the unity of self and of the immediate possession of the thing, which gives rise to desire.

In the Imaginary there is no desire. Self merges with Other in an unmediated unity. But with the Symbolic and the Oedipus comes a separation and interdiction that intrudes upon the dual relation of mother and child. This intrusion of what Lacan calls the "Law-of-the-Father" represents a necessary step in the formation of the subject. But it also marks the end of the Imaginary unity with the mother, causing the child to renounce and repress what—through naming and language—can now be called desire. Thus the child learns to accept the laws of limitation, to assume through the symbolic threat of castration his or her lack.[22] But at the same time, this Symbolic leads the subject into a quest for substitute objects that are increasingly removed from the original lost object. Any articulated demand is thus supported by an unconscious desire for the original lost object.[23]

In this context Mathieu's desire for Concha is only superficially the quest for physical consummation. Behind the notion of Concha the prick-tease, who will offer her mouth, her breasts, and any-

---

[21] Lemaire, *Jacques Lacan*, p. 41.

[22] Lacan, "The Direction of the treatment and principles of its power," *Ecrits*, p. 165.

[23] "Desire is situated in dependence upon demand which, by being articulated in signifiers, leaves a metonymic remainder that runs under it, an element that is not indeterminate, which is a condition both absolute and unapprehensible, an element naturally lacking, unsatisfied, impossible, misconstrued [*méconnu*], an element that is called desire." Lacan, *Four Fundamental Concepts of Psycho-analysis*, p. 154.

thing but the supposedly virginal hymen Mathieu desires, and of the elusive woman-object, who will allow herself to be seen but not touched, is the more fundamental and impossible quest of the human subject for fulfillment of a lack in its own being. Lacan writes, "In persuading the other that he has that which may complement us, we assure ourselves of being able to continue to misunderstand precisely what we lack." [24] Thus Concha herself is simply a figure of desire—an associated stand-in for Mathieu's own lost object. And the division she undergoes (the split between cool, ironic French actress Carole Bouquet and sultry Spanish Angela Molina) is nothing more than a projection of a more fundamental division within the desiring subject—the objectification of his own division within himself. Thus the patently false unity Mathieu desires and believes in in Concha is revealed by the film as the basic misrecognition of all desire.

Concha herself withholds her virginity in the name of an individual integrity that her very division into two women belies. "*Moi, c'est moi,*" she argues in both Loüys's novel and Buñuel's film, although the phrase only has this ironic resonance in the film. If Mathieu believes her, it is because this desired unity and integrity is the complement to his own lack. Thus the obscure object of desire is both an expression of the subject's desire to fill a lack and the revelation of the impossibility of ever really doing so. What first appears to be a reduction of frustrated erotic pursuit to the bare essentials of a penis denied entrance to the vagina of its choice turns out to have all the complexity and abstraction of a medieval allegory, a psychomachia of desire exploring the respective positions of subject and object.

In the Loüys novel Concha does eventually give herself to Don Mateo but only after she has frustrated him to such an extent that he nearly beats her to death. With this beating Concha the original sadist becomes Concha the converted masochist, and the novel itself degenerates into an antifeminine tract. [25] Her passion finally aroused by the dramatic proof of his suffering, Concha discovers a

---

[24] Ibid., p. 133.

[25] Michael Wood's discussion of both film and novel stresses Loüys's misogynist message that women must be kept in their place by force. "Buñuel's Private Lessons," *New York Review of Books,* February 23, 1978, p. 39.

sadomasochistic wellspring of desire more powerful and perverse than Don Mateo's.

In Buñuel's film, however, Concha never gives herself to Mathieu. Her own desire remains always a mystery. As Mathieu grows increasingly enslaved, Concha grows ever more elusive, casually quiting temporary jobs, slipping in and out of Mathieu's life at will, as first one woman then another. In both Loüys's novel and von Sternberg's film, the final revelation of Concha's own desire puts an end to her status as an enigma. In these works the enigma of woman-as-object is lessened by the eventual climactic revelation of woman-as-subject.[26] Thus Loüys's Concha looses her status as *mocita* (virgin) to become in turn a sexually desiring subject; while von Sternberg's Concha, though clearly never *mocita*, finally reveals a perverse but apparently genuine desire for the man who has the greatest reason to hate her.

Buñuel's version provides us with two physical stereotypes, the virgin (Bouquet is blond, cool, haughty, and intellectual) and the whore (Molina is dark, sultry, and earthy), and with a similar dichotomy on the level of the scenario (the valet thinks women are "sacks of excrement," while Mathieu is inclined to believe in a purity that he is only too eager to sully). But the film never allows us to conclude that Concha is either one or the other.

Thus where Loüys and von Sternberg titillate with alternate mystification and revelation in an erotic striptease of the woman's soul, Buñuel's eroticism is strangely chaste[27] and intellectual, more in the style of a medieval allegory than a modern love story. In the medieval allegory *Roman de la Rose*,[28] the unitary subject or Lover dreams of the object of his desire, whose attributes are separated into a multitude of allegorical figures—e.g., Shame, Fair Welcoming, and Modesty—who surround and protect the central metaphor, the rose, which the lover desires to pluck. This allegorical structure, in

---

[26] These eleventh-hour glimpses into a woman's soul are typical of a great many boy-meets-girl films presented from a predominantly male point of view. It is interesting that many of these films seem to validate their objectification of women through just such last-minute revelations of what the woman *really* wants. Buñuel does not objectify Concha in this sense.

[27] Buñuel once described *Belle de Jour* as a chastely erotic film.

[28] Guillaume de Lorris and Jean de Meun (pseud.), *The Romance of the Rose*, trans. Charles Dahlberg (Princeton: Princeton University Press, 1969).

which debates between the lover and the lady's various attributes dominate the action, encourages an understanding on the part of the reader of the various stages of love, both carnal and divine. The poem can be read either as a dirty-joke parody of the courtly and religious ideals of love or as a commentary on the narcissistic nature of the fantasy that propels the lover toward the figure of his desire.[29]

Buñuel's film encourages a similar double reading, both dirty-joke and intellectual commentary on the structure of desire. The one thing this story is not is a realistic depiction of a man and woman in love. Since Concha is entirely a figure of Mathieu's desire, she is as open to interpretation, as multiple and diverse as are the dreamer's projections of his lady in the allegory.

In the course of the film we are given several possible interpretations of the enigmatic figure of desire. The first is suggested in a verbal metaphor spoken by Mathieu's valet, "Women are sacks of excrement." This metaphor represents one extreme of the seesaw of interpretation that constitutes Mathieu's involvement with Concha. Either she is pure and untouched—in which case Mathieu will delight in being the first to "spoil" her—or as the valet claims, she is a sack of excrement. Mathieu can never be sure if she is one or the other. The point is (and this is where Buñuel radically differs from both Loüys and von Sternberg) that she is neither.

One way Buñuel reveals the virgin/whore dichotomy for the ridiculous and (literally) cumbersome burden it is, is through a very sly literalization of the valet's metaphor that women are sacks of excrement. Early in the film a man in work clothes appears carrying a large burlap sack. Later, as Concha and Mathieu walk along a Paris street, they pass this same man with the same sack. In yet another scene, as Concha and Mathieu walk along the Seine, Mathieu himself casually picks up the sack from a park bench and continues with it slung over his shoulder. Later in Seville, where he has once again run into Concha, a porter reminds Mathieu that he has forgotten his sack. The sack functions as a literalization of a figure of speech, mocking the absurdity of the valet's pronouncement through an emphasis on the quality of burden inherent in the figure. Mathieu appears under the weight of this burden and thus metaphorically un-

---

[29] The lover first becomes enamored as he gazes at the same fountain where Narcissus died. Ibid., ll. 1425–36.

der the weight of these preconceived notions of the supposed purity or filth of women. Like the weight of the pianos and rotting donkeys pulled by the cyclist in *Un Chien andalou*, the sack is an unnatural and constraining cultural burden ludicrously assumed at the very height of an erotic quest.

But this is not the last we see of the sack or of the figural possibilities of Mathieu's object of desire. After the train arrives at the Paris station and Mathieu has completed his account of the supposed end of his affair with Concha, the story is resumed in the present tense as Concha in turn douses Mathieu with a bucket of water and the whole affair begins again. A wet Mathieu and battered Concha leave the station, together with Mathieu's valet. Near the fashionable streets of the Place de la Concorde, they enter an elegant skylit gallery, where a shopwindow catches Mathieu's eye. At the same time, a radio announcement interrupts operatic music to say that the forces of P. R. I. Q. U. E. and R. U. T. are increasing their terrorist acts. A woman in the window unties a burlap sack identical to the one we have come to associate with the excremental metaphor for women. She pulls out a delicate, long white gown with a bloodied hole in its center. Seating herself in the window, she begins to mend the hole. Mathieu stares in fascination at the gown and hole in much the same way Modot stared at the erotic window displays in *L'Age d'or*. The operatic music from the radio grows louder, building to a dramatic crescendo. Concha drifts off to one side, no longer receiving Mathieu's interest. A great explosion in the vicinity of the window fills the screen and obliterates everything. The film ends as red-letter credits appear over the smoke of the explosion.

The young terrorists, who are the obvious perpetrators of the explosion that seems to obliterate both Mathieu and the figure of his desire, achieve a parody of the earth-shaking orgasm Mathieu has sought all along. As before, it is Mathieu who watches and is the victim of someone else's satisfaction. This explosion is also a movement back to the nothingness from which the subject and his desire were originally formed. As in the final tableau of implanted corpses in *Un Chien andalou* or the final image of sadistic murder in *L'Age d'or*, Buñuel's most recent film ends at the only place ending is possible, in the movement from Eros to Thanatos.

The woman in the store window has finally revealed what is

Mathieu stares in fascination at the bloodied gown and its hole.

really in the sack—not excrement at all but something infinitely
more complex and resonant not only in terms of this film but also in
relation to the many figures of desire throughout all Buñuel's Surrealist films. For this final metaphor completes that initial metaphorical moment in *Un Chien andalou* when the flesh of the eyeball was slit to open up the film to the figural discourse of desire. We
have seen how this initial stroke of the razor opened up the first
wound, symbolic not only of castration but of the fundamental lack
in the subject. In so doing it gave rise to a dizzying series of metaphoric and metonymic associations, all of which attempted to fill
in, cover over, or deny an original lack.

Now, fifty years later, in a film whose studio-pretty, professional
veneer and smooth narration bear almost no relation to the aggressive, dreamlike, experimental short that began it all, Buñuel presents the complementary figural response to the assertion of lack in
the image of the woman mending the hole in the gown. This gesture perfectly captures the always-imperfect attempt to deny lack
through the efforts of suture.[30] In both films we are confronted with
texts whose main thrust is the figural attempt to fill an absence,

[30] I use the term *suture* in the normal sense of surgically joining the opening of a wound.
But it is worth noting that the word has recently taken on a more specific psychoanalytic
construction. Briefly, the notion of suture as applied to film studies has developed out of an
article by Jacques-Alain Miller entitled "Suture (elements of the logic of the signifier)," trans.
Jacqueline Rose, *Screen* 18 (Winter 1977–78): 24–34. Although the term is never mentioned
by Lacan himself, Miller proposes that it is inherent in Lacan's "logic of the signifier." He
offers it as a further development of Lacan's idea that the unconscious does not preexist but is
instead formed at the same time as the effect of the signifier creates the subject. The "I" created by language is thus both a division and a joining, and suture names the process by which
the fundamental division of the I is overcome through the Imaginary projection of a unitary
ego—the subject. As applied to film, the notion of suture has been appropriated by Jean-
Pierre Oudart in an article originally published in *Cahiers du cinema* 211–12 (April–May
1969). In Oudart's article "Cinema and Suture," trans. Kari Hanet, *Screen* 18 (Winter–Spring 1977–78): 35–47, suture becomes the logic of the cinematic signifier. It is the
process by which the spectator as subject fills in the discontinuities and absences of the cinematic discourse that proceeds by cuts, framings, and the absence of the signifier itself.

I am not altogether convinced of the value of adding yet another psychoanalytic term
(which my definition has grossly simplified) to this analysis. It seems to me that the concepts
of Imaginary and Symbolic—at which juncture suture seems to be located—are adequate to
the description of the processes of Surrealist film. But to appropriate the concept of suture to
Surrealist film would be to find in it striking literal representations of what Miller and Oudart
found only as metaphor for the disunity that gives rise to the desire for fictional unity in the
subject. Nowhere is this more apparent than in the incomplete attempt to mend the tear in
the soiled and bloodied garment at the end of this film.

cover a gap, mend a tear. In this final image Mathieu faces the truth of a desire born of the fundamental lack in the subject. Like the cyclist in *Un Chien andalou*, who stares at the hole in his hand, Mathieu stands transfixed before the final figure of his desire—a simple, bloodied hole. This bloodied rent in the gown, like the similar wounds in the eye and hand of *Un Chien andalou*, is an obvious metaphor for castration. But, as we have seen in this earlier film, castration is itself a metaphor for the fundamental disjunction of self and world created by the subject's entrance into language and the Law-of-the-Father. Castration, in this sense, represents the basic signifier of the difference that irremediably separates subject and object, giving rise to the simultaneous desire to retrieve the lost object and to cover over or fill the original lack-in-being with substitute objects.

We have already seen how the fetish functions as a metonymic substitute that attempts to disavow the fear of castration. Freud describes it as the substitute for the "penis that the little boy once believed in, a disavowal of the biological fact that women have no penis."[31] Typical fetish objects either cover or are adjacent to the part of the body the child fears has undergone castration. The fetish is thus a figure of presence used to hide a contiguously associated absence.

The torn dress pulled out of the sack at the end of *That Obscure Object of Desire* is not the first fetish in this film. Earlier, in one of Mathieu and Concha's many chance encounters, Concha deliberately dropped a white handkerchief before disappearing with her terrorist friends. Mathieu, finding the handkerchief, raised it to his face for an erotic sniff reminiscent of Professor Rath's similar sniff of Lola-Lola's panties in *The Blue Angel*. Like the handkerchief, the woman's gown is a metonymic stand-in for the absent woman. But if the gown and handkerchief function as the fetishistic disavowal of lack, then the bloodied hole in the center of the dress is the disavowal of a disavowal, the insidious reassertion of the lack or wound in the very fabric of the material which attempts to cover that lack.

In this film a transparently simple narrative soon becomes a complex chain of figural associations, whereby Concha, the woman-as-

---

[31] Freud, "Fetishism," *Complete Psychological Works*, 21:153.

object, stands for a number of contradictory figural qualities. The tension created by these contradictory visions of woman and by the random alternation of the two actresses who play the part suggests that it is precisely this opposition which creates desire. Thus the film leads us back through a complex chain of figural associations, each of which seems about to define the "nature" of woman as object of desire. But what the film reveals is not simply that this mysterious object is undefinable, but that, once again, a certain structure of opposition in the unconscious of the subject has engendered this desire in the first place.

The first set of oppositions is that of the virgin and the whore. We have seen that Concha is at different times associated with each in the satirically cumbersome symbols of the chastity belt on the one hand and the sack of excrement on the other. But with the sack of excrement in particular, we encounter a tongue-in-cheek parody of both the misogynist content of the valet's metaphor that women are sacks of excrement and the process of making film metaphors out of verbal ones. In the valet's original verbal metaphor, we obviously are meant to believe, not that women literally are sacks of excrement, but that, as in all metaphors, these two objects share certain semantic features: for the valet, both are filthy and both are mere receptacles. As in all verbal metaphors, the obvious denotative meaning is supressed, while the semantic features shared by the tenor and vehicle are stressed to create a new connotation.

Buñuel's joke is, however, that in film the image of a sack of excrement stubbornly remains just that. Film metaphors cannot operate as redundant translations of verbal metaphors. We see this, first of all, in the extreme awkwardness with which this verbal similarity is visualized. To render visual the verbal image of the sack of excrement is to defeat the point of the verbal metaphor: to find similarity in dissimilar things. Among other things, the sack becomes a joke on the difficulty of translating verbal metaphors to visual ones. Thus also, as we have seen, Buñuel forges an ironic metaphoric comment on the dull "burden" of such misogynist beliefs and the nature of the metaphoric process itself.

But the final joke is, of course, that the sack does not contain excrement at all but, instead, yet another figure—the fetish object that covers the feared wound of castration (the famous Buñuelian

1. Although this still of Concha's face reflected in a mirror became the primary publicity image for the film, the image itself—another absent figure of desire—is nowhere to be found in the film.

2. Mathieu sniffs Concha's handkerchief, one of the many fetish objects that stand in for the elusive Concha.

3. The woman in the shop window mends the torn and bloodied lace.

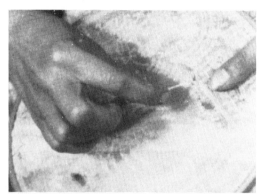

4. Close-up of the mending.

5. Vermeer's *The Lacemaker* from Buñuel and Dalí's *Un Chien andalou*.

penchant for Chinese boxes is here exercized with great flair). Thus one figural association leads to another, as the illusory sack of excrement gives way to another stand-in for the woman: the gown that is taken from the sack. But once again this metonymic figure of the gown—the fetish substitute for the woman that both evokes her and covers the disturbing absence that constitutes her difference from the male—contains a contradictory metaphor at its center: the bloodied hole that reasserts the disturbing threat of absence and lack inherent in castration.

This hole and the contradictory act of mending it are the final links in a complex chain of figural associations that began with the opposition between the two physical types of women in the random substitutions of the two Conchas, continued through the ludicrous opposition of the symbolic accoutrements of virgin and whore—the chastity belt and sack of excrement—and further continued in the metonymic fetish of the dress and the metaphoric absence at its center. With this final opposition, *That Obscure Object of Desire* shifts the ground of the original opposition between the virgin and whore and returns to the same fundamental opposition of presence and absence, castration and disavowal of castration, that animated the figural associations of *Un Chien andalou*.

The attempt to mend the tear in the dress is a final metaphor of suture, an attempt to close the gap or division at the very center of being. It recalls yet another figure from *Un Chien andalou*, the book that mysteriously fell open to a reproduction of Vermeer's *The Lacemaker*.[32] The Vermeer painting shows a seated woman intently working a piece of lace. This lacemaker, like the seated woman mending the tear in the fabric of the dress at the end of *That Obscure Object of Desire*, joins the threads of a material that, by its very nature, can never be totally joined. For lace can only partially veil the flesh beneath. Lacemaking is thus the permanent inscription of absence and lack in the very act of joining together threads of an imperfect suture. It is a fetishistic disavowal whose attempt to close the gap inevitably asserts it as well.

Similarly, the woman in the window, who mends the hole in the dress, attempts impossibly to connect the two lips of the wound that

[32] See ch. 2, p. 76.

stands in for the eternal incompleteness of the desiring subject. This final image is the last link in the chain of associations that leads from the original misrecognition of the illusory unity of Concha herself back to this most elementary figure of division and suture.

It is wonderfully appropriate that this final figure of desire should be framed by the window of an advertising display and that Mathieu, ever the voyeur, should regard it as any window-shopper would regard other banal objects of desire. As in *L'Age d'or* where Modot's erotic desire for Lys is triggered by shopwindow displays for women's toiletries, Buñuel reminds us of the similarity between erotic desire and desire for a consumer product. Both lover and consumer are governed by an awareness of lack that the erotic or consumer object gives the illusion of being able to fill, thus offering a new image of the self as a completed being.

Like the elusive phantom of liberty, the object of desire is also an illusion. But if this object is an obscure illusion, Buñuel's presentation of the oppositions that structure it is wonderfully clear. There are no true objects of desire; there are only perpetual substitutions of figures that stand in for the original lack in the subject.

# CHAPTER FIVE

# Conclusion:
# The Figures of Desire

BOTH the aesthetic enterprise of Surrealist film and the interpretive enterprise of Lacanian psychoanalysis isolate the phenomenon of an absence that is infinitely desirable because never attainable. The Surrealists took pleasure in the paradoxical fact that the unparalleled visual perceptivity of the film image is only a projected illusion—an absence that creates the illusion of presence. The relation of the spectator to the cinematic image thus parallels the relation of the human subject to the *other scene* of the unconscious. For the unconscious, too, is a scene that is never directly present and is only indicated—as in dreams—by an illusory image. Thus the film and the dream resemble each other most in their ability to project desire. This is so precisely because in both cases the projected image of this desire is radically not there.

As Lacan has shown, desire is produced in the human subject through the subject's situation in language—in the fact that an original need, when articulated to the Other through language, becomes a demand, which every time it is uttered opens up an entire chain of signification that is not under its control. Through language, need is addressed to the Other in the form of a demand. It is a demand *for* something, but when this demand is satisfied, there is something left over that is not satisfied. This something cannot be satisfied by the thing itself, because through language the demand to the Other has become something more—a demand for recognition by that Other.

Thus there is always something left over that is not satisfied. This residue, which lodges in the *other scene* of the unconscious and which can be evoked through the association of signifiers, is desire. Desire can never be achieved because it is always the desire for an unpossessable fantasy of the Other. The imaginary signifier of the cinematic image parallels this linguistic structuring of desire because it, too, is posited upon a fundamentally unpossessable absence. But Lacan's theory of linguistic alienation and of the construction of the subject in the place of the Other does not just explain the Surrealists' fascination with the cinema's imaginary signifier, it also elucidates many of the *uses* the Surrealists made of this signifier. For, although the Surrealists initially tried simply to cultivate divergent responses to the dominant mode of fictional films, they soon began to write and produce works that more systematically exploited the Imaginary processes at work in film.

Initially they did this within the framework of the fictional mode. Both Apollinaire in *La Bréhatine* and Artaud in *Eighteen Seconds* devised fictions in which their heroes identified with (imagined) images of themselves. In each of these works the self is revealed as a product of an identification with the Other. Both of these scenarios present fictional characters involved in situations that permit an exploration of the illusive unity of the self. But although they create situations that give cinematic form to an identification process based on the desire for the Other, they are still working within the confines of the fictional film and its representation of a previously existing time, space, and character. In *Eighteen Seconds*, however, the actual representation of this time, space, and character is reduced to a skeletal framing device—the man standing under the street lamp at beginning and end. In between is the portrayal of his subjective mindscreen—a whole realm of unconscious associations that obeys none of the rules of traditional fictional diegesis.

With *Un Chien andalou* and *L'Age d'or*, Surrealist film found a way to rupture the film's fictional and conventional unity of the self without resorting to the usual devices of dream sequences or subjective fantasies—devices that only preserve the supreme fiction of the unity of the self while giving access to its partial fracturings. The eye-cutting of the *Un Chien andalou* prologue can be seen as the definitive rupture with this fictional unity—not only the unity of character, but even the minimal physical unity of the human body.

So there are really several kinds of unity ruptured by the *Chien* prologue: first, the unity of the human subject itself, which, beginning in the prologue and continuing throughout the rest of the film, undergoes repeated splittings; second, the fictional unity of the diegetic worlds of balcony, apartment, forest, and beach; and third, the unity of the viewers' identification with the person on the screen. It is this last identification that the razor so ruthlessly severs. Everything that follows from this prologue is predicated upon this rupture of Imaginary identification so crucial in Lacan's mirror stage. These ruptures create a series of literal and figural gaps that give rise to a text whose images depict the processes of desire rather than the external image of its object. Again and again, in this film and in *L'Age d'or* as well, a violent rending of human flesh opens a gap on the surface of the body. These gaps—in both eye and hand in both films—are grotesque parallels to natural body apertures marked by their dual role as loci of both biological function and erotic pleasure.

As prologue to the entire film, the slashed eye of *Un Chien andalou* posits a gap that opens the way to a continual flux of male and female signifiers—the marks of difference from which desire is generated. Thus the feminine frills and masculine tie of the cyclist follow directly upon the eye-cutting. Similarly, the hole in the hand is followed by a metaphoric elaboration of male and female, convex and concave, shapes. In both cases these gaps in the flesh lead to new figurations of desire. Desire arises out of the rupture, in this case a very physical rupture, of the unified surface of the human body. It results from the destruction of the literal and physically present flesh—the same flesh that gets in the way of the lovers in *L'Age d'or*—and generates subsequent progressions to imaginary figures.

In a characteristically overdetermined way—overdetermination itself being an important feature of dreams—this rending of the flesh is also a figure of castration. Chapter 2 shows that symbolic castration is a culturally determined initial loss that structures desire and the relations between the sexes. All the subsequent figures of the film act alternately to cover or deny this initial loss. Thus castration functions not as the complex of a given character but as the opening up of the text to a new level of signification. This is another way in which Surrealist film dramatizes the fundamental loss that characterizes the position of the subject in a world of difference.

Thus we are confronted with two very similar kinds of losses, both of which make desire possible: the loss of the phallus in the assumption of castration and the loss of the self through the construction of the self in language. *Un Chien andalou* presents both aspects of this loss. It presents a self that is constantly splitting and is constantly the focus of an evolving series of oppositions between the sexual signs of male and female, death and love, sight and blindness. And it presents a related loss of unity through the realization of sexual difference afforded by repeated allusions to castration beginning with the prologue metaphor.

Lacan has shown how each of these related experiences of loss involves a movement from the illusory misrecognition of unity in the Imaginary, to the awareness of difference contained in the Symbolic. The Imaginary is the illusory misrecognition of satisfaction, a relationship of identity between the self and the Other that desire has not yet entered, whereas the Symbolic is the entrance into a whole system of differences to which the self is subjected (and from which it is produced), resulting in the impossibility of ever finding satisfaction. Thus *Un Chien andalou* exposes the misrecognitions of the Imaginary, making the viewer experience the loss that the assumption of language—and castration—inaugurates.

Where the fiction film employs the symbolic codes of narrativity to encourage identification with the Other on the screen and thus to exploit what is ultimately the dual relations of the Imaginary and its illusion of satisfaction, *Un Chien andalou* does quite the contrary. It establishes an initial Imaginary relation of identification with the Other so as to expose the fundamental misrecognition at its heart. Both castration and the structural oppositions of male/female, love/death, blindness/sight come to rupture these Imaginary dreams of undifferentiation. Desire intrudes as a function of the Symbolic, and satisfaction is forever lost.

In *L'Age d'or* desire arises out of a similar structure of loss. Only when Lys and Modot are apart does desire begin to operate. It operates precisely to move the filmic discourse to a new level in which what is desired—the figure of Lys masturbating or the fetish objects of the dress and foot—is never the love object itself but an associated and sometimes fetishized signifier of it. It is thus an essential absence that here, too, engenders the particular figures of desire. Thus, in its own way, *L'Age d'or* dramatizes the structure of a desire predicated upon an initial loss or absence. Here, too, the gaps in the surface unity of the body—Modot's bleeding eye and severed hand—give access to previously unspoken desires—the lovers' interior dialogue. But, as chapter 3 shows, in a larger sense the gaps between the film's five different sections also give access to the articulation of underlying relations between sex and violence, murderers and victims elaborated throughout the film, culminating in the final condensation of Christ/Blangy.

The attention I have given throughout this work to the disturbed hierarchy between figure and diegesis is of central importance to the special dramatization of desire in Surrealist film. The peculiar emphasis of figure over diegesis in both works reverses the usual function of the figure in narrative film. In these Surrealist films, the figure does not momentarily move to the foreground to make connotative comments on the denotation of the diegesis. The eye-cutting in *Un Chien andalou* does not just comment on the story; in a peculiar way it generates what there is of a story. Neither do any of the five sections of *L'Age d'or* function as an immediate connotative comment on the other sections: each remains part of the diegesis while being also figural. Similarly, in *The Phantom of Liberty*, figures do not serve the diegesis; they, too, take on the *generative* qualities that are usually associated with diegesis. In all these films the emphasis shifts away from the present fictive illusion of a time, place, and character to an elusive elsewhere, an *other scene* constructed out of mechanisms analogous to those in dream work.

By virtue of their dominant generative function, the figures of metaphor and metonymy have taken on the features of the dream procedures of condensation and displacement as described by Freud.[1] But, as we have seen, this figural dominance happens differently in each film. In *Un Chien andalou* the most memorable figures are, for the most part, extradiegetic metaphors that associate

[1] Freud, *Interpretation of Dreams*, pp. 311–44. As shown in ch. 1, *condensation* is the association of several ideas in one single dream representation. *Displacement* is the decentering of psychic values onto insignificant or indifferent but often more figurable elements. As ch. 2 indicates, Jacques Lacan has suggested that condensation and displacement in dreams are ways of binding the psychic energy of desire in a manner similar to the poetic binding of meaning in metaphor and metonymy. Since many aspects of this analogy between dream figuration and the figuration of more conscious texts still remain to be explored, I have preferred to retain the poetic and rhetorical terms *metaphor* and *metonymy* in my own analysis. But I have done so (as stated in ch. 2) with the purpose of showing how these figures have taken on some of the qualities of condensation and displacement in the unconscious.

the formal similarities of such distinctly divergent objects as clouds and razors, swarming ants, underarm hair, and sea urchin tentacles. The illogic of these surreal juxtapositions of very distant realities is strongly felt by the viewer.

In *L'Age d'or* and *The Phantom of Liberty*, however, the viewer registers a greater sense of logical and narrative coherence, because an increased use of metonymic rather than metaphoric figures gives the impression of reality. In these films, links between different sections are usually based on peculiarly displaced, partial contiguities. This greater reliance on metonymic associations of contiguity (rather than metaphoric associations of similarity) lends a stronger sense of realistic concretion to both films. But this greater concretion does not ultimately give precedence—as Jean Mitry[2] would have it—to their diegesis, for we have seen that these mostly metonymic figures neither comment upon nor entirely become the diegesis.

Thus, even though they are differently structured, the overall function of the figures in all these films remains the same. The ultimate effect is that of a disturbed hierarchy between diegesis and figure. The shift from metaphoric figuration in *Un Chien andalou* to metonymic figuration in *L'Age d'or* and *The Phantom of Liberty* is simply another aspect of the movement already observed in the early stages of Surrealist film's development out of Expressionistic, Fantastic and Dadaistic modes. In this early development, Surrealist filmmakers elaborated their own brand of paradoxical realism, consisting of a reduction of realism on the level of the fiction or represented instance (signified) and compensated for by an increase in realism on the level of the image that does the representing (signifier). As shown in chapter 1, this means that even such obviously unrealistic effects as the ants in the hand or the cutting of the eye in *Un Chien andalou* are nevertheless highly realistic with regard to the viewer's initial perception of the image. Unlike camera or laboratory effects such as slow-motion or superimposition, these particular distortions of reality are comparatively believable because the viewer experiences no distortion in the immediate perception of the object, no matter how bizarre that object might be.

Just as Surrealist film discovered a visual style that renders our

[2] *Esthétique et psychologie du cinéma*, 2:447.

belief in the strangeness of the dream as we dream it rather than our surprise at its strangeness when we *represent* it to ourselves and others in an awakened state, so too did it approximate the discourse of the unconscious through an increasing use of metonymic over metaphoric figures. In other words, we accept and believe in the literal existence of the elements composing a metonymic figure more readily than we do the similarities and contrasts of metaphors. This is so because, as Christian Metz[3] explains, the associations of metonymy have a greater quality of prefabrication in the real world. They are based on impressions that enter the preconscious system already linked by the very real phenomenon of spatial contiguity.

Thus contiguity is a more immediately perceptible and believable quality than are the similarities or contrasts of pure metaphors, which in reality are never prefabricated but always established by the juxtaposition of elements rarely found together in the real world. Metz explains that since the psychic apparatus must forge these metaphoric connections itself, such associations tend to lodge in the unconscious, where they are experienced as constructions.

Thus, even though metaphor would seem to be more intrinsically surreal by virtue of its tendency to be forged by the unconscious rather than perceived as reality, it seems to have been a feature of the development of Surrealist film that metonymic figures become increasingly important. This is another aspect of the process by which an avant-garde movement seeks to complicate obvious signs of its own avant-gardeness. By inscribing the film's discourse in apparent conformity with diegetic norms in which the diegesis gives the appearance of dominance, Surrealist filmmakers provide a semblance of realism analogous to the process of secondary revision in dreams. As in secondary revision, this semblance is a cover for what is still a profound rupture with logical coherence, but one that is not initially recognized as such.

The point is not just to label these filmic figures as either metaphoric or metonymic but to observe the way in which they differ from other figures in more conventionally diegetic films. Whether metaphors or metonymies, these peculiarly surreal figures resemble the rhetorical figures of the unconscious because of the overwhelm-

[3] "Métaphore/Métonymie," p. 244.

ing dominance of figure over diegesis. This rupture with the diegetic illusion of previously existing time, place, and character gives access to the *other scene* of the unconscious—to a discourse whose fictional illusions are only there to *be* disrupted. It is the rupture itself that indicates there is something else to be said, something that cannot be said except through rupture. This something is unconscious desire—a quality that can never be present in the same way in which the people and events of the diegesis are present. Through this emphasis on the figure's disruption of the diegesis, Surrealist film places desire as a metaphorical hole at the center of its discourse.

Nowhere is this more evident than in *That Obscure Object of Desire*. In this most recent of Surrealist films, an apparently realistic diegesis about the pursuit of an elusive object soon reveals that this object is divided into two persons. This radical division of the object is metaphorically similar to the fundamental division and lack in the subject doing the desiring. But the smooth connections of the narrative and the fact that Mathieu does not notice the difference tend to minimize this division. The two Conchas glide effortlessly in and out of the narrative, as also does the sack, which is a metaphorical stand-in for the (supposed) significance of the woman-as-object. Finally, both woman and sack are displaced by yet another figure—the bloodied hole in the garment that is mended by the woman in the window. In this final image, metaphor and metonymy converge in the contradictory assertion and denial of hole and suture. Buñuel thus turns the usual quest for the object of desire on its head. Instead of the usual quest for the object, he examines a series of figural associations which lead us back to the lack-in-being of the subject—once again revealing more about the structure of desire as it operates within the subject than about its always unknowable object.

### FILM FETISH

Christian Metz has shown how the cinema itself, considered in its dominant role as the creator of believable fictions, aims all of its

technical prowess at the disavowal of the lack on which it is based—
the absence of the object the imaginary signifier replaces.[4] As we
have seen, the whole apparatus of the fiction film aims precisely to
cover up this fundamental absence by creating the illusion of presence. Just as the fetish that covers a lack takes on the erotic desirability of the whole love-object, so the entire cinematic institution—considered especially in its technical prowess—becomes
erotogenic.[5]

It is perhaps the final paradox of Surrealist film that, although
it gives concrete form to the fetish within its narrative, it simultaneously ruptures the fetish function of the cinematic institution as
a whole. Everything about the Surrealist attitude toward film, from
the early film-going habits of Breton, Vaché, and Desnos to the de-
emphasizing of technical prowess (Buñuel's statement, for example,
that camera effects do not interest him) and the surprisingly nonero-
tic nature of the films themselves, aims at a defetishizing of the cinematic institution. The Surrealists exposed what other filmmakers
tried to hide: the underlying structure of the fetish and its role in the
creation of desire. When the cinema *is* a fetish, when it only ma-
nipulates the desires of its audience, it cannot possibly reveal its
fetish structure as well. But when the cinema ruptures the identification between spectator and image, the fetish function of the institution crumbles as well. This crumbling is replaced by a new awareness of the fetish in the mind of the spectator. Thus Surrealist film's
imitation of the discourse of the unconscious once again has the
paradoxical effect of making the spectator more conscious of the
processes that produce desire.

[4] "The Imaginary Signifier," pp. 67–75.

[5] The fetish function of the camera itself is only the most obvious manifestation of this
phenomenon. Long-lens cameras worn by amateur photographers at waist-level are perhaps a
most blatant and amusing instance. A scene in *Blow-Up*, in which David Hemmings
"shoots" his camera repeatedly at a writhing model, is a recent and very explicit example of
the way in which the camera—the most important element of cinematic prowess—acts as a
fetish replacement for the photographer's penis. The pleasure of the film buff lodges precisely
in the contemplation of this gap between "the force of presence the film has and . . . the
absence of which this force is constructed." Metz, "The Imaginary Signifier," p. 72. But for
this pleasure to be maintained, the film image must always be straining to cover this absence,
to convince viewers that it really is there.

# Bibliography

Abel, Richard. "The Contribution of the French Literary Avant-Garde to Film Theory and Criticism (1907–1924)." *Cinema Journal* 14 (Spring 1975).

Alexandrian, Sarane. *Le Surréalisme et le rêve*. Paris: Gallimard, 1974.

Althusser, Louis. *Positions*. 1st ed. Paris: Editions sociales, 1976.

Apollinaire, Guillaume. "Interview avec Guillaume Apollinaire." *Sic* 8, 9, 10 (1916).

———, and André Billy. *La Bréhatine. Archives des lettres modernes* 7 (1971).

Aragon, Louis. "Du Décor." *Le Film* (Sept. 1918). Reprinted in *Le Point* 59 (1962).

———. "Cinéma et C$^{ie}$." *Littérature* 4 (1919).

———. *Traité de Style*. Editions de la Nouvelle Revue Française. Paris: Gallimard, 1928.

Aranda, Francisco. *Luis Buñuel: A Critical Biography*. Trans. and ed. David Robinson. New York: Da Capo Press, 1976.

Artaud, Antonin. *Oeuvres complètes*. 5 vols. Paris: Gallimard, 1961. Vol. 3. *Collected Works*. 5 vols. Trans. Alastair Hamilton. London: Calder & Boyars, 1972. Vol. 3.

———. "L'Activité du Bureau de Recherches Surréalistes," *La Révolution surréaliste* 3 (April 15, 1925).

Balakian, Anna. *André Breton: Magus of Surrealism*. New York: Oxford University Press, 1971.

———. *Surrealism: The Road to the Absolute*. New York: Dutton, 1970.

Balazs, Bélla. *Theory of Film*. Trans. Edith Bone. New York: Dover, 1970.

Barthes, Roland. "L'Ancienne rhétorique: Aide-mémoire." *Communications* 16 (1970).

Bataille, Georges. *Erotisme*. Paris: Minuit, 1957.

Bazin, André. *What Is Cinema?* 2 vols. Trans. Hugh Gray. Berkeley: University of California Press, 1971.

Beaujour, Michel. "La poétique de l'automatisme chez André Breton." *Poétique* 25 (1976). Paris: Seuil.

Beckett, Samuel. *Oh, les beaux jours*. Paris: Editions de minuit, 1963.

*Happy Days*. London: Faber & Faber, 1962.

Benveniste, Emile. *Problèmes de linguistique générale*. Paris: Gallimard, 1966. *Problems in General Linguistics*. Trans. Mary Elizabeth Meek. Coral Gables, Fla.: University of Miami Press, 1971.

Blanchot, Maurice. *La Part du feu*. 5th ed. Paris: Gallimard, 1949.

Bonitzer, Pascal. "Le Gros orteil: 'Realité' de la denotation." *Cahiers du cinéma* 232 (October 1971).

Bonnet, Marguerite. "L'Aube du surréalisme et le cinéma." *Etudes cinématographiques: Surréalisme et cinéma* 1 (Spring 1965).

Breton, André. *L'Amour fou*. Paris: Gallimard, 1937.

———. "Comme dans un bois." *L'Age du cinéma* 4–5 (August–November, 1951). Trans. Paul Hammond, "As in a Wood," in *The Shadow and Its Shadow*. London: British Film Institute, 1978.

———. *Manifestes du surréalisme*. Paris: Editions Jean-Jacques Pauvert, 1962. *Manifestoes of Surrealism*. Trans. Richard Seaver and Helen R. Lane. Ann Arbor: University of Michigan Press, 1974.

———. *Position politique du surreálisme*. Paris: Sagittaire, 1935.

———. *Le Surréalisme et la peinture suivi de Genèse et perspective artistiques du surréalisme et de Fragments inédits*. New York: Brentano's, 1945.

———. *Les vases communicants*. Paris: Gallimard, 1955.

———, and Philippe Soupault. *Les Champs magnétiques*. Paris: Gallimard, 1971.

Buache, Freddy. *The Cinema of Luis Buñuel*. Trans. Peter Graham. New York: A. S. Barnes, 1973.

Buñuel, Luis. *Un Chien andalou, L'Age d'or, L'ange exterminateur*. *L'Avant Scène du Cinéma* 27–28 (July 1963).

———. Preface to *Un Chien andalou*. *La Révolution surréaliste* 12 (15 Dec. 1929).

Carrouges, Michel. *André Breton et les donneés fondamentales du surréalisme*. Paris: Gallimard, 1967.

Cook, David. "Some Structural Approaches to Cinema: A Survey of Models," *Cinema Journal* 14 (Spring 1975).

Crevel, René. "Notes en vue d'une psycho-dialectique." *Surréalisme au service de la révolution* 5 (1933).

Dalí, Salvadore. "L'Ane pourri." *Surréalisme au service de la révolution* 1 (July 1930). "The Stinking Ass." Trans. J. Bronowsky, *This Quarter* 5 (September 1932). Reprinted in Lucy Lippard, ed. *Surrealists on Art*. Englewood Cliffs, N.J.: Prentice-Hall, 1970.

———. "Interprétation paranoiaque-critique de l'image obsédante *L'Angélus de Millet*." *Minotaure* 1 (February 15, 1933).

————. *La Vie secrète de Salvadore Dalí.* French adapt. Michel Déon. Paris: La Table Ronde, 1952.

Décaudin, Michel. "Les Poètes découvrent le cinéma." *Etudes cinématographiques* 38–39 (1965).

Delteil, Joseph. "Le Cinéma." *La Revue européene,* (March 1, 1925).

Derrida, Jacques. *L'Ecriture et la différence.* Paris: Seuil, 1967. *Writing and Difference.* Trans. Alan Bass. Chicago: University of Chicago Press, 1978.

Desnos, Robert. *Cinéma.* Ed. André Tchernia. Paris: Gallimard, 1966.

Drummond, Philip. "Textual Space in *Un Chien andalou,*" *Screen* 18 (Autumn 1977).

Durgnat, Raymond. *Luis Buñuel.* Berkeley: University of California Press, 1968.

*Edinburgh '76 Magazine: Psycho-Analysis/Cinema/Avante-Garde* 1 (1976).

Eisenstein, Sergei. *Film Form.* Trans. Jay Leyda. New York: Harcourt, Brace, 1949.

Eliade, Mircea. *Myth and Reality.* Trans. Willard Trask. New York: Harper & Row, 1963.

Eliot, T. S. *Selected Poems.* New York: Harcourt, Brace & World, 1964.

Eluard, Paul. "Le Baillon sur la table." *La Vie immédiate.* Paris: Editions des cahiers libres, 1932.

————. "Recherches expérimentales." *Le Surréalisme au service de la révolution* 6.

————. Untitled note about his dreams. Ibid., 1 (July 1930).

Farges, Joel. "L'Image d'un corps." *Comunications* 23 (May 1975).

Foucault, Michel. *Les Choses et les mots.* Paris: Gallimard, 1966. *The Order of Things.* New York: Pantheon Books, 1971.

Freud, Sigmund. *Civilization and Its Discontents.* Trans. and ed. James Strachey. New York: W. W. Norton, 1961.

————. *The Standard Edition of the Complete Psychological Works of Sigmund Freud.* 23 vols. Trans. and ed. James Strachey. 3d ed. London: Hogarth Press, 1953–66.

————. "Fetishism." Ibid. Vol. 21.

————. "Screen Memories." Ibid. Vol. 3.

————. "The Uncanny." Ibid. Vol. 17.

————. *The Interpretation of Dreams.* Trans. and ed. James Strachey. New York: Avon Books, 1965.

————. "Metapsychological Supplement to the Theory of Dreams." *General Psychological Theory: Papers on Metapsychology.* Ed. Philip Rieff. New York: Collier Books, 1963.

Gauthier, Xavière. *Surréalisme et sexualité*. Paris: Gallimard, 1971.

Genette, Gérard. *Figures III*. Paris: Seuil, 1972.

————. "La Rhétorique restreinte." *Communications* 16 (1970).

Goudal, Jean. "Surréalisme et cinéma." *La Revue hébdomadaire*, 8 (February 21, 1925). Reprinted as "Surrealism and Cinema," in Paul Hammond, trans. and ed., *The Shadow and Its Shadow*. London: British Film Institute, 1978.

Gould, Michael. *Surrealism and the Cinema*. New York: A. S. Barnes, 1976.

Guillaume de Lorris and Jean de Meun (pseud.). *The Romance of the Rose*. Trans. Charles Dahlberg. Princeton: Princeton University Press, 1969.

Green, Naomi. *Poet without Words*. New York: Simon & Schuster, 1970.

Hammond, Paul, trans. and ed. *The Shadow and Its Shadow*. London: British Film Institute, 1978.

Harcourt, Peter. *Six European Directors: Essays on the Meaning of Film Style*. Baltimore: Penguin Books, 1974.

Jakobson, Roman. "Aphasia as a Linguistic Topic." "Two Aspects of Language and Two Types of Aphasic Disturbances." *Selected Writings*. 2 vols. The Hague: Mouton, 1971. Vol. 2.

Jenny, Laurent. "La Surréalité et les signes narratifs." *Poétique* 16 (1973).

Johnston, Claire. "Towards a Feminist Film Practice: Some Theses," *Edinburgh '76 Magazine: Psycho-Analysis/Cinema/Avant-Garde* 1 (1976).

Kael, Pauline. "The Cutting Light." *New Yorker*, December 19, 1977.

————. "Taking a Chance." Ibid., October 28, 1974.

Kawin, Bruce. *Mindscreen: Bergman, Godard, and First-Person Film*. Princeton: Princeton University Press, 1978.

Kehr, Dave. "The Poetry of Paradox," *Chicago Reader*, March 31, 1978.

Kelman, Ken. "The Other Side of Realism." *The Essential Cinema: Essays on the Films in the Collection of Anthology Film Archives*. 2 vols. Ed. P. Adams Sitney. New York: Anthology Film Archives & New York University Press, 1975. Vol. 1.

Kinder, Marsha. "The Tyranny of Convention in *The Phantom of Liberty*." *Film Quarterly* 28 (Summer 1975).

Kyrou, Ado. "*L'Age d'or* centre et tremplin du cinéma surréaliste." *L'Age du Cinéma* 4–5 (August–November, 1951).

————. *Amour, érotisme et cinéma*. Paris: Le Terrain Vague, 1957.

————. *Luis Buñuel*. 1st ed. Paris: Seghers, 1962.

————. *Le Surréalisme au cinéma*. 1st ed. Paris: Editions Arcanes, 1953.

Lacan, Jacques. *Ecrits*. Paris: Editions du seuil, 1966. *Ecrits: A Selection*.

Trans. Alan Sheridan. New York: Norton, 1977.

———. *Le Séminaire de Jacques Lacan.* 20 vols. Paris: Seuil, 1972– . Vol. 1: *Les Ecrits techniques de Freud* (1972). Vol. 11: *Les Quatre concepts fondamentaux de Freud* (1973).

———. *The Four Fundamental Concepts of Psycho-Analysis.* Trans. Alan Sheridan. New York: Norton, 1978.

———. *The Language of the Self: The Function of Language in the Unconscious.* Trans., with notes and commentary, Anthony Wilden. New York: Dell, 1975.

———. "Les problèmes du style et les formes paranoiaques de l'expérience." *Minotaure* 1 (February 15, 1933).

Laplanche, Jean, and Serge Le Claire. "L'Inconscient: Une Etude psychanalytique." *Les Temps Modernes* 183 (July 1961).

———, and J. B. Pontalis. *Le Vocabulaire de la psychanalyse.* Bibliothèque de la psychanalyse. Paris: Press universitaires, 1967.

Lautréamont. *Maldoror.* Trans. Guy Wernham. New York: New Directions, 1965.

———. *Oeuvres complètes.* Paris: Librairée Générales Française, 1963.

Lawder, Standish D. *The Cubist Cinema.* New York: New York University Press.

Lemaire, Anika. *Jacques Lacan.* Brussels: Charles Denart, 1970. *Jacques Lacan.* Trans. David Macey. London: Routledge & Kegan Paul, 1977.

Levi-Strauss, Claude. *Structural Anthropology.* Trans. Claire Jacobson and Brooke Grundfest Schoepf. New York: Doubleday, 1967.

Loüys, Pierre. *La Femme et le pantin.* Paris: Albin Michel, 1959.

MacCabe, Colin. "Presentation of 'The Imaginary Signifier.'" *Screen* 16 (Summer 1975).

Larkin, David, ed. *Magritte.* New York: Random House, 1972.

Manonni, Octave. *Clefs pour l'imaginaire ou l'autre scène.*

Mathews, J. H. *Surrealism and Film.* Ann Arbor: University of Michigan Press, 1971.

Metz, Christian. *Essais sur la signification au cinéma.* 2 vols. Paris: Editions Klincksieck, 1972. Vol. 2.

———. "The Fiction Film and Its Spectator: A Metapsychological Study." Trans. Alfred Guzzetti. *New Literary History* 8 (Autumn 1976).

———. *Film Language.* Trans. Michael Taylor. New York: Oxford University Press, 1974.

———. "The Imaginary Signifier." Trans. Ben Brewster. *Screen* 16 (Summer 1975).

———. *Language and Cinema.* Trans. Donna Jean Umiker-Sebeok. The Hague: Mouton, 1974.

————. *Le Signifiant imaginaire: Psychanalyse et cinéma*. Paris: Union générale d'éditions, 1977.

Mitry, Jean. *Le Cinéma expérimental*. Paris: Seghers, 1974.

————. *Esthétique et psychologie du cinéma*. 2 vols. Paris: Editions universitaires, 1963. Vols. 1 and 2.

Mulvey, Laura. "Visual Pleasure and Narrative Cinema." *Screen* 16 (Autumn 1975).

Münsterberg, Hugo. *The Film: A Psychological Study*. New York: Dover Publications, 1970.

Nadeau, Maurice. *Histoire du surréalisme suivi de Documents surréalistes*. Paris: Seuil, 1964.

Oudart, Jean-Pierre. "Cinema and Suture." Trans. Kari Hanet. *Screen* 18 (Winter 1977).

Reverdy, Pierre. "L'Image." *Nord-Sud* 13 (March 1918).

————. "Cinématograph." Ibid. 16 (1918).

Richards, I. A. *Principles of Literary Criticism*. New York: Harcourt, Brace, 1925.

Ricoeur, Paul. *The Rule of Metaphor: Multidisciplinary Studies of the Creation of Meaning in Language*. Trans. Robert Czerny. Toronto: University of Toronto Press, 1977.

Riffaterre, Michel. "La Métaphore filée dans la poésie surréaliste." *Langue Française* (Sept. 1969).

Ropars-Wuilleumie, Marie-Claire. "Fonction de la métaphore dans 'Octobre' d'Eisenstein." *Littérature* 11 (Oct. 1973).

Sade, Donatien Alphonse François. *Oeuvres complètes*. 16 vols. Vols. 13–14, *120 Journées de Sodome: Ou l'école du libertinage*. Paris: Cercle du livre précieux, 1966.

Sala, Carlo. *Max Ernst et la démarche onirique*. Paris: Klincksieck, 1970.

*Screen* 16 (Summer 1975). Special issue on psychoanalysis and cinema.

Soupault, Philippe. "L'Indifférence." "Note I sur le cinéma." *Sic* 25 (January 1918).

Suleiman, Susan. "Freedom and Necessity: Narrative Structure in *The Phantom of Liberty*." *Quarterly Review of Film Studies* 3 (Summer 1978).

Truffaut, François. Interview. *Arts*, July 21, 1955. Reprinted in Kyrou, *Luis Buñuel*. Paris: Seghers, 1962.

Virmaux, Alain. *Antonin Artaud et le théâtre*. Paris: Seghers, 1970.

————. "Artaud and Film." *Tulane Drama Review* 2 (Fall 1966).

————. "*La Bréhatine* et la cinéma: Apollinaire en quête d'un langage neuf." *Archives des lettres modernes* 7 (1971).

———. "Une Promesse mal tenue." *Etudes cinématographiques: Surréalisme et cinéma* 1 (1965).

——— and Odette. *Les Surréalistes et le cinéma*. Paris: Seghers, 1976.

Wood, Michael. "Buñuel's Private Lessons." *New York Review of Books*, February 23, 1978.

# Supplementary Bibliography

The following bibliography contains selected books and articles related to Surrealist cinema and art, film theory and criticism, and feminist criticism which have been published since 1981.

Abel, Richard. *French Cinema: The First Wave, 1915–1929*. Princeton: Princeton University Press, 1984.

———. *French Film Theory and Criticism: A History/Anthology, 1907–1939*. 2 vols. Princeton: Princeton University Press, 1988.

Andrew, Dudley. "On Figuration." *iris* (1983): 121–132.

Aranda, J.F. "Cinema experimental e de vanguarda." *Celuloide* 28.348 (May 1983): 126–29.

Buñuel, Luis. *My Last Sigh*. New York: Knopf, 1983.

Doane, Mary Ann. *The Desire to Desire: The Woman's Film of the 1940's*. Bloomington: Indiana University Press, 1984.

Doane, Mary Ann, Patricia Mellencamp, and Linda Williams, eds. *Re-Vision: Essays in Feminist Film Criticism*. American Film Institute Monograph Series, vol. 3. Frederick, Md.: University Publications of America, 1984.

Hedges, Inez. *Languages of Revolt: Dada and Surrealist Literature and Film*. Durham, N.C.: Duke University Press, 1983.

Krauss, Rosalind. "The Photographic Conditions of Surrealism." *October* 19 (Winter 1981):3–34.

———. "Photography in the Service of Surrealism." In *L'Amour Fou*, ed. Rosalind Krauss and Jane Livingston. New York: Abbeville, 1985. 15–54.

Kuenzli, Rudolf, ed. *Dada and Surrealist Film*. New York: Willis Locker and Owens, 1987.

Flitterman-Lewis, Sandy. *To Desire Differently: Feminism and the French*

*Cinema.* Urbana: University of Illinois Press, 1990.

Metz, Christian. *The Imaginary Signifier.* Bloomington: Indiana University Press, 1982.

Mulvey, Laura. *Visual and Other Pleasures.* Bloomington: Indiana University Press, 1989.

Oswald, L. "Figure/Discourse: Configurations of Desire in *Un Chien andalou.*" *Semiotica* 33.1–2 (1981): 105–22.

Penley, Constance, ed. *Feminism and Film Theory.* New York: Routledge, 1988.

Polan, Dana. *The Political Language of Film and the Avant Garde.* Ann Arbor: UMI Research Press, 1985.

Rose, Jacqueline. *Sexuality in the Field of Vision.* London: Verso, 1986.

Sandro, Paul. *Diversions of Pleasure and the Crises of Desire.* Columbus: Ohio State University Press, 1987.

Wills, David. "Language surrealiste, langage cinematographique." *La Siècle éclate* 3 (1985): 67–84.

# Index

Abraham, Karl, 50
*L'Amour fou*, 24*n*
*Amour fou* (mad love): defined, 24; in Desnos, 24, 26; in *L'Age d'or*, 133, 137, 145; in *The Phantom of Liberty*, 175
Apollinaire, Guillaume: *esprit nouveau*, 6; on film theory, 6; review *Les Soirées de Paris*, 6; scenario of *La Bréhatine*, 7, 42, 51, 143, 211
Aragon, Louis, 5–6; "Contre-Chant" (poem), 45, 149*n*; signed *L'Age d'or* support manifesto
Artaud, Antonin: *The Seashell and the Clergyman*, xii*n*, 19*n*, 22, 31, 45, 51, 110; on model of dream in film, 15, 54, 101; scenarios of, 20, 32, 33, 42, 101; Derrida on, 20; on language, 20, 31; theater of cruelty, 21; *Eighteen Seconds* (scenario), 28–30, 31, 42–43, 51, 211
Automatic writing, 10, 13

Beckett, Samuel, *Happy Days*, 99
*Belle de jour*, 154
*The Blue Angel*, 204
*La Bréhatine*. *See* Apollinaire, Guillaume
Breton, André: criticism as love, xi; *Manifestoes of Surrealism*, 10, 11; on plastic arts and Surrealism, 11; Surrealist poetic image, 12–13; *Poisson soluble* (*Soluble Fish*), 13, 18; *L'Amour fou*, 24; *Les Vases communicants*, 33, 41, 74*n*; moviegoing habits, 45–46, 218; on Lautréamont, 74; simplest Surrealist act, 94*n*, 171; *L'Age d'or* support manifesto
Buñuel, Luis: on fancy camera effects, 48; direction of *Un Chien andalou*, 53ff; as actor in *Un Chien andalou*, 72; sexual desire in films of, 87, 89, 90, 201; fetishes in films of, 149–50; two poles of Surrealism in, 153
Bureau de Recherches Surréalistes, 19

*Cabinet of Dr. Caligari*, 51, 102
*Les Carabiniers*, 46
Chaplin, Charles, 58, 60, 61, 62

Chirico, Giorgio de, 11, 12
*Cinéma pur* (pure cinema), 25–26
Cocteau, Jean, 20
Condensation. *See* Freud, Sigmund
Crevel, René, 43
*The Criminal Life of Archibaldo de la Cruz*, 151, 154
Cubism, 3*n*, 12

Dadaism, xii, 7, 48
Dalí, Salvadore: meeting with Lacan, 44; on paranoia and creativity, 44; canvases attacked, 47, 107; and direction of *Un Chien andalou*, 53ff
Delteil, Joseph, 46
*Dépaysement* (Surrealist disorientation), 11, 13
Desire: content vs. form, 14; as articulated by unconscious, 33; defined, 37; phantom object of, 175
Desnos, Robert: on dreams and film, 15, 23ff, 26; "Etoile de Mer" (poem), 20; *Minuit à quatorze heures* (screenplay), 27, 30; screenplays of, 28, 32, 33, 42, 101; on spectator identification with film, 46; film-going habits, 218
*The Devil Is a Woman*, 186, 188, 199, 200
Difference (in language), 21, 144–45
*The Discreet Charm of the Bourgeoisie*, 134*n*, 152, 154, 185
Displacement. *See* Freud, Sigmund
Dreams: similarity to film, xiii, 15–17, 143, 210; as models for Surrealist film, 14, 26, 32, 33, 54; manifest and latent content in, 16; wish-fulfilment in, 33; condensation and displacement in, 33, 55; discourse in, 75; logic of, 84–85; overdetermination in, 212
Duchamp, Marcel, 11, 12
Dulac, Germaine, director, *The Seashell and the Clergyman*, 19*n*, 31*n*, 110*n*

Eggeling, Viking, 25
Eisenstein, Sergei: metaphoric films, 58; *Potemkin*, 59, 77, 98, 139, 181; *The*

227

A NOTE ON THE AUTHOR

LINDA WILLIAMS received a bachelor's degree from the University of California at Berkeley in 1969 and a doctorate from the University of Colorado in 1977, both in comparative literature. *Figures of Desire* was begun with the aid of a grant from the French government for graduate study in 1975–76 under Christian Metz at the Ecole des Hautes Etudes in Paris. It was completed later with a faculty grant from the Research Board of the University of Illinois at Chicago Circle. Williams has written articles on film and literary criticism for leading film journals and also serves as an assistant editor of *Jump Cut*. She has codirected several films, the most recent of which is *Maxwell Street Blues*, a documentary about blues musicians who perform at Chicago's Maxwell Street market. She is an assistant professor of English at the University of Illinois at Chicago Circle.